The Alchemy of Race and Rights

The Alchemy
of Race and Rights

PATRICIA J. WILLIAMS

HARVARD UNIVERSITY PRESS
Cambridge, Massachusetts, and London, England

Library of Congress Cataloging-in-Publication Data

Williams, Patricia J., 1951–
   The alchemy of race and rights / Patricia J. Williams.
     p. cm.
   Includes bibliographical references and index.
   ISBN 0-674-01470-7
   1. Afro-Americans—Civil rights. 2. United States—Race relations.
3. Williams, Patricia J., 1951–   . 4. Law teachers—United States—Biography.
5. Critical legal studies—United States. 6. Feminist criticism—
United States. I. Title.
KF4757.W53 1991
342.73'0873—dc20
[347.302873]   90-48439
                                        CIP

Designed by Gwen Frankfeldt

For Sophie, Marjorie, and the three bears

Contents

*O*nce upon a time there was a society of priests who built a Celestial City with gates secured by word-combination locks. The priests were masters of the Word and, within the City, ascending levels of power and treasure became accessible to those who could learn ascendingly intricate levels of Word Magic. At the very top level, the priests became gods; and because they then had nothing left to seek, they engaged in games with which to pass the long hours of eternity. In particular, they liked to ride their strong, sure-footed steeds around and around the perimeter of heaven: now jumping word hurdles, now playing polo with concepts of the moon and the stars, now reaching up to touch that pinnacle, that splinter of Refined Understanding called Superstanding, which was the brass ring of their merry-go-round.

In time, some of the priests-turned-gods tired of this sport, denounced it as meaningless. They donned the garb of pilgrims, seekers once more, and passed beyond the gates of the Celestial City. In this recursive passage they acquired the knowledge of Undoing Words.

Beyond the walls of the City lay a Deep Blue Sea. The priests built small boats and set sail, determined to explore the uncharted courses and open vistas of this new terrain. They wandered for many years in this manner, until at last they reached a place that was half a circumference away from the Celestial City. From this point the City appeared as a mere shimmering illusion; and the priests knew that they had finally reached a place Beyond the Power of Words. They let down their anchors, the plumb lines of their reality, and experienced godhood once more.

Under the Celestial City, dying mortals cried out their rage and suffering, battered by a steady rain of sharp hooves whose thundering, sound-drowning path described the wheel of their misfortune.

At the bottom of the Deep Blue Sea, drowning mortals reached silently and desperately for drifting anchors dangling from short chains far, far overhead, which they thought were lifelines meant for them.

I

Excluding Voices

**A Necklace of Thoughts on
the Ideology of Style**

The Brass Ring
and the Deep Blue Sea

(some parables about learning to think like a lawyer)

Since subject position is everything in my analysis of the law, you deserve to know that it's a bad morning. I am very depressed. It always takes a while to sort out what's wrong, but it usually starts with some kind of perfectly irrational thought such as: I *hate* being a lawyer. This particular morning I'm sitting up in bed reading about redhibitory vices. A redhibitory vice is a defect in merchandise which, if existing at the time of purchase, gives rise to a claim allowing the buyer to return the thing and to get back part or all of the purchase price. The case I'm reading is an 1835 decision from Louisiana, involving the redhibitory vice of craziness:

> The plaintiff alleged that he purchased of the defendant a slave named Kate, for which he paid $500, and in two or three days after it was discovered the slave was crazy, and run away, and that the vices were known to the defendant . . .
>
> It was contended [by the seller] that Kate was not crazy but only stupid, and stupidity is not madness; but on the contrary, an apparent defect, against which the defendant did not warrant . . .
>
> The code has declared, that a sale may be avoided on account of any vice or defect, which renders the thing either absolutely useless, or its use so inconvenient and imperfect, that it must be supposed the buyer would not have purchased with a knowledge of the vice. We are satisfied that the slave in question was wholly, and perhaps worse than, useless.[1]

As I said, this is the sort of morning when I hate being a lawyer, a teacher, and just about everything else in my life. It's all I can do to feed the cats. I let my hair stream wildly and the eyes roll back in my head.

So you should know that this is one of those mornings when I refuse to compose myself properly; you should know you are dealing with someone who is writing this in an old terry bathrobe with a little fringe of blue and white tassles dangling from the hem, trying to decide if she is stupid or crazy.

Whenever I'm in a mood like this, it helps to get it out on paper, so I sit down to write even when I'm afraid I may produce a death-poem. Sometimes I can just write fast from the heart until I'm healed. Sometimes I look at my computer keyboard and I am paralyzed, inadequate—all those letters of the alphabet, full of random signification. I feel like a monkey. Those mornings, and this is one, I need a little extra push to get me started, and if I turn on the television, almost any story will do. I switch channels through a sea of news programs with the coopting, carnivorous eagerness of catharisis.

Conditions are bad, very bad, all over the world. The newscasters tell me that everyone is afraid of black men these days, even black women. Black people are being jailed in huge numbers, and the infant-mortality rate is staggering. Courts have authorized the custody removal of children at birth from mothers who are drug-addicted. Drugs bring pleasure to the biological catastrophe of having been born in the fearsome, loathesome packaging of an "other" body. Editorials talk about the efficiency of apartheid. Bigger better prisons. Spy satellites. Personnel carriers in Harlem. Door-to-door searches. State-sanctioned castration. Some neutral market thing devouring the resources of the earth at a terminally reckless rate. The Ku Klux Klan and the Aryan Brotherhood are the major unions among prison guards. Eastern Europe wants more freedom in the form of telephone-answering machines and video cassettes. AIDS spreads and spreads and spreads, among black and brown communities in particular. Subsistence farmers and indigenous people are dying all over the world, their ways and knowledge devoured and lost forever. According to the most authoritative scientists, the greenhouse effect is supposed to raise the temperature of the earth by two or three degrees over the next millennium. The winter of 1989 was five, ten, sometimes fifteen degrees above normal, all over the earth. It is the spring of 1990, and we are all worried about the summer to come.

I don't know how to find something to write about in the panic of this deadly world. There is more in the news than even my depression can consume.

Then I see it. A concise, modular, yet totally engaging item on the "MacNeil/Lehrer News Hour": Harvard Law School cannot find one black woman on the entire planet who is good enough to teach there, because we're all too stupid. (Well, that's not precisely what was said. It was more like they couldn't find anyone smart enough. To be fair, what Associate Dean Louis Kaplow actually said was that Harvard would have to "lower its standards," which of course Harvard simply cannot do.[2])

So now you know: it is this news item, as I sit propped up in bed with my laptop computer balanced on my knees, clad in my robe with the torn fringe of terry bluebells, that finally pushes me over the edge and into the deep rabbit hole of this book.

When I dust myself off, I am sitting with my sister at my parents' kitchen table. Grown now, she and I are at home for Christmas. We chat, catching up on each other's lives. My sister tells me how her house is haunted by rabbits. I tell her how I'm trying to write a book on law and liberation.

"The previous owner had hundreds of them," she says. "You can hear them dancing in the dining room after midnight."

"It will be a book about the jurisprudence of rights," I respond. "I will attempt to apply so-called critical thought to legal studies. I believe that critical theory has valuable insights to contribute to debates about the ethics of law and the meaning of rights; yet many of those insights have been buried in relatively arcane vocabulary and abstraction. My book will concern itself with the interplay of commerce and constitutional protections and will be organized around discussion of three basic jurisprudential forces: autonomy, community, and order. My chapters will address such issues as surrogate motherhood and ownership; neighborhood and homelessness; racially motivated violence and disownedness. I will try to write, moreover, in a way that bridges the traditional gap between theory and praxis. It is not my goal merely to simplify; I hope that the result will be a text that is multilayered—that encompasses the straightforwardness of real life *and* reveals complexity of meaning."

"But what's the book *about?*" my sister asks, thumping her leg against the chair impatiently.

"Howard Beach, polar bears, and food stamps," I snap back. "I am interested in the way in which legal language flattens and confines in absolutes the complexity of meaning inherent in any given problem; I am trying to challenge the usual limits of commercial discourse by using an intentionally double-voiced and relational, rather than a traditionally legal black-letter, vocabulary. For example, I am a commercial lawyer as well as a teacher of contract and property law. I am also black and female, a status that one of my former employers described as being 'at oxymoronic odds' with that of commercial lawyer. While I certainly took issue with that particular characterization, it is true that my attempts to write in my own voice have placed me in the center of a snarl of social tensions and crossed boundaries. On the one hand, my writing has been staked out as the exclusive interdisciplinary property of constitutional law, contract, African-American history, feminist jurisprudence, political science, and rhetoric. At the same time, my work has been described as a 'sophisticated frontal assault' on laissez-faire's most sacred sanctums, as 'new-age performance art,' and as 'anecdotal individualism.' In other words, to speak as black, female, *and* commercial lawyer has rendered me simultaneously universal, trendy, and marginal. I think, moreover, that there is a paradigm at work, in the persistent perceptions of me as inherent contradiction: a paradigm of larger social perceptions that divide public from private, black from white, dispossessed from legitimate. This realization, while extremely personal, inevitably informs my writing on a professional level."

"What's so new," asks my sister, losing interest rapidly, "about a schizophrenic black lady pouring her heart out about food stamps and polar bears?"

I lean closer to her. "Floating signifiers," I whisper.

I continue: "Legal writing presumes a methodology that is highly stylized, precedential, and based on deductive reasoning. Most scholarship in law is rather like the 'old math': static, stable, formal—rationalism walled against chaos. My writing is an intentional departure from that. I use a model of inductive empiricism, borrowed from—and parodying—systems analysis, in order to enliven thought about complex social problems. I want to look at legal issues within a framework inscribed not just within the four corners of a document—be it contract or the Constitution—but by the disciplines of psychology, sociology, history, criticism, and philosophy. The advantage of this approach is that it highlights factors that would otherwise go unremarked. For example, *stare decisis* (the judicial practice of deciding cases in a manner limited by prior court decisions in factually analogous situations), rather than remaining a silent, unquestioned 'given,' may be analyzed as a filter to certain types of systemic input. Another advantage is that this sort of analytic technique can serve to describe a community of context for those social actors whose traditional legal status has been the isolation of oxymoron, of oddity, of outsider. I am trying to create a genre of legal writing to fill the gaps of traditional legal scholarship. I would like to write in a way that reveals the intersubjectivity of legal constructions, that forces the reader both to participate in the construction of meaning and to

7

be conscious of that process. Thus, in attempting to fill the gaps in the discourse of commercial exchange, I hope that the gaps in my own writing will be self-consciously filled by the reader, as an act of forced mirroring of meaning-invention. To this end, I exploit all sorts of literary devices, including parody, parable, and poetry."

". . . as in polar bears?" my sister asks eagerly, alert now, ears pricked, nose quivering, hair bristling.

"My, what big teeth you have!" I exclaim, just before the darkness closes over me.

It is my deep belief that theoretical legal understanding and social transformation need not be oxymoronic. I want this book to occupy the gaps between those ends that the sensation of oxymoron marks. What I hope will be filled in is connection; connection between my psyche and the readers', between lived experience and social perception, and between an encompassing historicity and a jurisprudence of generosity.

"Theoretical legal understanding" is characterized, in Anglo-American jurisprudence, by at least three features of thought and rhetoric:

(1) The hypostatization of exclusive categories and definitional polarities, the drawing of bright lines and clear taxonomies that purport to make life simpler in the face of life's complication: rights/needs, moral/immoral, public/private, white/black.

(2) The existence of transcendent, acontextual, universal legal truths or pure procedures. For example, some conservative theorists might insist that the tort of fraud has always existed and that it is part of a universal system of right and wrong. A friend of mine demanded of a professor who made just such an assertion: "Do you mean to say that when the first white settlers landed on Fiji, they found tortfeasors waiting to be discovered?" Yes, in a manner of speaking, was the professor's response. This habit of universalizing legal taxonomies is very much like a cartoon I once

saw, in which a group of prehistoric fish swam glumly underwater, carrying baseball bats tucked beneath their fins, waiting to evolve, looking longingly toward dry land, where a baseball was lying in wait on the shore. The more serious side of this essentialized world view is a worrisome tendency to disparage anything that is nontranscendent (temporal, historical), or contextual (socially constructed), or nonuniversal (specific) as "emotional," "literary," "personal," or just Not True.

(3) The existence of objective, "unmediated" voices by which those transcendent, universal truths find their expression. Judges, lawyers, logicians, and practitioners of empirical methodologies are obvious examples, but the supposed existence of such voices is also given power in romanticized notions of "real people" having "real" experiences—not because real people have experienced what they really experienced, but because their experiences are somehow *made* legitimate—either because they are viewed as empirically legitimate (directly corroborated by consensus, by a community of outsiders) or, more frequently, because those experiences are corroborated by hidden or unspoken models of legitimacy. The Noble Savage as well as the Great White Father, the Good-Hearted Masses, the Real American, the Rational Consumer, and the Arm's-Length Transactor are all versions of this Idealized Other whose gaze provides us either with internalized censure or externalized approval; internalized paralysis or externalized legitimacy; internalized false consciousness or externalized claims of exaggerated authenticity.

The degree to which these three features of legal thought are a force in laws ranging from contracts to crimes, from property to civil liberties, will be a theme throughout the rest of this book. For the moment, however, a smaller example might serve to illustrate the interpretive dynamic of which I am speaking.

A man with whom I used to work once told me that I made too much of my race. "After all," he said, "I don't even think of you as black." Yet sometime later, when another black woman became engaged in an ultimately unsuccessful tenure battle, he confided to me that he wished the school could find more blacks like me. I felt myself slip in and out of shadow, as I became nonblack for purposes of inclusion and black for purposes of exclusion; I felt the boundaries of my very body manipulated, casually inscribed by definitional demarcations that did not refer to me.

The paradox of my being black yet notblack visited me again when, back to back, the same (white) man and then a (black) woman wondered aloud if I "really identified as black." When the white man said this, I was acutely aware that the choice of identifying as black (as opposed to white?) was hardly mine; that as long as I am identified as black by the majority of others, my own identifying as black will almost surely follow as a simple fact of human interdependency. When the black woman told me the very same thing, I took it to heart as a signpost of self-denial; as possible evidence within myself of that brand of social distress and alienation to which blacks and oppressed people are so peculiarly subject; and as a call for unity in a society that too often helps us turn against ourselves.

I heard the same words from each, and it made no difference to me. I heard the same words from each, but differently: one characterized me as more of something I am not, white; the other called for me to be more conscious of something I am, black. I heard the same-different words addressed to me, a perceived white-male-socialized black woman, as a challenge to mutually exclusive categorization, as an overlapping of black and female and right and male and private and wrong and white and public, and so on and so forth.

That life is complicated is a fact of great analytic importance. Law too often seeks to avoid this truth by making up its own breed of narrower, simpler, but hypnotically powerful rhetorical truths. Acknowledging, challenging, playing with these *as* rhetorical gestures is, it seems to me, necessary for any conception of justice. Such acknowledgment complicates the supposed purity of gender, race, voice, boundary; it allows us to acknowledge the utility of such categorizations for certain purposes and the necessity of their breakdown on other occasions. It complicates definitions in its shift, in its expansion and contraction according to circumstance, in its room for the possibility of creatively mated taxonomies and their wildly unpredictable offspring.

I think, though, that one of the most important results of reconceptualizing from "objective truth" to rhetorical event will be a more nuanced sense of legal and social responsibility. This will be so because much of what is spoken in so-called objective, unmediated voices is in fact mired in hidden subjectivities and unexamined claims that make property of others beyond the self, all the while denying such connections. I remember A., a colleague, once stating that he didn't like a book he had just read because he had another friend who was a literary critic and he *imagined* that this critical friend would say a host of negative things about the book. A. disclaimed his own subjectivity, displacing it onto a larger-than-life literary critic; he created an authority who was imaginary but whose rhetorical objectivity was as smooth and convincing as the slice of a knife. In psychobabble, this is known as "not taking responsibility." In racial contexts, it is related to the familiar offensiveness of people who will say, "Our maid is black and *she* says that blacks want . . ."; such statements both universalize the lone black voice and disguise, enhance, and "objectify" the authority of the individual white speaker. As a legal tool, however, it is an extremely common device by which not just subject positioning is obscured, but by which agency and responsibility are hopelessly befuddled.

The propagated mask of the imagined literary critic, the language club of hyperauthenticity, the myth of a purely objective perspective, the godlike image of generalized, legitimating others—these are too often reified in law as "impersonal" rules and "neutral" principles, presumed to be inanimate, unemotional, unbiased, unmanipulated, and higher than ourselves. Laws like masks, frozen against the vicissitudes of life; rights as solid as rocks; principles like baseballs waiting on dry land for us to crawl up out of the mud and claim them.

This semester I have been teaching a course entitled Women and Notions of Property. I have been focusing on the semantic power and property of individualistic gendered perspectives, gender in this instance having less to do with the biology of male and female than with the semiotics of power relations, of dominance and submission, of assertion and deference, of big and little; as well as on gender issues specifically based in biology, such as reproductive rights and the complicated ability of women in particular to live freely in the territory of their own bodies. An example of the stories we discuss is the following, used to illustrate the rhetoric of power relations whose examination, I tell my students, is at the heart of the course.

Walking down Fifth Avenue in New York not long ago, I came up behind a couple and their young son. The child, about four or five years old, had evidently been complaining about big dogs. The mother was saying, "But why are you afraid of big dogs?" "Because they're big," he responded with eminent good sense. "But what's the difference between a big dog and a little dog?" the father persisted. "They're *big*," said the child. "But there's really no difference," said the mother, pointing to a large slathering wolfhound with narrow eyes and the calculated amble of a gangster, and then to a beribboned Pekinese the size of a roller skate, who was flouncing along just ahead of us all, in that little fox-trotty step that keep Pekinese from ever being taken seriously. "See?" said the father. "If you look really closely you'll see there's no difference at all. They're all just dogs."

And I thought: Talk about your iron-clad canon. Talk about a static, unyielding, totally uncompromising point of reference. These people must be lawyers. Where else do people learn so well the idiocies of High Objectivity? How else do people learn to capitulate so uncritically to a norm that refuses to allow for difference? How else do grown-ups sink so deeply into the authoritarianism of their own world view that they can universalize their relative bigness so completely that they obliterate the subject positioning of their child's relative smallness? (To say nothing of the position of the slathering wolfhound, from whose own narrow perspective I dare say the little boy must have looked exactly like a lamb chop.)

I used this story in my class because I think it illustrates a paradigm of thought by which children are taught not to see what they see; by which blacks are reassured that there is no real inequality in the world, just their own bad dreams; and by which women are taught not to experience what they experience, in deference to men's ways of knowing. The story also illustrates the possibility of a collective perspective or social positioning that would give rise to a claim for the legal interests of groups. In a historical moment when individual rights have become the basis for any remedy, too often group interests are defeated by, for example, finding the one four-year-old who has wrestled whole packs of wolfhounds fearlessly to the ground; using that individual experience to attack the validity of there ever being any generalizable four-year-old fear of wolfhounds; and then recasting the general group experience as a fragmented series of specific, isolated events rather than a pervasive social phenomenon ("You have every right to think that that wolfhound has the ability to bite off your head, but that's just your point of view").

My students, most of whom signed up expecting to experience that crisp, refreshing, clear-headed sensation that "thinking like a lawyer" purportedly endows, are confused by this and all the stories I tell them in my class on Women and Notions of Property. They are confused enough by the idea of property alone, overwhelmed by the thought of dogs and women as academic subjects, and paralyzed by the idea that property might have a gender and that gender might be a matter of words.

But I haven't been able to straighten things out for them because I'm confused too. I have arrived at a point where everything I have ever learned is running around and around in my head; and little bits of law and pieces of everyday life fly out of my mouth in weird combinations. Who can blame the students for being confused? On the other hand, everyday life is a confusing bit of business. And so my students plot my disintegration, in the shadowy shelter of ivy-covered archways and in the margins of their notebooks . . . . .

Gilded Lilies
and Liberal Guilt

(a reflection on law-school pedagogy)

I am sitting on a train rushing from my old home in New York to my new home in California. In the dining car of the Broadway Bomber, or some other Amtrak name like that, with my pens and notebook spread out on the table, I am writing a speech for a program sponsored by the University of Maryland Law School. About all I have done is pick a title: Contract and Communion. This much I can do without difficulty, because contract and something like communion are pretty much what I always write about. Most of my work is concerned with the division between the commercial and the communitarian, or the legal and the illegal, the righted and the outlawed, the legitimate and the illegitimate, the propertied and the dispossessed.

In this piece, I plan to make an analogy between social and private contract. My conviction is that aspects of the social contract are characterized by strategies of evasion or control embedded in American symbology, a symbology that is rooted in a certain ahistoricism. I want to use the model of private contract to illustrate the problematics of social contract because it seems a manageable way to test my hypotheses. At issue is a structure in which a cultural code has been inscribed; if I am inside the bell jar of the culture, my dilemma becomes how I can situate myself in order to evaluate it. Thus I am attempting to reduce the all-encompassing social contract to a manageable private context (or is it that I am using the all-encompassing private contract to examine what our social contract has become?).

Suspended in travel, encapsulated in perpetual motion between speeches, I have no time to waste when I travel. Writing furiously to keep up with the pace of my movement, I scribble into my notebook:

> Private contract is based on will theory, in which individual will and private acts of interpretation are joined to fulfill the expectations of not the larger but the smaller society of the parties. If one looks at documents like the Declaration of Independence and the Constitution, one can see how they marry aspects of consent and aspects of symbology—for example, concepts like the notion of freedom. On the one hand there is the letter of the law exalted in these documents, which describes a specific range of rights and precepts. On the other hand there is the spirit of the law, the symbology of freedom, which is in some ways utterly meaningless or empty—although at the same time the very emptiness provides a vessel to be filled with possibility, with a plurality of autonomous yearnings.

I pause for a moment and gaze out the train window. My life, I think, has become one long stream of text, delivered on the run to gatherings of mostly strangers. It is a strange period in my life, watching the world whiz by, these brazen moments of intimate revelation to no one in particular in my declared challenge to the necessary juxtaposition of the personal with the private. In some odd way, it is as though the question with which I began—Who Am I—has become reconstituted into Where Am I.

It is lunchtime. The dining car is starting to fill up, and an Amtrak attendant politely intrudes into my reveries. She brings me a menu, some silverware, and another traveler with whom I am to share the table. My new companion is a stockbroker from New York. He says he travels a lot too, and we talk about uprootedness. Then we talk about homelessness.

"I never give money when people beg from me," he says. "I tell them I have nothing. But I always stop to chat."

"Why?" I ask, meaning why doesn't he give money, but he misunderstands and proceeds to explain why he stops to talk.

"Finding out a little about who they are," he explains, "helps me remember that they're not just animals."

"Are you at risk of forgetting that?" I ask, wondering exactly whom it helps when he stops to reassure himself of a humanity unconnected to any concerted recognition of hunger or need.

"Yes," he replies to my surprise. "Over time, my conversations have helped me not to resent their presence on the streets in my neighborhood so much." He seems anxious to prove the benignity of his neglect. It is an awkward, dangerous moment in our short acquaintance; we chew in silence for a while, each not wanting to offend the other. I ponder the notion of speech as propertizing, and the silly irony, given the circumstance, of metaphors like eating one's words.

A little while later we part, not much more said, cordially enough. A small thing: I can't help noticing that he does not tip our waitress at all.

The original vehicle for my interest in the intersection of commerce and the Constitution was my family history. A few years ago, I came into the possession of what may have been the contract of sale for my great-great-grandmother. It is a very simple but lawyerly document, describing her as "one female" and revealing her age as eleven; no price is specified, merely "value exchanged." My sister also found a county census record taken two years later; on a list of one Austin Miller's personal assets she appears again, as "slave, female"—thirteen years old now with an eight-month infant.

Since then I have tried to piece together what it must have been like to be my great-great-grandmother. She was purchased, according to matrilineal recounting, by a man who was extremely temperamental and quite wealthy. I try to imagine what it would have been like to have a discontented white man buy me, after a fight with his mother about prolonged bachelorhood. I wonder what it would have been like to have a thirty-five-year-old man own the secrets of my puberty, which he bought to prove himself sexually as well as to increase his livestock of slaves. I imagine trying to please, with the yearning of adolescence, a man who truly did not know I was human, whose entire belief system resolutely defined me as animal, chattel, talking cow. I wonder what it would have been like to have his child, pale-faced but also animal, before I turned thirteen. I try to envision being casually threatened with sale from time to time, teeth and buttocks bared to interested visitors.

Family legend has it that my great-great-grandmother was very lazy, that she sat on the bank of the river all day and fished. According to the census, she was at least two decades younger than any other slave on the estate; family legend says that no one liked her. What could it have been like for my stunned, raped great-great-grandmother—an unwed teenage mother in today's parlance—so disliked and isolated from even her own children that the stories they purveyed were of her laziness? Her children were the exclusive property of their father (though that's not what they called him). They grew up in his house, taken from her as she had been taken from her mother. They became haughty, favored, frightened house servants who were raised playing with, caring for, and envying this now-married man's legitimate children, their half brothers and sister. Her children grew up reverent of and obedient to this white man—my great-great-grandfather—and his other children, to whom they were taught they owed the debt of their survival. It was a mistake from which the Emancipation Proclamation never fully freed any of them.

Her children must have been something of an ultimate betrayal; it could not have been easy to see in them the hope of her own survival. Freed from slavery by the Civil War, they went on to establish respected black Episcopal churches and to learn to play the piano. They grew up clever and well-bred. They grew up to marry other frightened, refined, master-blooded animals; they grew up good people, but alien.

Austin Miller, one of Tennessee's finest lawyers according to other records, went on to become a judge; and the sons by his wife went on to become lawyers as well. There is no surviving record of what happened to my great-great-grandmother, no account of how or when she died.

This story is what inspired my interest in the interplay of notions of public and private, of family and market; of male and female, of molestation and the law. I track meticulously the dimension of meaning in my great-great-grandmother as chattel: the meaning of money; the power of consumerist world view, the deaths of those we label the unassertive and the inefficient. I try to imagine where and who she would be today. I am engaged in a long-term project of tracking his words—through his letters and opinions—and those of his sons who were also lawyers and judges, of finding the shape described by her absence in all this.

I see her shape and his hand in the vast networking of our society, and in the evils and oversights that plague our lives and laws. The control he had over her body. The force he was in her life, in the shape of my life today. The power he exercised in the choice to breed her or not. The choice to breed slaves in his image, to choose her mate and be that mate. In his attempt to own what no man can own, the habit of his power and the absence of her choice.

I look for her shape and his hand.

When I get to California, I read this much of this chapter to an audience of law professors. The response is generally warm, but a friend of mine tells me that in the men's room he heard some of them laughing disparagingly: "All this emotional stuff just leaves me cold." Since the one who is reported to have said this is not only in love with power but is also powerful, I go back to my computer to find a way of saying it just for him.

I type random quotations onto my hard disk, thinking I'll find a place to use them somewhere. I write from a temporary office at a university in Southern California where I have come for a conference. It overlooks a plaza called The Marketplace. Pink-tiled and stuccoed, it seems too neat to be real. In it are the university bookstore, a couple of restaurants and juice bars, the accounting offices for the university, colorful boutiques that advertise for salespeople who are "bright, creative, and love to smile," and a movie theater, now showing *Pet Sematary, Friday Night, Part II,* and *Honey, I Shrunk the Kids!* which theater the university uses as a lecture hall by day. It is, I think, a literal marketplace of ideas. I sit and long for the messy complication of New York.

I miss my street in New York. I can always see, just by stepping outside my apartment, the dimension of meaning in my great-great-grandmother's being a chattel: the life-or-death contrast of lifestyles. On my street there are lots and lots of mercenary mothers, black women mostly, pushing white children in strollers, taking them to and from school. They are modern mammies who give up their own families to tend to the modern master's brood, just as slave mothers became mothers to whatever child was at hand. The black nanny is the direct descendant of the mammy described by W.E.B. DuBois "as 'one of the most pitiful of the world's Christs . . . She was an embodied Sorrow, an anomaly crucified on the cross of her own neglected children for the sake of the children of masters who bought and sold her as they bought and sold cattle.'"[1] This exploitation persists today, in the familiar image of grossly underpaid but ever-so-loved black female "help." The going rate for black female full-time live-in babysitter/maids in New York City is as low as $150 a week. "Haitians come cheaper. Their starting salary ranges from $100 to $125 a week . . . A Hispanic woman . . . is likely to start at $200 a week, since she's white."[2]

I type more random words into the computer: the rage of black mothers washes back in the rage of black children.

I am sitting in the library preparing a class on homelessness and the law. A student of mine, B., interrupts my writing. She is angry at me because she says my class is "out of control." She has been made to feel guilty, by the readings and the discussion, that her uncle is, as she describes him, "a slumlord." She says that the rich can't help who they are. I resent this interruption and snap at her: "They can help who they are as much"—and here I give B. back her own words of only a day or so before—"as poor people who are supposed to 'help' themselves out of poverty (as distinguished, of course, from helping themselves to any of the 'unearned' goodies of the wealthy)." I am very angry and it shows. I can feel how unprofessorial I must seem; looking into her eyes, I know I'll have to pay.

A few days later I receive a memo from the associate dean, expressing his concern about the way in which certain inappropriate "trumping moves" are being employed to "silence the more moderate members of the student body."

After the Civil War, when slaves were unowned—I hesitate to use the word emancipated even yet—they were also disowned: they were thrust out of the market and into a nowhere land that was not quite the mainstream labor market, and very much outside the marketplace of rights. They were placed beyond the bounds of valuation, in much the same way that the homeless are or that nomads and gypsies are, or tribal people who refuse to ascribe to the notion of private space and who refuse or are refused traditional jobs or stationary employment; they became like all those who cannot express themselves in the language of power and assertion and staked claims—all those who are nevertheless deserving of the dignity of social valuation, yet those who are so often denied survival itself.

I have been thinking about the unowning of blacks and their

consignment to some collective public state of mind, known alternatively as "menace" or "burden"—about the degree to which it might be that public and private are economic notions, i.e., that the right to privacy might be a function of wealth. I wonder, still smarting from my encounter with B., if the concept of intimacy (assuming privacy is related to the drive for intimacy) is premised on socioeconomic status. B. was upset, I think, not because I actually insulted an uncle whom she loved and of whose existence I had no knowledge, but because the class discussion had threatened the deeply vested ordering of her world. She was saying: haves are entitled to privacy, in guarded, moated castles; have-nots must be out in the open—scrutinized, seen with their hands open and empty to make sure they're not pilfering. The rationale went something like: the poor are envious of the rich; the rich worked hard to get where they are or have more valuable social characteristics and therefore deserve it; they have suffered. B. kept saying just that: "My family suffered for what they have."

Perhaps, I finally decided, the best way to overcome all these divisions is indeed to acknowledge the suffering of the middle and upper classes. I think, in an odd moment of connection, of my Great-Aunt Mary who, back in the 1920s, decided that her lot in life would be better if she pretended to be a white woman. She left home, moved to Cambridge, Massachusetts, and married into one of the state's wealthiest families. While the marriage lasted, she sent her decidedly black daughter by a previous marriage to live with her sister, my Great-Aunt Sophie. Thirty years later, I grew up under the rather schizophrenic tutelage of these two aunts, one of whom had been a charwoman at Harvard University even as the other lived in splendor with one of its largest contributors. The gulf and yet the connection between the sisters is almost indescribable. The explicit sacrifice of family for money by each; the bonds, the tendrils, the need seeping up in odd, nonfamilial and quasi-familial ("just like family" is how the aunt who was the maid was described by the rich young men whose rooms she cleaned) expectations that were denied, in guilt, in half-conscious deference to the corruption of real family bonds. Their only contact with love, attention, and intimacy was always at the expense of their own children or family—each was in peonage to the other. There was in this a real exchange of mutual suffering.

I think about B.'s uncle the slumlord and the tax I seem to have extorted in her life's bargain not to think about him with guilt. I wonder at the price her uncle must have charged to begin with, in the agreement not to think of him in unheroic terms. And if the consideration in such an exchange is more than just money and material gain—if the real transaction is not for "salary" but for survival itself, for love and family and connection, then this becomes a contract of primal dimensions.

If both rich and poor are giving up life itself and yet both are deeply dissatisfied, even suffering, they will never feel paid enough for their lot in life: what has gone on is not a trade or exchange, but a sacrifice. They have been victimized by a social construction that locks money into an impossible equation with "pricelessness," uniqueness. They have been locked into a socially constructed life-disappointment by the carrot of hope that somewhere, just ahead, there is satisfaction or sufficiency of payment. In the insistence on equation, more money eventually comes to equal the right to more intimacy, to have family. Yet since there is never "enough" money, family becomes out of reach, increasingly suspect as un-deserved. Family becomes not figurative wealth (as in "my children are my jewels"), but the sign of literal wealth—that is, those who have family have money, or they are suspect, their welfare seen as undeserved theft. Such a bargain is nothing more than a trade of self-esteem for money. Money buys self-esteem. If you're poor, you can't be happy because you're the object of revulsion and ridicule; if you're poor, you can't be satisfied because that's equated with laziness; if you're poor, you can't accept it as fate because poverty is your fault; and if you're poor, you have to resent the upper classes because competition—or economic revenge—is the name of the game, the only way out.

This is not merely a description of a class system; it is a formula for class war. Ideology aside, it is a formula bought by hopes of a lifestyle that will release us all from serfdom, show us into the promised land, and open the secrets of wealth and belonging. It is a formula that sprang forth from a hypothetical world in which the streets were paved with gold and where there were infinite resources. It is not a formula for a real world in which the reality of proximity comes crashing in on the illusion of privacy; or in which the desperation of isolation explodes into the mindless pleasantry of suburban good times. It is not a formula that works in a finite world.

I continue to ponder the equation of privacy with intimacy and of publicity with dispossession. Is not homelessness a metaphor for, as well as the manifestation of, collective disownership? I take my wondering to class and place it before my students. There are, I tell them, by conservative estimates 70,000 homeless people in New York City alone.[3] Although a disproportionate number of the homeless are black, this is not essentially a racial problem. Still I do see it as interwoven with the legacy of slavery, in its psychology of denial, in the notions of worth and unworthiness that go into the laws dealing with the homeless, in the ranking of "legitimate" needy and "illegitimate" homeless—these are familiar, cruel, blind games that make bastards and beggars of those who are in fact our family.

There are many homeless people on my street in New York, I tell my class full of non-New Yorkers. From the window of my home, I watch the well-heeled walk by the homeless. Some give money, most do not. From time to time, something especially visible or controversial happens with reference to the homelessness issue, and then the well-heeled give more or less, depending upon which way the sentiments are twisted. Mayor Koch puts up signs in the subway telling travelers not to give to panhandlers, that it's bad for tourism. Someone writes an editorial to say that the streets belong to taxpayers and that the homeless should pay rent for their use. A homeless child dies in her mother's arms. Small disenfranchisements give birth to large disenfranchisements, sympathies come and go.

There was a particularly well-publicized story about a homeless woman who gave birth to her child in the subway.[4] The state intervened and took away the child, saying that the mother was unfit because of her economic circumstances. The American Civil Liberties Union represented the mother in her attempt to maintain custody of the child. Although there is some law in New York to protect a newborn child from a mother's destitute circumstances, there is no law in the United States to provide a mother with the housing or health care or economic rights by which to provide for her child:

> While many European constitutions and the European Convention on Human Rights guarantee everyone the right to an education, the right to health care and even the right to a job or welfare payments, our Constitution does not.
>
> Our Bill of Rights guarantees the individual's right to be free of Governmental intrusions, not the individual's entitlements to Governmental support. The Supreme Court has uniformly rejected all claims to constitutional entitlements.[5]

My students always fight with me on this point. They tell me that this is the land of opportunity and everyone who works hard can get anything they want. (My students are all very hard workers.) I am not arguing, I tell them, that there are not laws that provide her with the opportunity to seek out a job and be successful at it. But if she does not find a job or is not successful at it, then she will have very little recourse, since the government has no obligation to provide for her. Friends working in the Department of Social Welfare in New York have told me that food stamps, for those lucky enough to get them (and most frequently this does not include the homeless), provided as of 1988 only 48 cents a meal. And in the wake of the October 1989 San Francisco earthquake, the Federal Emergency Management Agency actually turned the pre-quake homeless away from shelters, arguing that they were not the "crisis" homeless—those with homes destroyed by the quake—which FEMA was designed to serve. "'They have to differentiate between the quake-victim homeless and the pre-quake homeless,' [Barry Del Buono, executive director of the southern bay area's Emergency Housing Consortium] said, an exercise that underlines in his mind the inadequacy of federal response to homelessness in general."[6] It was also a distinction, conspicuous in the wake of the Reagan Administration's Housing and Urban Development Agency scandal, in which those privileged enough to have had comfortable property interests to begin with became the "truly needy" after all.

It is thus, I tell my angry students, that the homeless have no real right to conjugal benefits, to family of their own, to anything like happiness, or to the good health that is necessary in order to enjoy life, appreciate liberty, and pursue happiness. Furthermore, our national and collective failure to provide guaranteed rights to food, shelter and medical care has significant costs that they will have to deal with in their lifetimes: both as a constitutional or a public matter, and in the overwhelming power of specialized economic interests, the power of so-called private interests.

It is the last few minutes of class, and my students are hungry and edgy. They growl with the restless urge to go shopping. I, who also love to shop, nevertheless run on and on: I am concerned, I say, about the way in which hunger, lack of education, and homelessness are devastating our communities, and particularly women, children, and black communities. I am alarmed by the denial that the very right to survive is being withheld, through untextualized constitutionalisms, governmental restraint, states rights, to say nothing of indigency's being characterized as a matter of choice.

I tell stories of the deep-rooted commonplaceness of our economically rationalized notions of humanity. Once I took the F train to 14th Street, where I saw an old beggar woman huddled against a pillar. Behind me, a pretty little girl of about six exclaimed, "Oh, daddy, there's someone who needs our help." The child was then led off by the hand, by her three-piece-suited father who patiently explained that giving money to the woman directly was "not the way we do things." Then he launched into a lecture on the United Way as succor for the masses. It was a first lesson in distributive justice: conditioned passivity, indirection, distance— statistical need positioned against actual need. I walked behind them for a little way, listening to him teach: responsiveness to immediate need was being devalued as wrong.

A few moments later, I saw another homeless person lying on a bench in the subway. He lay extended along its length, one leg bent to the floor, the other stretched out on the bench; one arm flung across his chest, the other crooked under his head. He was dressed poorly, but not as badly as some street people. He had a little beard and a complacent face. His mouth hung open, and his eyes—his eyes were half closed, yet open. His eyes were a startlingly vacant blue, heavy-lidded yet staring at the subway station ceiling, intense yet with no particular focus. They were the eyes, I thought, of a dead man. Then, I rationalized, no, he couldn't be. He's just sleeping as my mother used to, with the whites of her eyes showing, when she was sitting in her chair and didn't really want to fall asleep.

Then I looked at the face of another man who had seen what I saw, both of us still walking, never stopping for a second. I tried to flash worry at him. But he was seeking reassurance, which he took from my face despite myself. I could see him rationalize his concern away, in the flicker of an eye. We walked behind each other upstairs and three blocks down Broadway before I lost him and the conspiracy of our solidarity. Thus the man on the subway bench died twice: in body and in the spirit I had murdered.

(Deep inside, I am made insecure by the wandering gazes of my students. I wonder, as they obviously do, if all this is really related to law.) I think all this is related, I say aloud, to our ability to interpret laws. What we had engaged in was not merely a rationalization but an imposition of order—the ironclad imposition of a world view requiring adherence to fictional visions cloaked in the comfort of familiar truth-denying truisms: "I know a black family and they're making it"; "My grandfather came to this country with nothing and . . ."; "He'll just use it for booze or drugs," even though "he" looks hungry and asks for money for food. We, the passersby of the dispossessed, formed a society of sorts. We made, by our actions, a comfortable social compact whose bounds we did not transgress. We also made a bargain of the man who lay dead. We looked at each other for confirmation that he was not dead; we, the grim living, determined to make profit of the dead. There is great power in being able to see the world as one will and then to have that vision enacted. But if being is seeing for the subject, then being seen is the precise measure of existence for the object.

After class, my students rush to the dean to complain. They are not learning real law, they say, and they want someone else to give them remedial classes. How will they ever pass the bar with subway stories? I am called to the dean's office. (Even in his distress, he does not forget to offer me sherry.) I explain: The discussion of economic rights and civil liberties usually assumes at least two things—that equal protection guarantees equality of opportunity "blindly" for the benefit of those market actors who have exercised rational choices in wealth-maximizing ways; and that those who make irrational non-profit-motivated choices have chosen, and therefore deserve, to be poor. But I take as given two counterfacts: that in the United States we subsidize the wealthy in all kinds of ways, and we do so in a way that directly injures the poor; and that neither the state of indigency nor the state of wealth is necessarily or even frequently the result of freely exercised choice. I think that this wide divergence of professed ideals and day-to-day reality creates in us some costly degree of social schizophrenia. Over time, our relation to both the marketplace and to a sense of liberty—our view of ourselves as both free and free agents—has become tremendously complicated.

The dean offers me biscuits and a soft white cheese. This past summer, I tell him, I drove across the country with a friend who had never visited the United States before. His conclusion was that "*Free* is a magic word in America." At that moment we were on the highway just outside Las Vegas. He pointed to a sign on a roadside diner: "Free! All you can eat, only $7.99."

The sign was more than a joke. It symbolized the degree to which much of what we call "freedom" is either contradictory or meaningless. For example, when the Supreme Court, in the case of *Buckley v. Valeo,* held not only that it is undesirable to constrain the expenditure of money in political elections, but that such expenditure *is speech,*[7] what did that mean? The *Buckley* court seems to have gone one step beyond holding that money is related to access to expensive media; it seems to imply that if one could speak freely (without pecuniary cost, that is) but could not spend money, then one would still be "censored." But if expression is commodified in this fashion, then can it not be bought and sold? Is money itself communicative and of what? Is the introduction of money as a concept of expression something like introducing usury into our love lives? Can speech be usurious? Is money a form of language, in the way we think of speech as language? What does this imply for oaths, rituals, the swearing of attachments? Can we now say "political money" and "artistic money" and mean the same as when we say "political speech" and "artistic expression"? What does free speech or freedom itself mean, if it really has a price?

Here's what troubles me: we use money to express our valuation of things. We express equivalencies through money, and in that process of laying claim we introduce a powerful leveling device. Through reducing to commodifiied equivalencies, we can bargain away what is undesirable; we can purchase and create a market for what is desirable. But given the way we use money, we also dispense with the necessity of valuing or considering (for this is, at heart, the definition of "consideration"[8] in our economically derived conception of contract) whatever is outside the market.

The sherry is beginning to go to my head. If, I demand somewhat sharply of the dean, political discourse is a market phenomenon, what happens to those members of the polis who are outside the market—who cannot or will not be bought and sold? And what indeed is the impact of buying and selling on the polis that is within the marketplace of ideas? I say, jabbing the air with my finger, that the answer to all of this is increasingly apparent in the construction of American political discourse, not just in things like political action committees lobbying for legislation but in the pernicious degree to which advertising agencies and wheel-of-fortune popularity polls determine the course of world events— elections, health care, invasions, and whole wars. The focus of politics is shifted, in other words, from concepts such as service and duty to purchasers and the buying public. It is wealth-representative politics, the equivalent of what Robert Ellickson so appallingly endorsed in his article "Cities and Homeowners' Associations."[9] The focus of politics is shifted from amassing the greatest amount of intellectual or social or erotic capital to the simple amassing of capital.

It enables the wealthiest presidential candidates to purchase the soft fuzzy image of "I am a real American" and to hoard it like commodity wealth. It allows us to spurn those who do not express themselves through expenditure as undeserving. It allows speechwriters to become the property of presidents, almost like wives. And the harm I see in all of this is that it puts reality up for sale and makes meaning fungible: dishonest, empty, irresponsible.

An image that comes to mind is that of movie star Jessica Lange, who testified to Congress about the condition of farms in the United States because she had *played* a farmer's wife.[10] What on earth does "testimony" mean in that context? Similarly, the movie *Mississippi Burning,* in making history subservient to sales, purchased wholesale a new rendering of reality, of history, of experience; it provided a profound illustration of this commodity quantification, as mercenarily motivated political *re*presentation. Public discourse becomes privatized, speech becomes moneyed, money becomes the measure of our lives.

I pause for breath. The dean says quietly, "But money is real," and refills my glass.

I fail to heed the warning in his voice and continue rashly: Jean Baudrillard has said that the "secret of gambling is that money does not exist as a value."[11] It seems to me that the secret of the Madison Avenue stakes for which our legal and political futures are played, is that words do not exist as a value in the constitution of political currency.

In our legal and political system, words like "freedom" and "choice" are forms of currency. They function as the mediators by which we make all things equal, interchangeable. It is, therefore, not just what "freedom" means, but the relation it signals between each individual and the world. It is a word that levels difference.

Similarly, money itself signals a certain type of relationship. So perhaps it is not just money that is the problem, but the relationship it signals. The Tit for Tat. The purchasing of our liberties; the peonage of our citizenship. As one analyst describes it,

> In bourgeois ideology, history is negated by the process of exchange; in the equalization brought about by the need to determine that one ware is worth another ware, and everything has its price, that this equals that, history is replaced by an eternal stasis where values remain constant in an ideological tit for tat where the equal sign ensures a never-ending binary equilibrium in which a change on one side of the equation is always balanced by the algebraically obligatory change on the other. Everything becomes a perfect metaphor for everything else, for in the end all equations say the same

thing and all equations say nothing. The emptiness behind the binary opposition is the emptiness behind the equation $0 = 0$. One thing is opposed to another thing in a two-fold opposition incapable of accommodating marginalities, third forces, or syntheses.[12]

The next day I get a note from the dean: he has received a variety of complaints about the polemical nature of my teaching and feels that my style is inappropriate in "the" law-school classroom. That night I go home, pour my own sherry, and write up my lecture notes for the next day's class, which on the next day I give, out of neither defiance nor defeat but because I don't have anything else to say.

In Brazil, I start, women are being asked to provide proof of sterilization before they can be hired. This comes in the wake of new legislation granting pregnant women four months of maternity leave. The law mostly affects poor rather than middle-class women, who "are able to return to work almost as quickly as they want because they can draw on a vast pool of poorly paid domestic servants, few of whom have social benefits . . . Such servants . . . also earned the right to maternity leave under the new laws. The Association for Domestic Workers in Rio De Janeiro believes this city alone has at least 300,000 nannies and maids, and the group has said it will now watch out for these women's interests."[13] In the United States we disguise the brutal directness of such bargains. We have employers in the private sector who, using arguments of fetal rights and protection, refuse to hire any woman capable of bearing a child.[14]

More troubling still, in the public sector we have the increasing phenomenon of sentencing hearings in which defendants in such cases as child abuse or rape are offered a "choice" between time in jail and sterilization.[15] The defendant is positioned as a purchaser, as "buying" her freedom by paying the price of her womb. And because that womb is in the position of money in this equivalence, it seems to many to be a form of expression, a voluntary and willing expenditure in the commerce of free choice.

One of the more peculiar examples of this last is the case of Roscoe Brown, a black South Carolinian convicted of rape.[16] In an arrangement styled to resemble contract, Brown was offered a commutation of his thirty-year prison sentence if he agreed to be castrated. (Castration is not merely male sterilization, as in a vasectomy; it is the actual removal of the testes and was outlawed in South Carolina, even for slaves, in 1789.[17]) After spending some time in prison, Brown asked to be castrated. Civil libertarians intervened, and the case was appealed to the Supreme Court of South Carolina. Fortunately, the court ruled that the castration "option" would amount to cruel and unusual punishment. But the issue is not settled in other states.[18]

The question this case raised for me was the interpretation of the words "contract," "freedom of choice," and "autonomy." "In 1985," wrote the *New York Times*, "three convicted rapists in South Carolina were resentenced after the state Supreme Court said a judge's decision to *let* them *choose* castration over prison violated their rights to be free from cruel and unusual punishment" (emphasis added).[19] The vocabulary of allowance and option seems meaningless in the context of an imprisoned defendant dealing with a judge whose power is absolute. Yet in January 1989, on the Oprah Winfrey show, I saw Roscoe Brown's white lawyer vehemently arguing that Brown should be *allowed* to be castrated, that the refusal to allow the arrangement to go forward was unwarranted state intrusion into his privacy.

I have some difficulty in getting my students to understand why this might not be good private contract. There is a siege of questions, from faces full of sincerity, mouths round with worried wonder. "Why do you want to rob the defendant of his last little bit of freedom," asks one. "But the defendant chose the castration," says another.

I continue: It is true that the transaction was structured as a contract. The power of that structure, however, transforms the discourse from one of public obligation and consensus into one of privatized economy. This positioning renders invisible the force of the state, and invisible the enormous judicial whimsy exercised in the selection of such a currency. It allows us to think that the state is not putting the cut on its citizenry; it allows us to sustain the fiction, the half truth, that the cut is coming from the defendant's own mouth. It is he who is begging to be castrated. It is, as Sacvan Bercovitch has observed, Ahab's notion of covenant: "I do not order ye: ye will it."[20]

"But what if the defendant really, really wanted it?" insists another student. I respond by asking: what does the defendant's "really, really" wanting mean in such a context? Is there room to distinguish desire as a matter of autonomy and free will from the desire to submit? After all, the scenario of someone's really, really imploring to be castrated is very close to what, in another realm of sexual affairs, is called "dominance and submission." But is what the defendant wants the issue anyway? What else is at stake in a case that bears the name *People [the public] v. Roscoe Brown*?

I don't think it serves any interest to window-dress the enormous power and dominance of the state in transforming the public interest in consistent and fair sentencing into one of private desire. The private desire that comes out of the defendant's mouth is in fact the private whimsy of the judge. The inversion of having the defendant beg to be dominated does not make the state any less dominating; nor does the inversion serve to make the state submissive. The force of the state remains: the backdrop of incarceration is generally understood as signifying something quite different from an invisible hand or an economic incentive. Yet what does seem to be obscured is the fact that the state is creating a situation where it determines who shall have children or not; and the fact that judges are exercising unprecedented latitude to impose sentences without statutory authority. The problem with this is not simply that it breaks the rules but that it substitutes for the public discourse and full airing of what sort of force the state should use. Yet it is all of us who are on trial in criminal sentencing proceedings: do we really, really want the state to require a ransom of body parts?

This notion of privately purchased public rights comes out at a more complicated level in the recent Supreme Court decision to permit a state to choose whether or not it will protect its children from abuse[21]—this from a court that does not hesitate to "protect" minors from information about birth control and abortion. Here governmental responsibility is less rooted in the jurisprudence of enduring social compact than in that of short-term private contract. This view would impose no duty at all unless the state, like some arm's-length private transactor, has undertaken the obligation, has assumed the debt. The logical corollary is that if the state has not been paid, if there has been no consideration to support the state's activity for its citizens, then there is no obligation.

What does the state have to be paid in order to intervene in protecting a citizen from abuse? It is not as simple as taxes. What would a child have to introduce as currency by which care of the state would be made a right? This begins to resemble the argument advanced by Carl Wellman in "The Growth of Children's Rights," where he maintains that children have no rights until they are grown enough to make the claim themselves.[22] Doesn't this mean that children don't have the price? Children and the poor make no considered bargains, and therefore they don't exist until they can buy and sell property. Before their emergence as property manipulators, there is no inducement, no exchange. The child's interests and the indigent's welfare become an incidental commodity to be purchased or not, an obligation for the government only if the right price is paid and the right laissez-faire subcontractors can be found to produce the thing purchased.

It is as if we lived in some supermarket state, a rich array of opportunities lining the shelves, the choices contingent only on the size of our budget. By this analogy, governmental goods and services all become fungible, equivalent. If there is no independent duty to provide welfare for our citizens, or if there is no community inspiration to provide it as a right, as a gift as some have characterized it, then the legislature becomes not the servant of the long-term public interest, but a slave to the buying public. Governmental actions become guided not by necessity but by trend. A municipal golf course, by such momentary consumerist vision, is as good a choice as child welfare (and certainly easier).

These bargained freedoms are perhaps nowhere better exemplified than in the words of President Bush's failed nominee for secretary of defense, John Tower. He promised, if you recall, to give up drinking if he got the job.[23] Not that he would give up drinking, period, or that he would give up drinking because it wrecked his homelife or because of public pressure, but that he would give it up *if*. Tit for tat. His sobriety was positioned as a commodity that we the public, through Congress, could purchase for the low, low price of our national defense. Like a used car-salesman who will throw in air conditioning if you write the check Now, he dangled his sobriety like a bribe. The overexpended mental state we call "privacy" is destructive, not just as a concern about constitutional protections or civil liberties but also in the marketplace. It shifts emphasis from commerce among people for real things and becomes instead a system that transforms, in Francis Bacon's imagery, the idol of the marketplace into the idol of the theater.

When I first started teaching consumer protection a decade ago, the mathematics of false advertising was simple. If the box or brochure said "100% cotton," you merely took the item in question and subtracted it from the words: any difference was the measure of your legal remedy. Sometimes you had to add in buyer's expertise or multiply the whole by seller's bad faith, but generally the whole reason people even took a class in consumer protection was that you didn't have to learn logarithms. Today, however, advertisers almost never represent anything remotely related to the reality of the product—or the politician—they are trying to sell; misrepresentation, the heart of false-advertising statutes, is very hard to prove. Increasingly, television ads are characterized by scenarios that neither mention the product nor contain a description of any sort. What fills the sixty seconds are "concepts" and diffuse images—images that used to be discursive, floating in the background, creating a mellow consumerist backdrop—which now dominate and direct content. Nothing is promised, everything evoked: warm fuzzy camera angles; "peak" experiences; happy pictures, mood-shaping music; almost always a smarmy, soft-peddling overvoice purring "This magic moment has been brought to you by . . ."

An example, in the form of another anecdote: about a year ago, I was sitting at home, installed before the television set. I was preparing for a class in consumer protection. The next day's assignment was false advertising, and I was shopping for an advertisement whose structure I could use as a starting point for discussion. An ad for Georges Marciano clothing flashed on the screen and dragged me in, first with the music, South African music of haunting urgency, the echoing simultaneity of nonlinear music, the syncopation of quickening-heartbeat percussive music, dragging the ear. In the picture, a woman with long blond hair in sunglasses ran from a crowd of photographers and an admiring public. The film was black and white, a series of frames jaggedly succeeding each other, like a patchwork of secretly taken stills. Sliced into the sequence of her running away were shots of the blond and her manager/bodyguard/boyfriend packing. He packed the passports and the handgun, she packed the Georges Marciano jeans. The climax came when she burst into a room of exploding flashbulbs—a blazing bath of white light.

The effect of this particular visual and aural juxtaposition was the appearance of the music as being inside the woman's head or her heart. The music was primal, dangerous, desperate. The woman's crisis of adoration framed the burning necessity of this pro-

37

found music, and the soaring universality of sound became white, female, privatized. The pulsing movement of the music elevated this event of narcissistic voyeurism to elemental importance. The music overflowed boundaries. Voices merged and surged; mood drifted and soared in the listening. African voices swelled and rose in the intricate music of knowledge, the wisdom of rhythm, the physics of echoing chasms bounded in intervals, the harmonic bells of voices striking each other in excitement and the wind, black African voices making music of the trees, of groundhogs, of whistling birds and pure chortling streams. It was generous shared music, open and eternal.

The pictures presented sought privacy. The chase was an invasion; the photographers pursued her private moments; she resisted even as her glamour consented. The viewer was drawn into desire to see her never-quite-revealed face, swept along by the urgency of her running to privacy, even as we never quite acknowledged her right to it. Thus the moment of climax, the flashing of cameras in her face (and ours, so completely have we identified with her), was one of release and relief. The music acted against the pictures. The mind resolved it queerly. The positive magnetic boundlessness of the music was turned into negative exposure. The run for privacy became an orgasmic peep show, the moment of negative exposure almost joyful.

In my lap, my textbook lay heavy, unattended pages drifting open to the Lanham Act:

False designations of origin and false descriptions forbidden:
. . . any person who shall affix, apply, or annex, or use in connection with any goods or services . . . a false designation of origin, or any false description or representation, including words or other symbols tending falsely to describe or represent the same, and shall cause such goods or services to enter into commerce, and any person who shall with knowledge of the falsity of such . . . description or representation cause or procure the same to be transported or used

in commerce . . . or used, shall be liable to a civil action . . . by any person who believes that he is or is likely to be damaged by the use of any such false description or representation.[24]

I have recounted this story at some length, not just for its illustrative contrast between the sight and the sound of an advertisement, but also because the relationship between the music and the pictures can serve as a metaphor for the tension between the political and marketplace dynamic that is my larger subject. I think that the invisible corruption of one by the other has consequences that are, ultimately, dehumanizing.

Ours is not the first generation to fall prey to false needs; but ours is the first generation of admakers to realize the complete fulfillment of the consumerist vision through the fine-tuning of sheer hucksterism. Surfaces, fantasies, appearances, and vague associations are the order of the day. So completely have substance, reality, and utility been subverted that products are purified into mere wisps of labels, floating signifiers of their former selves. "Coke" can as easily add life plastered on clothing as poured in a cup. Calculating a remedy for this new-age consumptive pandering is problematic. If people like—and buy—the enigmatic emptiness used to push products, then describing a harm becomes elusive. But it is elusive precisely because the imagery and vocabulary of advertising have shifted the focus from need to disguise. With this shift has come—either manipulated or galloping gladly behind—a greater public appetite for illusion and disguise. And in the wake of that has come an enormous shift of national industry, national resources, and national consciousness.

Some years ago, when I first started teaching, most of my students agreed that a nice L. L. Bean Baxter State Parka delivered without a label saying "L. L. Bean" was minor default indeed. Today I have to work to convince them that the absence of the label is not a major breach of contract; I have to make them think about what makes the parka "an L. L. Bean": its utility or its image? Its service to the wearer or its impact on those around the wearer? If masque becomes the basis of our bargains, I worry that we will forget the jazzy, primal King Lear-ish essence of ourselves from which wisdom springs and insight grows. I worry that we will create new standards of irrelevance in our lives, reordering social relations in favor of the luxurious—and since few of us can afford real luxury, blind greed becomes the necessary companion.

On a yet more complicated level, I worry that in accustoming ourselves to the emptiness of media fictions, we will have reconstructed our very notion of property. If property is literally the word or the concept used to describe it, then we have empowered the self-willed speaker not just as market actor but as ultimate Creator. If property is nothing more than what it evokes on the most intimate and subjective levels, then the inherence of its object is denied; the separateness of the thing that is property must be actively obliterated in order to maintain the privately sensational pleasantry of the mirror image. A habituated, acculturated blindness to the inherent quality of the people and things around us grows up, based on our safety from having to see. Our interrelationships with these things is not seen; their reasons for being are rendered invisible.

At the simplest level of market economics, the modern algebra of advertising deprives society of a concept of commodities as enduring. Sales of goods are no longer the subject of express or long-term promissory relationships—there is at best an implied warranty of merchantability at the fleeting moment of contract and delivery. Contract law's historic expectation interest[25] becomes even more thoroughly touch and go, in the most virulent tradition of caveat emptor. It is an unconscious narrowing of expectation to the extent that we lose our expectations. Thus, in some way, Coke and Pepsi lead us to obliterate the future, not just with empty calories but with empty promises. The illusion of a perky, sexy self is meaningless as to the reality of a can of corn syrup: but this substitution, this exchange of images, is a harm going beyond wasted money, tooth decay, or defeated notions of utility. The greater harm is that it is hypnotic, and culturally addictive.

In theory, contract doctrine is the currency of law used to impose economic order on human beings for certain purposes; defenses to contract formation such as fraud, duress, and undue influence are, I think, a theoretical attempt to impose an ordered humanity on economics. Increasingly, however, the day-to-day consumer purchases that form most of what is governed by contract have been characterized by a shift in popular as well as legal discourse: contract is no longer a three-party transliterative code, in which law mediates between profit and relationship, and in which property therefore remains linked to notions of shared humanity. Instead, consumerism is locked into a two-party, bipolar code that is little more mediative than a mirror. Money reflects law and law reflects money, unattached to notions of humanity. The neat jurisprudence of interpretive transposition renders the whole into a system of equations in which money = money, words = words (or law = law). The worst sort of mindless materialism arises. The worst sort of punitive literalism puts down roots.

Some time ago, my friend and colleague Dinesh Khosla traveled to Costa Rica for a conference. On his way back to the United States, he found himself in the airport behind throngs of Costa Ricans pushing five or six huge suitcases apiece. Dinesh stopped often to assist several different people; each time he was surprised by how light the suitcases felt. After this much of the story, I already imagined its end, filling the suitcases with media images of feathery coca leaves and dusty white powders. But I was wrong; it turned out that these travelers were all wealthy Costa Ricans going to Miami for the sole purpose of shopping. They planned to load up the suitcases with designer clothes and fancy consumables and cart them back home. I was reminded of the Sufi tale of the customs official who for years scrutinized the comings and goings of a man famed as a smuggler. For years he subjected each parcel to thorough searches, but all he ever found was straw. Many years later when they were both retired, he asked the smuggler where he had hidden the contraband all that time. The man replied: "I was smuggling straw." Dinesh's account made the conspicuous luxury of North American commodities into a similar form of invisible contraband, a sinfully expensive and indulgent drug.

One last anecdote: a little way down Broadway from the 14th Street subway station in Manhattan, there is a store called the Unique Boutique. Yards from the campus of New York University, it is a place where stylish coeds shop for the slightly frumpy, punky, slummy clothes that go so well with bright red lipstick and ankle-high black bootlets. One winter day I saw a large, bright, fun-colored sign hanging in the window: "Sale! Two-dollar overcoats. No bums, no booze." Offended, and not wanting to feel how offended I was, I turned my head away toward the street. There, in the middle of the intersection of Broadway and Washington Place, stood a black man dressed in the ancient remains of a Harris Tweed overcoat. His arms were spread-eagled as if to fly, though he was actually begging from cars in both directions. He was also drunk and crying and trying to keep his balance. Drivers were offended, terrified of disease or of being robbed. Traffic slowed as cars described wide avoiding arcs around him and his broad-winged pleading.

So the sign was disenfranchising the very people who most needed two-dollar overcoats, the so-called bums. Moreover, it was selling the image of the disenfranchised themselves. The store is a trendy boutique aimed at NYU's undergraduate population. It was selling an image of genteel poverty, of casual dispossession. It attracted those who can afford to slum in style: yet it simultaneously exploited the slum itself. It was segregationist in the same way that "whites only" signs are. And it was not just segregationist along race and class lines; it also stole the images of those who had nothing and styled it as a commodity (slumminess) to be sold to those who have much. It was the ultimate in short-term consumerist redundance: clothes do not just make the man, they would admit him into the clothing store itself.

In discussing the tension between liberty and authority, John Stuart Mill observed that self-government means "not the government of each by himself but of each by all the rest." Mill feared what he called the "tyranny of the majority" and cautioned,

> Protection . . . against the tyranny of the magistrate is not enough; there needs protection also against the tyranny of prevailing opinion and feeling; against the tendency of society to impose, by other means than civil penalties, its own ideas and practices as rules of conduct on those who dissent from them . . . how to make the fitting adjustment between individual independence and social control—is a subject on which nearly everything remains to be done.[26]

The tyranny of the majority has survived in liberal political theory as a justification for all manner of legislative restraint, particularly economic restraint. But what Mill did not anticipate was that the persuasive power of the forum itself would subvert the polis, as well as the law, to the extent that there is today precious little "public" left, just the tyranny of what we call the private. In this nation there is, it is true, relatively little force in the public domain compared to other nations, relatively little intrusive governmental interference. But we risk instead the life-crushing disenfranchisement of an entirely owned world. Permission must be sought to walk upon the face of the earth. Freedom becomes contractual and therefore obligated; freedom is framed by obligation; and obligation is paired not with duty but with debt.

From these notes, from the thoughts that eventually become this chapter, I condense an article for the *University of Maryland Law Review*. I mention neither deans nor the dissatisfaction of my students. It is quite warmly received, I am pleased to note, even when I press my ear to the men's room door for a long time afterwards.

The Death of the Profane

(a commentary on the genre of legal writing)

Buzzers are big in New York City. Favored particularly by smaller stores and boutiques, merchants throughout the city have installed them as screening devices to reduce the incidence of robbery: if the face at the door looks desirable, the buzzer is pressed and the door is unlocked. If the face is that of an undesirable, the door stays locked. Predictably, the issue of undesirability has revealed itself to be a racial determination. While controversial enough at first, even civil-rights organizations backed down eventually in the face of arguments that the buzzer system is a "necessary evil," that it is a "mere inconvenience" in comparison to the risks of being murdered, that suffering discrimination is not as bad as being assaulted, and that in any event it is not all blacks who are barred, just "17-year-old black males wearing running shoes and hooded sweatshirts."[1]

The installation of these buzzers happened swiftly in New York; stores that had always had their doors wide open suddenly became exclusive or received people by appointment only. I discovered them and their meaning one Saturday in 1986. I was shopping in Soho and saw in a store window a sweater that I wanted to buy for my mother. I pressed my round brown face to the window and my finger to the buzzer, seeking admittance. A narrow-eyed, white teenager wearing running shoes and feasting on bubble gum glared out, evaluating me for signs that would pit me against the limits of his social understanding. After about five seconds, he mouthed "We're closed," and blew pink rubber at me. It was two Saturdays before Christmas, at one o'clock in the afternoon; there were several white people in the store who appeared to be shopping for things for *their* mothers.

I was enraged. At that moment I literally wanted to break all the windows of the store and *take* lots of sweaters for my mother. In the flicker of his judgmental gray eyes, that saleschild had transformed my brightly sentimental, joy-to-the-world, pre-Christmas spree to a shambles. He snuffed my sense of humanitarian catholicity, and there was nothing I could do to snuff his, without making a spectacle of myself.

I am still struck by the structure of power that drove me into such a blizzard of rage. There was almost nothing I could do, short of physically intruding upon him, that would humiliate him the way he humiliated me. No words, no gestures, no prejudices of my own would make a bit of difference to him; his refusal to let me into the store—it was Benetton's, whose colorfully punnish ad campaign is premised on wrapping every one of the world's peoples in its cottons and woolens—was an outward manifestation of his never having let someone like me into the realm of his reality. He had no compassion, no remorse, no reference to me; and no desire to acknowledge me even at the estranged level of arm's-length transactor. He saw me only as one who would take his money and therefore could not conceive that I was there to give him money.

In this weird ontological imbalance, I realized that buying something in that store was like bestowing a gift, the gift of my commerce, the lucre of my patronage. In the wake of my outrage, I wanted to take back the gift of appreciation that my peering in the window must have appeared to be. I wanted to take it back in the form of unappreciation, disrespect, defilement. I wanted to work so hard at wishing he could feel what I felt that he would never again mistake my hatred for some sort of plaintive wish to be included. I was quite willing to disenfranchise myself, in the heat of my need to revoke the flattery of my purchasing power. I was willing to boycott Benetton's, random white-owned businesses, and anyone who ever blew bubble gum in my face again.

My rage was admittedly diffuse, even self-destructive, but it was symmetrical. The perhaps loose-ended but utter propriety of that rage is no doubt lost not just to the young man who actually barred me, but to those who would appreciate my being barred only as an abstract precaution, who approve of those who would bar even as they deny that they would bar *me*.

The violence of my desire to burst into Benetton's is probably quite apparent. I often wonder if the violence, the exclusionary hatred, is equally apparent in the repeated public urgings that blacks understand the buzzer system by putting themselves in the shoes of white storeowners—that, in effect, blacks look into the mirror of frightened white faces for the reality of their undesirability; and that then blacks would "just as surely conclude that [they] would not let [themselves] in under similar circumstances."[2] (That some blacks might agree merely shows that some of us have learned too well the lessons of privatized intimacies of self-hatred and rationalized away the fullness of our public, participatory selves.)

On the same day I was barred from Benetton's, I went home and wrote the above impassioned account in my journal. On the day after that, I found I was still brooding, so I turned to a form of catharsis I have always found healing. I typed up as much of the story as I have just told, made a big poster of it, put a nice colorful border around it, and, after Benetton's was truly closed, stuck it to their big sweater-filled window. I exercised my first-amendment right to place my business with them right out in the street.

So that was the first telling of this story. The second telling came a few months later, for a symposium on Excluded Voices sponsored by a law review. I wrote an essay summing up my feelings about being excluded from Benetton's and analyzing "how the rhetoric of increased privatization, in response to racial issues, functions as the rationalizing agent of public unaccountability and, ultimately, irresponsibility." Weeks later, I received the first edit. From the first page to the last, my fury had been carefully cut out. My rushing, run-on-rage had been reduced to simple declarative sentences. The active personal had been inverted in favor of the passive impersonal. My words were different; they spoke to me upsidedown. I was afraid to read too much of it at a time—meanings rose up at me oddly, stolen and strange.

A week and a half later, I received the second edit. All reference to Benetton's had been deleted because, according to the editors and the faculty adviser, it was defamatory; they feared harassment and liability; they said printing it would be irresponsible. I called them and offered to supply a footnote attesting to this as my personal experience at one particular location and of a buzzer system not limited to Benetton's; the editors told me that they were not in the habit of publishing things that were unverifiable. I could not but wonder, in this refusal even to let me file an affadavit, what it would take to make my experience verifiable. The testimony of an independent white bystander? (a requirement in fact imposed in U.S. Supreme Court holdings through the first part of the century[3]).

Two days *after* the piece was sent to press, I received copies of the final page proofs. All reference to my race had been eliminated because it was against "editorial policy" to permit descriptions of physiognomy. "I realize," wrote one editor, "that this was a very personal experience, but any reader will know what you must have looked like when standing at that window." In a telephone conversation to them, I ranted wildly about the significance of such an omission. "It's irrelevant," another editor explained in a voice

47

gummy with soothing and patience; "It's nice and poetic," but it doesn't "advance the discussion of any principle . . . This is a law review, after all." Frustrated, I accused him of censorship; calmly he assured me it was not. "This is just a matter of style," he said with firmness and finality.

Ultimately I did convince the editors that mention of my race was central to the whole sense of the subsequent text; that my story became one of extreme paranoia without the information that I am black; or that it became one in which the reader had to fill in the gap by assumption, presumption, prejudgment, or prejudice. What was most interesting to me in this experience was how the blind application of principles of neutrality, through the device of omission, acted either to make me look crazy or to make the reader participate in old habits of cultural bias.

That was the second telling of my story. The third telling came last April, when I was invited to participate in a law-school conference on Equality and Difference. I retold my sad tale of exclusion from Soho's most glitzy boutique, focusing in this version on the law-review editing process as a consequence of an ideology of style rooted in a social text of neutrality. I opined:

> Law and legal writing aspire to formalized, color-blind, liberal ideals. Neutrality is the standard for assuring these ideals; yet the adherence to it is often determined by reference to an aesthetic of uniformity, in which difference is simply omitted. For example, when segregation was eradicated from the American lexicon, its omission led many to actually believe that racism therefore no longer existed. Race-neutrality in law has become the presumed antidote for race bias in real life. With the entrenchment of the notion of race-neutrality came attacks on the concept of affirmative action and the rise of reverse discrimination suits. Blacks, for so many generations deprived of jobs based on the color of our skin, are now told that we ought to find it demeaning to be hired, based on the color of our skin. Such is the silliness of simplistic either-or inversions as remedies to complex problems.
>
> What is truly demeaning in this era of double-speak-no-evil is

going on interviews and not getting hired because someone doesn't think we'll be comfortable. It is demeaning not to get promoted because we're judged "too weak," then putting in a lot of energy the next time and getting fired because we're "too strong." It is demeaning to be told what we find demeaning. It is very demeaning to stand on street corners unemployed and begging. It is downright demeaning to have to explain why we haven't been employed for months and then watch the job go to someone who is "more experienced." It is outrageously demeaning that none of this can be called racism, even if it happens only to, or to large numbers of, black people; as long as it's done with a smile, a handshake and a shrug; as long as the phantom-word "race" is never used.

The image of race as a phantom-word came to me after I moved into my late godmother's home. In an attempt to make it my own, I cleared the bedroom for painting. The following morning the room asserted itself, came rushing and raging at me through the emptiness, exactly as it had been for twenty-five years. One day filled with profuse and overwhelming complexity, the next day filled with persistently recurring memories. The shape of the past came to haunt me, the shape of the emptiness confronted me each time I was about to enter the room. The force of its spirit still drifts like an odor throughout the house.

The power of that room, I have thought since, is very like the power of racism as status quo: it is deep, angry, eradicated from view, but strong enough to make everyone who enters the room walk around the bed that isn't there, avoiding the phantom as they did the substance, for fear of bodily harm. They do not even know they are avoiding; they defer to the unseen shapes of things with subtle responsiveness, guided by an impulsive awareness of nothingness, and the deep knowledge and denial of witchcraft at work.

The phantom room is to me symbolic of the emptiness of formal equal opportunity, particularly as propounded by President Reagan, the Reagan Civil Rights Commission and the Reagan Supreme Court. Blindly formalized constructions of equal opportunity are the creation of a space that is filled in by a meandering stream of unguided hopes, dreams, fantasies, fears, recollections. They are the presence of the past in imaginary, imagistic form—the phantom-roomed exile of our longing.

It is thus that I strongly believe in the efficacy of programs and paradigms like affirmative action. Blacks are the objects of a constitutional omission which has been incorporated into a theory of neutrality. It is thus that omission is really a form of expression, as oxymoronic as that sounds: racial omission is a literal part of original intent; it is the fixed, reiterated prophecy of the Founding Fathers. It is thus that affirmative action is an affirmation; the affirmative act of hiring—or hearing—blacks is a recognition of individuality that re-places blacks as a social statistic, that is profoundly interconnective to the fate of blacks and whites either as sub-groups or as one group. In this sense, affirmative action is as mystical and beyond-the-self as an initiation ceremony. It is an act of verification and of vision. It is an act of social as well as professional responsibility.

The following morning I opened the local newspaper, to find that the event of my speech had commanded two columns on the front page of the Metro section. I quote only the opening lines: "Affirmative action promotes prejudice by denying the status of women and blacks, instead of affirming them as its name suggests. So said New York City attorney Patricia Williams to an audience Wednesday."[4]

I clipped out the article and put it in my journal. In the margin there is a note to myself: eventually, it says, I should try to pull all these threads together into yet another law-review article. The problem, of course, will be that in the hierarchy of law-review citation, the article in the newspaper will have more authoritative weight about me, as a so-called "primary resource," than I will have; it will take precedence over my own citation of the unverifiable testimony of my speech.

I have used the Benetton's story a lot, in speaking engagements at various schools. I tell it whenever I am too tired to whip up an original speech from scratch. Here are some of the questions I have been asked in the wake of its telling:

Am I not privileging a racial perspective, by considering only the black point of view? Don't I have an obligation to include the "salesman's side" of the story?

Am I not putting the salesman on trial and finding him guilty of racism without giving him a chance to respond to or cross-examine me?

Am I not using the store window as a "metaphorical fence" against the potential of his explanation in order to represent my side as "authentic"?

How can I be sure I'm right?

What makes my experience the real black one anyway?

Isn't it possible that another black person would disagree with my experience? If so, doesn't that render my story too unempirical and subjective to pay any attention to?

Always a major objection is to my having put the poster on Benetton's window. As one law professor put it: "It's one thing to publish this in a law review, where no one can take it personally, but it's another thing altogether to put your own interpretation right out there, just like that, uncontested, I mean, with nothing to counter it."[5]

II

Trial by Text

A Sequence of Sublimation

4

Teleology on the Rocks

(or spirit-murdering the messenger)

My abiding recollection of being a student at Harvard Law School is the sense of being invisible. I spent three years wandering in a murk of unreality. I observed large, mostly male bodies assert themselves against one another like football players caught in the gauzy mist of intellectual slow motion. I stood my ground amid them, watching them deflect from me, unconsciously, politely, as if I were a pillar in a crowded corridor. Law school was for me like being on another planet, full of alienated creatures with whom I could make little connection. The school created a dense atmosphere that muted my voice to inaudibility. All I could do to communicate my existence was to posit carefully worded messages into hermetically sealed, vacuum-packed blue books, place them on the waves of that foreign sea, and pray that they would be plucked up by some curious seeker and understood.

Perhaps there were others who felt what I felt. Perhaps we were all aliens, all silenced by the dense atmosphere. Thinking that made me feel, ironically, less isolated. It was not merely that I was black and female, but a circumstance external to myself that I, and the collective, could not help internalizing.

When I became a law professor, I found myself on yet another planet: a planet with a sun as strong as a spotlight and an atmosphere so thin that my slightest murmur would travel for miles, skimming from ear to ear to ear, merrily distorting and refracting as it went. Again I comforted myself that my sense of alienation and now-heightened visibility were not inherent to my blackness and my femaleness, but an uncomfortable atmospheric condition afflicting everyone. But at the gyroscopic heart of me, there was and is a deep realization that I have never left the planet earth. I know that my feelings of exaggerated visibility and invisibility are the product of my not being part of the larger cultural picture. I know too that the larger cultural picture is an illusion, albeit a powerful one, concocted from a perceptual consensus to which I am not a party; and that while these perceptions operate as dictators of truth, they are after all merely perceptions.

My best friend from law school is a woman named C. For months now I have been sending her drafts of this book, filled with many shared experiences, and she sends me back comments and her own associations. Occasionally we speak by telephone. One day, after reading the beginning of this chapter, she calls me up and tells me her abiding recollection of law school. "Actually it has nothing to do with law school," she says.

"I'll be the judge of that," I respond.

"Well," she continues, "it's about the time I was held at gunpoint by a SWAT team."

It turns out that during one Christmas vacation C. drove to Florida with two friends. Just outside Miami they stopped at a roadside diner. C. ordered a hamburger and a glass of milk. The milk was sour, and C. asked for another. The waitress ignored her. C. asked twice more and was ignored each time. When the waitress finally brought the bill, C. had been charged for the milk and refused to pay for it. The waitress started to shout at her, and a highway patrolman walked over from where he had been sitting and asked what was going on. C. explained that the milk was sour and that she didn't want to pay for it. The highway patrolman ordered her to pay and get out. When C. said he was out of his jurisdiction, the patrolman pulled out his gun and pointed it at her.

("Don't you think" asks C. when I show her this much of my telling of her story, "that it would help your readers to know that the restaurant was all white and that I'm black?" "Oh, yeah," I say. "And six feet tall.")

Now C. is not easily intimidated and, just to prove it, she put her hand on her hip and invited the police officer to go ahead and shoot her, but before he did so *he* should try to drink the damn glass of milk, and so forth and so on for a few more descriptive rounds. What cut her off was the realization that, suddenly and silently, she and her two friends had been surrounded by eight SWAT team officers, in full guerrilla gear, automatic weapons drawn. Into the pall of her ringed speechlessness, they sent a local black policeman, who offered her twenty dollars and begged her to pay and be gone. C. describes how desperately he was perspiring as he begged and, when she didn't move, how angry he got—how he accused her of being an outside agitator, that she could come from the North and go back to the North, but that there were those of "us" who had to live here and would pay for her activism.

C. says she doesn't remember how she got out of there alive or why they finally let her go; she supposes that the black man paid for her. But she does remember returning to the car with her two companions and the three of them crying, sobbing, all the way to Miami. "The damnedest thing about it," C. said, "was that no one was interested in whether or not I was telling the truth. The glass was sitting there in the middle of all this, with the curdle hanging on the sides, but nobody would taste it because a black woman's lips had touched it."

I think of C. a lot when I write, and of her truth-telling glass of sour, separated milk. The curd clinging to the sides; her words curdled in the air. The police with guns drawn, battlelines drawn, the contest over her contestation; the proof of the milk in the glass inadmissible, unaccounted for, unseen. The insolent fact of her words; defiant presumption as the subject for a war over the invisible. The thing I like best about C. is her insistence always to be exactly wherever she is in the universe. I am thankful she survives the messes she gets herself into.

In the early morning hours of December 20, 1986, three black men left their stalled car on Cross Bay Parkway, in Queens, New York, and went to look for help. They walked into the neighborhood of Howard Beach, entered a pizzeria, ordered pizzas, and sat down to eat. An anonymous caller to the police reported their presence as "black troublemakers"; a patrol car came, found no trouble, and left. After the men had eaten, they left the pizzeria and were immediately surrounded by a group of eight to ten white teenagers who taunted them with racial epithets. The white youths chased the black men a distance of approximately three miles, beating them severely along the way. One of the black men died, struck by a car as he tried to flee across a highway; another suffered permanent blindness in one eye.[1]

In the heated public controversy that ensued, as much of the attention centered on the community of Howard Beach, where the assault took place, as on the assaulters themselves. The chief cause of such attention was a veritable Greek chorus (composed of lawyers for the defendants as well as resident after resident of Howard Beach) repeating and repeating that the mere presence of three black men in that part of town at that time of night was reason enough to drive them out: "They had to be starting trouble"; "We're a strictly white neighborhood"; "What were they doing here in the first place?"[2] The pinnacle of legitimacy to which these particular questions rose is, to me, the most frightening aspect of this case. When Mayor Ed Koch was asked why he thought the young men were walking around Howard Beach, he dignified the question with the following answer: "I don't know ... And neither did the 12 or so people who beat them. Because they didn't ask them. They didn't talk to them." One is left to speculate: if the attackers, those self-appointed gatekeepers, *had* asked and got an answer like "none of your business," would they then have been entitled to beat and attack out of public-spirited zeal? And, one wonders further, what explanation would have been sufficient to allow black males continued unmolested passage into the sanctified byways of Howard Beach?

Although the immensely segregationist instincts behind such statements may be evident, it is worth making explicit some of the presuppositions behind them:

> Everyone who lives here is white.
>
> No black could live here.
>
> No one here has a black friend.
>
> No white would employ a black here.
>
> No black is permitted to shop here.
>
> No black is ever up to any good.

Moreover, these presuppositions themselves are premised on certain lethal philosophies of life:

Better safe than sorry. "Are we supposed to stand around and do nothing, while these blacks come into our area and rob us?" asked one woman of a reporter, in the wake of the Howard Beach attack. " 'We ain't racial,' said 20-year old Michael Habe, who has lived in Howard Beach all his life. 'We just don't want to get robbed.' "[3] The hidden implication of such statements is that to be safe is not to be sorry; and to be safe is to be white and to be sorry is to be associated with blacks. Thus safety and sorrow, which are inherently alterable and random, are linked to inalterable essences. The expectation that uncertain conditions are immutable is a formula for frustration, a belief that feeds a sense of powerlessness. The rigid determinism of placing in the disjunctive things that are not in fact is a setup for betrayal by the very nature of reality.

The national repetition that white neighborhoods are safe and blacks bring sorrow is an incantation of powerlessness. And with the upsidedown logic of all irrational incantations, it imports a concept of white safety that necessarily endangers the lives as well as the rights of blacks.

It is also an incantation of innocence and guilt, related to the accusations that affirmative-action programs allow (presumably guilty?) blacks to displace innocent whites.[4] (Although even assuming that "innocent whites" are being displaced by blacks, does that make blacks less innocent in the pursuit of education and jobs?) In fact, in the wake of Howard Beach, police and the press rushed to service the public's interest in showing what unsavory dispositions the victims had. But the point that gets overlooked in all this is how racial slurs and attacks objectify people: "the incident could have happened to any black person who was there at that time and place. This is the crucial aspect of the Howard Beach affair that is now being muddied in the media. Bringing up Griffith's [the dead man] alleged involvement in a shooting incident a couple of years ago is another way of saying 'He was a criminal who deserved it.'"[5] It is thus that a pernicious game of Victim Responsibility was set in motion, itself slave to society's stereotypes of good and evil.

It does no one much good, however, to make race issues contests for some Holy Grail of innocence. In my own lifetime, segregation and antimiscegenation laws were still on the books in many states. During the lifetimes of my parents and grandparents, and for several hundred years before them, laws were used to prevent blacks from learning to read, write, own property, or vote; blacks were, by constitutional mandate, outlawed from the hopeful, loving expectations that come from being treated as a whole, rather than three-fifths of a person. When every resource of a wealthy nation is put to such destructive ends, it will take more than a few generations to mop up the mess.

We are all inheritors of that legacy, whether new to this world or new to this country, for it survives as powerful and invisibly reinforcing structures of thought, language, and law. Thus generalized notions of innocence and guilt have little place in the struggle for transcendence; there is no blame among the living for the dimensions of this historic crime, this national tragedy.[6] There is, however, responsibility for never forgetting another's history, for making real the psychic obliteration that does live on as a factor in shaping relations not just between blacks and whites (Mayor Koch asserted, during a trip to Howard Beach intended to promote racial harmony, that "most robberies were committed by blacks"), or between blacks and blacks (the mayor went on, moreover, to reassure his all-white audience that "most of the victims were black, too"[7]), but between whites and whites as well. Whites must take into account how much this history has projected onto blacks all criminality and all of society's ills. It has become the means for keeping white criminality invisible.

A prejudiced society is better than a violent society. The attempt to split bias from violence has been this society's most enduring and fatal rationalization. Prejudice does hurt, however, just as absence of it can nourish and shelter. Discrimination can repel and vilify, ostracize and alienate. Any white person who doesn't believe it should spend a week telling everyone she meets that one of her parents or grandparents was black. I had a friend in college who discovered, having lived her life as a red-haired, gray-eyed white person, that she was one-sixteenth black (may-as-well-be-all-black, in other words). Before my eyes and despite herself, she began to externalize all the unconscious baggage that "black" bore for her, the self-hatred that racism is. She did not think of herself as a racist—nor had I—but she literally wanted to jump out of her skin, shed her flesh, start life over again. She confided that she felt fouled and betrayed. (She also asked me if I had ever felt this way. Her question dredged from some deep corner of my mind the recollection of feeling precisely that when, at the age of three or so, some white playmates explained that God had mixed mud with the pure clay of life in order to make me.)

In the Vietnamese language, "the word 'I' (*toi*) . . . means 'your servant'; there is no 'I' as such. When you talk to someone you establish a relationship."[8] Such a self-concept is a way of experiencing the other, of ritualistically sharing the other's essence and cherishing it. In our culture, seeing and feeling the dimension of harm done by separating self from other requires somewhat more work.[9] Very little in our language or culture encourages looking at others as parts of ourselves. With the imperviously divided symmetry of the marketplace, gains for whites are not felt as gains for blacks, and social costs to blacks are simply not seen as costs to whites. (One of the starkest examples of this has been the disastrous delay in responding to the AIDS epidemic: as long as it was seen to be an affliction of Haitians, Hispanics, Africans, and other marginalized groups such as drug users and homosexuals, its long-term implications were all but ignored.[10])

What complicates this structure of thought insofar as racism is concerned, however, is that the distancing does not stop with the separation of the white self from the black other. In addition, the cultural domination of blacks by whites means that the black self is placed at a distance even from itself, as in my example of blacks being asked to put themselves in the position of the white shopkeepers who scrutinize them. So blacks in a white society are conditioned from infancy to see in themselves only what others, who despise them, see.[11]

It is true that conforming to what others see in us is any child's—black or white—way of becoming socialized.[12] It is what makes children in our society appear so gullible, impressionable, "impolitely" honest, blindly loyal, and charming to the ones they imitate. Yet this conformity also describes a way of being that relinquishes the power of independent ethical choice. Although such a relinquishment can have desirable consequences, it presumes a fairly homogeneous social context in which values are collectively shared and enforced. (Is it any wonder that western anthropologists and ethnographers, for whom adulthood is manifested by the exercise of individual ethical judgment, are so quick to denounce tribal collective cultures as "childlike"?)

Our culture, in contrast, does not make all selves or I's the servants of others, but only some. Thus some I's are defined as "your servant," some as "your master." The struggle for the self becomes not a true mirroring of self-in-other, but a hierarchically inspired series of distortions, where some serve without ever being served; some master with no sense of what it is to be mastered; and almost everyone hides from the fact of this vernacular domination by clinging to the legally official definition of an I meaning "your equal."

In such an environment, relinquishing the power of individual ethical judgment to a collective ideal risks psychic violence, an obliteration of the self through domination by an all-powerful other. It is essential at some stage that the self be permitted to retreat into itself and make its own decisions with self-love and self-confidence. What links child abuse, the mistreatment of women, and racism is the massive external intrusion into psyche that dominating powers impose to keep the self from ever fully seeing itself.[13] Since the self's power resides in another, little faith is placed in the true self, in one's own experiential knowledge. It is thus that children's, women's, and blacks' power is actually reduced to the "intuitive" rather than to the real: social life is based primarily on the imaginary.[14] Furthermore, since it is difficult constantly to affirm the congruence of one's own self-imagining with what the other is thinking of the self—and since even that correlative effort is usually kept within limited family, neighborhood, or religious-racial boundaries—encounters cease even to be social, and are merely presumptuous, random, and disconnected.

This peculiarly distancing standpoint allows dramas—particularly racial ones like Howard Beach—to unfold in scenarios weirdly unrelated to the incidents that generated them: at one end

of the spectrum is a laissez-faire response that privatizes the self in
order to remain unassailably justified in any and all activities. At
the other is a pattern of generalizing particular others into terrifyingly uncontrollable "domains" of public wilderness against
whom proscriptive barriers must be built.

The prototypical scenario of the privatized response to issues
of racial accountability might be imagined as follows:

> *Cain:* Abel's part of town is tough turf.
>
> *Abel:* It upsets me when you say that; you have never been to my
> part of town. As a matter of fact, my part of town is a leading sup-
> plier of milk and honey.
>
> *Cain:* The news that I'm upsetting you is too upsetting for me to
> handle. You were wrong to tell me of your upset because now I'm
> terribly upset.
>
> *Abel:* I felt threatened first. Listen to me. Take your distress as a
> measure of my own and empathize with it. Don't ask me to recant
> and apologize in order to carry this conversation further.

What is problematic in this sort of discourse is that the issue of
Cain's calling Abel's turf tough gets transformed into a discussion
of how Abel challenges that statement. Though there is certainly
an obligation to be careful in addressing others, the obligation to
protect the feelings of the other gets put above the need to protect
one's own; the self becomes subservient to the other, with no rec-
iprocity; and the other becomes a whimsical master. Abel's feelings get deflected in deference to Cain's; and Abel bears the
double burden of raising his issue correctly and of being responsible for its impact on Cain should Cain take it wrong. Cain is
rendered unaccountable, as long as the deflection continues, for
both the care with which he expressed the initial statement and
his own response to Abel, because in the end it is all Abel's fault.

Morality and responsiveness thus become split as Abel
drowns in responsibility for valuative quality control; and Cain
rests on the higher ground of a value-neutral zone. For example,

here is more of the encounter between Mayor Koch and the black congregation in Queens: "In discussing the Howard Beach incident, Mr. Koch asked the people in Morning Star [Baptist Missionary Church] whether, if three white men were walking in Harlem after midnight, 'do you believe they would be absolutely safe?' 'Yes,' the congregation chorused. The Mayor did not think so, but said he was glad they did."[15] In reading this account, I had trouble figuring out what the mayor's motivation was in asking such a question. Was he implying that blacks would support racial violence if it occurred in reverse? And if he were implicitly asking for black understanding based on a presumed condoning of black-on-white violence, then wasn't he really asking blacks to understand that white-on-black violence isn't so hard to understand after all? That there is a sympathetic chord to be struck if only blacks would look deeply enough into themselves? If, as the story implies, Koch thought the congregation would say no, what he then would have "shown" (of himself, of institutional posture, if not of the teleological essence of things) is that racism is just human nature after all; that public absolution is simply a matter of pointing a finger and wailing "well, you did it too"; and that death in turf wars isn't racism but part of life.

Caught in conversations like this, blacks as well as whites will feel keenly circumscribed. Perhaps most people never intend to be racist or oppressive or insulting, but by describing zones of vulnerability, by setting up regions of conversational taboo and fences of rigidified politeness, the unintentional exile of individuals as well as races may be quietly accomplished and avoided indefinitely. A strong example of the degree to which racism may be transformed into issues of "courtesy" is the following: when Alan Hendrickse, the leader of the mixed-race chamber of the South African parliament, decided to go swimming at a "whites only" beach, President Botha demanded that he either apologize or resign, or else he would "have no choice but to dissolve the Parliament . . . When he started marching in on the beach, he embarrassed me and broke the rules of Parliament . . . It is a question of procedure."[16]

Another scenario of the distancing of the self from responsibility for racism is the inventing of some vast wilderness of others (composed, in the context of Howard Beach, of violent seventeen-year-old black males in running shoes and hooded sweatshirts) against which the self must barricade itself. It is this fear of the overwhelming other that animates many of the more vengefully racist comments from Howard Beach: "'We're a strictly white neighborhood,' Michelle Napolitano said. 'They had to be starting trouble.'"[17]

Not only do such attitudes set up angry, excluding boundaries, but they imply that the *failure* to protect and avenge is a bad policy, bad statesmanship, an embarrassment. They raise the stakes to a level beyond that of the unexpressed rage arising from the incident itself, as in the example of Cain and Abel. The need to avenge becomes a separate issue of protocol, of etiquette—not a loss of a piece of the self, which is the real cost of real tragedies, but a loss of self-regard. By "self-regard" I don't mean self-concept, as in self-esteem; I mean, again, that view of the self which is attained when the self steps outside to regard and evaluate the self; in which the self is watched by an imaginary other, a projection of the opinions of real others; in which "I" means "your master," not your servant; in which refusal of the designated other to be dominated is felt as a personal assault. Thus the failure to avenge is treated as a loss of self-regard; it is used as a psychological metaphor for whatever trauma or original assault constituted the real loss to the self.[18] It is more abstract, more illusory, more constructed, more invented—and therefore potentially less powerful than real assault, in that it can with effort be unlearned as a source of vulnerability. This is the real message of the attempt to distinguish between prejudice and violence: names, as in the old sticks-and-stones ditty, or structures of thought, while undeniably influential, can be unlearned—or undone—as motivations for future destructive action. But as long as they are not unlearned, the exclusionary power of free-floating emotions make their way into the gestalt of prosecutorial and jury disposition and into what the law sees as a crime, sees as relevant, justified, provoked, or excusable.[19] Laws become described and enforced in the spirit of our prejudices.

The evidentiary rules of legitimating turf wars. Here is a description of the arraignment of three of the white teenagers involved in the Howard Beach beatings:

> The three defense lawyers also tried to cast doubt on [the prosecutor's] account of the attack. The lawyers questioned why the victims walked all the way to the pizza parlor if, as they said, their mission was to summon help for their car, which broke down three miles away . . . At the arraignment, the lawyers said the victims passed two all-night gas stations and several other pizza shops before they reached the one they entered . . . A check yesterday of area restaurants, motels and gas stations listed in the Queens street directory found two eating establishments, a gas station and a motel that all said they were open and had working pay phones on Friday night . . . A spokesman for the New York Telephone Company, Jim Crosson, said there are six outdoor pay telephones along Cross Bay Boulevard on the way to the pizzeria.[20]

In the first place, lawyers must wonder about the relevance of all this. Does the answer to any of the issues raised by the defense team serve to prove that these black men assaulted, robbed, threatened, or molested these white men? Or even that the white men *reasonably* feared such a fate? The investigation into how many phone booths to a mile of the course establishes no reason why the white men would fear the black men's presence; its relevance is only to prove that there is no reason a black man should just walk, just wander, around Howard Beach. This is no mere semantic detail: it is central to understanding the real burdensomeness of proof in such cases. It is this unconscious restructuring of burdens of proof into burdens of white over black that permits people who believe they are not racist to condone and commit crimes of genocidal magnitude. It is easy to generalize all this away as linguistically technical or as society's sorrow ("I'm so tired of hearing blacks say that society's done them wrong," said a student of mine). But these gyrations kill with their razor-toothed presumption; it is we lawyers—who, with doctors, are the modern wizards and medicine people—who must define innocent murderousness as crime.

In addition, investigations into "closer" (really farther—from Howard Beach) alternatives eclipse the possibility of other explanations; they assume that the young black men were not headed for the subway, which in fact was not far from and in the same direction as the pizzeria; they assume that black people (and I have never heard the same public assumption about white people) need documented reasons for excursioning into neighborhoods where they do not live, for venturing beyond the bounds of the zones to which they are supposedly confined.

It is interesting to contrast this implicit requirement of documentation imposed on blacks walking down public streets in Howard Beach with the explicit lack of such a requirement in the contemporaneous public discussions of the murder of Eleanor Bumpurs. In that case, seven white officers burst into the private space of Mrs. Bumpurs' apartment and, while attempting an illegal eviction, shot and killed her (see Chapter 7). Here the availability of other, less intrusive options was consistently dismissed by lawmakers as presumption and idle hindsight; such rejection of other alternatives dismissed the burden that police officers have to use the least harmful method. In the context of Howard Beach, however, such an analysis implicitly imposes a burden on nonresidents of neighborhoods to stay out unless absolutely necessary; it implies that there is harm in the presence of those who do not "own" something specific there. Both analyses skirt the propriety and necessity of public-sector responsibility; both redefine public accountability in privatized terms. And whether those privatized terms operate to restrict or expand accountability is seemingly dichotomized according to the race of the actors.

Finally, this factualized hypothesizing was part of a news story, which means that the news—or what is purported to be fact—is in fact hypothesis, based on such silent premises as: they should have used the first phone they came to; they should have eaten at the first restaurant they found; they should have gone into a gas station and asked for help; surely they should have had the cash and credit cards to do any of the above or else not travel in strange neighborhoods. In elevating these to relevant issues, the *Times* only mirrored what was being done in the courtroom.

Privatized innocence and publicized guilt. In his ill-fated trip to the town of Jamaica in Queens, purportedly to soothe tensions, Mayor Koch asked black churchgoers to understand the disgruntlement of residents of Howard Beach about the interracial march, by fourteen hundred protestors, through "their" streets. He asked them how they would feel if fourteen hundred white people took to the streets of Jamaica (a mostly black neighborhood) in such a march.[21] This question, from the chief executive of New York City's laws, accepts a remarkable degree of possessiveness about public streets—possessiveness, furthermore, that is racially and not geographically bounded. Koch was, in effect, pleading for acceptance of the privatization of public space. This is the de facto equivalent of segregation; it is exclusion in the guise of deep-moated property "interests" and "values." Lost is the fact that the object of discussion, the street, is public.

Furthermore, the structure of Koch's question implies that fourteen hundred black people took to the streets of Howard Beach: in fact it was a well-integrated crowd, blacks, browns, and whites, Howard Beach residents and others. Apparently crowds in New York are subject to the unwritten equivalent of Louisiana's race statutes (1/72 black blood renders the whole black) or of the Ku Klux Klan's "contamination by association" ("blacks and white-blacks" was how one resident of Forsythe County, the Georgia equivalent of Howard Beach, described an interracial crowd of protestors there). If, on the other hand, Koch were directing attention to the inconvenience, the noise, the pollution of that many people in those small streets, then I am sympathetic. At the same time, I have no problem moving past my sympathy as insignificant in proportion to the emotions that provoked such a spontaneous, peaceful outpouring of rage, sorrow, and pain.

If, however, Koch was simply appealing to the "gut," asking blacks to conjure up the vision of fourteen hundred angry white people descending on a black community, then I would have to say that yes, I would be frightened. It would also conjure up visions of fourteen hundred hooded white people burning crosses, or of fourteen hundred Nazis marching through Skokie, or of fourteen hundred cavalry men riding into an American Indian neighborhood—and yes, that vision would inspire great fear in me of their doing grave harm to the residents. But there is a clear difference. It is important to distinguish mass protests of violence from organized hate groups who openly threaten violence. By failing to distinguish at this level, Mayor Koch effectively manipulated into the hearts of many blacks and whites the specter of unspecified mobs, sweeping through one's home in pursuit of vague and diffusely dangerous ends: from this perspective, his was an appeal to thoughtlessness, to the pseudo-consolation of hunkering down and bunkering up against the approach of the hordes, to a view of the unneighborhooded "public" world as glacially overgeneralized.

Finally, the mayor's comments reveal his ignorance of the degree to which black people *have* welcomed, endured, and suffered white people marching through their streets on one mission or another: white people have always felt free to cruise through black communities; most black neighborhoods have existed only as long as whites have permitted them to; blacks have been this society's perpetual tenants, sharecroppers, lessees. Blacks went from being owned by others to having everything around them owned by others. In a civilization that values private property above all else, this means a devaluation of person, a removal of blacks not just from the market but from the pseudo-spiritual circle of psychic and civic communion. As illustrated in microcosm by my exclusion from Benetton's,[22] this limbo of disownedness keeps blacks beyond the pale of those who are entitled to receive the survival gifts of commerce, the life, liberty, and happiness whose fruits our culture locates in the marketplace. In this way blacks are analogically positioned exactly as they were during slavery or Jim Crow.[23]

There is also a subtler level to the enactment of this dispossession. Not long ago, when I first moved back to New York after some twenty years, I decided to go on a walking tour of Harlem. The tour, which took place on Easter Sunday, was sponsored by the New York Arts Society and was, with the exception of me, attended exclusively by young white urban-professional real-estate speculators. They were pleasant-faced, with babies strapped to their backs and balloons in their hands, and seemed like very nice people. Halfway through the tour, the guide asked the group if they wanted to "go inside some churches. It'll make the tour a little longer; but we'll probably get to see some services going on . . . Easter Sunday in Harlem is quite a show." A casual discussion ensued about the time it might take.

What astonished me was that no one had asked the churches if they wanted to be stared at like living museums. I wondered what would happen if a group of blue-jeaned blacks were to walk uninvited into a synagogue on Passover or St. Anthony's of Padua during high mass—just to peer, not pray. My feeling is that such activity would be seen as disrespectful, at the very least. Yet the aspect of disrespect, intrusion, seemed irrelevant to this well-educated, affable group of people. They deflected my observation with comments like "We just want to look," "No one will mind," and "There's no harm intended." As well-intentioned as they were, I was left with the impression that no one existed for them who could not be governed by their intentions.[24] While acknowledging the lack of apparent malice in this behavior,[25] I can't help thinking that it is a liability as much as a luxury to live without interaction. To live so completely impervious to one's own impact on others is a fragile privilege, which over time relies not simply on the willingness but on the inability of others—in this case blacks—to make their displeasure heard.

Reflecting on Howard Beach brought to mind a news story, from my fragmentary grammar-school recollections of the 1960s. A black man working for some civil-rights cause was killed by a white man for racially motivated reasons; the man was stabbed thirty-nine times, which prompted a radio commentator to observe that the point was not just murder but something beyond. I wondered for a long time what it was that would not die, what could not be killed by the fourth, fifth, or even tenth knife blow; what sort of thing would not die with the body but lived on in the mind of the murderer. Perhaps, as psychologists have argued, what the murderer was trying to kill was a part of his own mind's image, a part of himself and not a real other. After all, generally, statistically, and corporeally, blacks as a group are poor, powerless, and a minority. It is in the minds of whites that blacks become large, threatening, powerful, uncontrollable, ubiquitous, and supernatural.

There are societies in which the limits of life and death are defined very differently from our own. For example, in Buddhism and Hinduism, death may occur long before the body ceases to function, and life may, in the proper circumstances, continue for a time after the body is carried to its grave. These non-body-bound, uncompartmentalized ideas recognize the power of spirit, or what we in our secularized society might describe as the dynamism of self-as-reinterpreted-by-the-perceptions-of-others. These ideas comprehend the fact that a part of ourselves is beyond the control of pure physical will and resides in the sanctuary of those around us; a fundamental part of ourselves and of our dignity depends on the uncontrollable, powerful, external observers who make up a society. Surely a part of socialization ought to include a sense of caring responsibility for the images of others that are reposited within us.

Taking the example of the man who was stabbed thirty-nine times out of the context of our compartmentalized legal system, and considering it in the framework of a legal system that would recognize the moral, religious, or psychological, I am moved to see this act as not merely body murder but as spirit murder. Only one form of spirit murder is racism—cultural obliteration, prostitution, abandonment of the elderly and the homeless, and genocide are some of its other guises. One of the reasons I fear what I call spirit murder—disregard for others whose lives qualitatively depend on our regard—is that it produces a system of formalized distortions of thought. It produces social structures centered on fear and hate, a tumorous outlet for feelings elsewhere unexpressed.[26] When Bernhard Goetz shot four black teenagers in a New York subway, J., an acquaintance of mine, said she could "understand his fear because it's a fact that blacks commit most of the crimes." Actually U.S. Bureau of Justice Statistics for 1986 show that whites were arrested for 71.7 percent of all crimes; blacks and all others (including American Indian, Alaskan Native, Asian, and Pacific Islander) account for the remaining 28 percent. Furthermore, there is evidence that "whites commit more crimes, and that white offenders have consistently lower probabilities of arrest, than do either blacks or Mexican-Americans. This is particularly striking for armed robbery and burglary." But, "Controlling for the factors most likely to influence sentencing and parole decisions, the analysis still found that blacks and Hispanics are less likely to be given probation, more likely to receive prison sentences, more likely to receive longer sentences, and more likely to serve longer time."[27]

What impressed me, beyond the factual inaccuracy of J.'s statement, was the reduction of Goetz's crime to "his fear," which I translate to mean *her* fear; the four teenage victims became all blacks everywhere; and "most of the crimes" clearly meant, in order for the sentence to make sense, that most blacks commit crimes. (Some have taken issue with my interpretation of J.'s remarks. They point out that what she must have meant was that young black men are arrested and convicted for a disproportionate number of the muggings committed in the New York subway system. Looking past the fact that this is not what she said, and that it is precisely the unframed nature of what she *did* say that is the source of my concern, I am left wondering what the real point of such a criticism is: should the assumed specificity of reference therefore give white subway riders a license to kill based on the empiricism of "statistical fear"?)

What struck me, further, was that the general white population seems, in the process of devaluing its image of black people, to have blinded itself to the horrors inflicted by white people. One of the clearest examples of this socialized blindness is the degree to which Goetz's victims were relentlessly bestialized by the public and by the media in New York: images of the urban jungle, with young black men filling the role of "wild animals," were favorite journalistic constructions; young white urban professionals were mythologized, usually wrapped in the linguistic apparel of lambs or sheep, as the tender, toothsome prey. A typical example is the front-page story of the *New York Post* of June 15, 1987, two days before the jury's verdict clearing Goetz of all but illegal gun possession. The article, excoriating the prosecutor's office for even bringing the case, ran under an enormous headline referring to the victims as "predators." The corollary to such imagery is that it

74

is the fate of domesticated white innocents to be slaughtered in meaningless and tragic sacrifice.[28] Locked into such a reification, the meaning of any act by the sheep against the wolves can never be seen as violent in its own right, for it is inherently uncharacteristic, brave, irresistibly and triumphantly parabolic. Thus, when prosecutor Gregory Waples cast Goetz as a "hunter" in his final summation, juror Michael Axelrod said that Waples "was insulting my intelligence. There was nothing to justify that sort of summation. Goetz wasn't a hunter."[29]

Nor do most white people seem to take as crime the dehumanizing cultural images of sterile, mindless white womanhood and expressionless, bored-but-righteous, assembly-line white manhood. (The short stories of Joyce Carol Oates and Raymond Carver often present characters who are prototypes of what I mean by this. They describe people of warmth, compassion, and variety trapped in flat sit-com lives. These people adjust to required expectations, but every now and then the repressed passion flares in sometimes wonderful but more often destructive ways.) I think, though this is hard to prove in any scientific way, that many whites do not expect whites (as compared to blacks) to rape, rob, or kill them (when in fact 54 percent of violent crimes are committed by friends, acquaintances, or relatives of the victims, according to 1987 Bureau of Justice Statistics.) They are surprised when it happens. Perhaps they blind themselves to the warning signals of approaching assault. Some do not even recognize white criminality when it does happen; they apologize for the assailant, think it must have been their fault; they misperceived the other's intent. A tragic example of this is the strangulation death in Central Park of college student Jennifer Levin, the "preppy murder case." If public response is a measure of anything at all, what fueled fascination was the fact that Robert Chambers, the wealthy WASP socialite who killed her, wasn't supposed to be the *type* of person who robbed, raped, or murdered.

To give another example, in the famous videotape Bernhard Goetz described to police in New Hampshire his intention to inflict as much harm as he could. He detailed his wish to see his victims dead; said if he had it to do over again, he'd do the same or worse; and expressed a retrospective desire to have gouged their eyes out. Yet in finding him not guilty of each of twelve counts of attempted murder, assault, and reckless endangerment, the jury discounted this confession entirely: "We felt he said a lot of things he was unsure about. He had nine days of thinking about what happened and reading newspapers, and combined with the guilt, we felt that he may have gotten confused. His own confusion coupled with his feelings of guilt might have forced him to make statements that were not accurate."[30]

This vignette may illustrate better what I mean:

> A lone black man was riding in an elevator in a busy downtown department store. The elevator stopped on the third floor, and a crowd of noisy white high school students got on. The black man took out a gun, shot as many of them as he could, before the doors opened on the first floor and the rest fled for their lives. The black man later explained to the police that he could tell from the "body language" of the students, from their "shiny eyes and big smiles," that they wanted to "play with him, like a cat plays with a mouse." Furthermore, the black man explained, one of the youths had tried to panhandle money from him and another asked him "how are you?"
>
> "That's a meaningless thing," he said in his confession, but "in certain circumstances, that can be a real threat." He added that a similar greeting had preceded the vicious beating of his father, a black civil rights lawyer in Mississippi, some time before. His intention, he confessed, was to murder the high school students.

My guess is that, in reading this tragic account, most white Americans would not hesitate to pronounce the severe contextual misapprehensions of the black gunman as a form of insanity. While degrees of sympathy might vary, I suspect that the consensus would be nearly unanimous that he presents a danger to himself and to others, that he should be institutionalized or imprisoned.

But the above story, with minor character alterations, is excerpted from Goetz's videotaped confession.[31] The public overwhelmingly presumed his innocence. Not only was it not proposed in most accounts that he be institutionalized—it was considered a failure of public institutions not to engage in more such punitive activities. This was reflected most blatantly in the fact that Goetz's defense was not that he was insane but that he acted *reasonably* in the circumstances.[32] It is reflected as well in the degree to which the public devoured, ex post facto, stories about the deviant behavior of the victims in this case. The victims' criminal propensities—allegations ranging from rape to robbery—were used not just to discuss whether deadly force should have been used defensively, but to show why the four young men deserved to be the objects of intent to kill. Imagine, moreover, again in the hypothetical case of the black gunman in the elevator, a public inquiry that focused attention on prior racist statements of the white high-schoolers, on their history of drinking and driving, on how they treated their girlfriends, on whether any of them had ever shoplifted and were only in the department store to do so again. Or imagine what might have happened if the black men in the Howard Beach case, even after the first few beatings, had decided to defend themselves by pulling guns and shooting repeatedly, to kill.

And it is reflected in the way in which Goetz became a cited authority and favorite interviewee on the subject of crime in New York: "Criminals," he declared, must realize that being shot is a "risk they are going to have to take."[33] I can think of no better example of the degree to which criminality has become lodged in a concept of the black "other."

If indeed Americans are subject to such emotional devastation, it is no wonder that the urge to act as victimizer is so irresistible, appears to be the only defensible thing to do—it is the defensive thing to do. It is no wonder that society has created in blacks a class (though not the only class, probably the most visible) of ready-made, prepackaged victims. To discount as much violence as we do must mean that we have a very angry population, suppressing explosive rage. Most white Americans, in urban areas at least, have seen the muttering "lunatic" black person who beats the air with his fists and curses aloud: most people cross the street; they don't choose him to satisfy their need to know the time of day. Yet for generations, and particularly in the wake of the foaming public response to incidents like Howard Beach, the Goetz shooting, and Forsythe County, that is precisely how white America has looked to many a black American.

There is a doorway on East 13th Street in New York that for months had a huge piece of brown paper taped to it, with the legend "Goetz." It reminded me of the banners hung in windows for the parades of astronauts and other heros. In fact, a parade was all the Goetz hoopla lacked to make it into a proper festive event. After delivering their verdict, "defense attorney Nark Baker said the jurors asked for and received Bernhard Goetz' autograph on their jury certificates."[34] In describing the degree to which subway gunman Bernhard Goetz was made a folk hero, Kenneth Clark has written: "As a society adjusts to, or rewards, its accepted cruelties and continues to deny their consequences, it makes heroes of lawless 'respectables' and in so doing develops a selective form of moral indignation and outrage as a basis for the anomaly of a civilization without a conscience."[35]

For these reasons I think that we need to elevate spirit murder to the conceptual—if not punitive—level of a capital moral offense.[36] We need to see it for the cultural cancer it is, for the spiritual genocide it is wreaking on blacks, in whites, and to the abandoned and abused of all races and ages. We need to eradicate its numbing pathology before it wipes out what precious little humanity we have left. As Timothy Mitchell, pastor of Ebenezer

Missionary Baptist Church, observed in 1986: "What happened to Michael Griffith [who was killed in the Howard Beach incident] can happen to any of us . . . The issue is whether we are free to walk around in our city and be seen and accepted and protected as God's children."

5

Crimes Without Passion

(some impersonal notes about personal politics)

It is early on a Tuesday morning. I am feeling most like a law professor—prolific, published, powerful. There is a knock on my office door. It is K., a first-year student, in tears.

"What's wrong?" I ask. A school administrator has called her an activist. My first instinct is to ask again, so what's wrong? But we're in the middle of a presidential election in which the word "liberal" has become a synonym for "better dead," so I try to put myself in tune with this upsidedown new world in which "activist" might mean something like "troublemaker." "Why?" I ask instead.

K. had gone to an administrator to complain about an exam she and her classmates were given by their criminal-law professor. The problem was an updated version of Shakespeare's *Othello,* in which Othello is described as a "black militaristic African leader" who marries the "young white Desdemona" whom he then kills in a fit of sexual rage. Othello is put on trial. The students were to identify the elements of murder. The model answer gives points for ability to "individualize the test" of provocation by recognizing that "a rough untutored Moor might understandably be deceived by the wiles of a more sophisticated European." K. had gone first to the professor and told him she thought the exam racist; the professor denied it, saying it was not he who had dreamed up the facts but Shakespeare. Then K. went to the administrator, who called her an activist but not before he said that she should be more concerned about learning the law and less about the package in which it comes.

As I read the exam, I think about this assertion that the exercise is not racist because, after all, it was Shakespeare who made race part of the problem. But the exam used race in a peculiarly gratuitous fashion; it seems to me that its offensiveness does not depend on whether race and cultural "unsophistication" play any part in the play *Othello;* the issue is what role they played in the fact pattern (Othello-as-legal-problem) that students had to resolve. In fact, the play is irrelevant to the resolution of Othello-as-defendant, and the opening paragraph of the exam says as much (that students don't need to have read the play to understand the dynamic contained in the problem). So the complex dramatic motivations, ironies, subtleties, and complications of character development in the original play are, again, rendered unimportant—gratuitous—in this context.

K. is crying softly in the background. I look up and offer her some tissue. As I continue to read, I reflect that one of the things I find most valuable about the insights of literary theory as applied to law is the recognition of some relation between reader and text, of looking at what the reader does to transform meaning: the issue of what you do with what you read is very important in textual interpretation. It challenges the notion that there is an easily identifiable objective meaning to something like *Othello* which can be sliced from the haunch of the play and served up, essentialism retained, on a law exam.

I grow angry as I continue to read. Even though the problem follows the facts of the original play, the analogy stops there. To say that this is "the same as" is to accept blindly the authority of "Shakespeare" as some universalized canon. Moreover, it does not acknowledge the fact that, while Shakespeare may have produced great literature, he was also a historical being, a product of an Elizabethan world that was in some ways quite as racist as our own. This is not to say that we should therefore suppress *Othello,* for it allows us to view ourselves and to evaluate a range of still valid human dilemmas.

Unfortunately, those human dilemmas do not seem to be the subject of this problem; instead there is a flattening of universal emotions and events to mere stereotype because all the artful, evocative context of the original is missing. The problem presents a defendant who is black, militaristic, unsophisticated, insecure, jealous, and sexually enraged. It reduces the facts to the very same racist generalizations and stereotypes this nation has used to subjugate black people since the first slave was brought from Africa. Moreover, it places an enormous burden on black students in particular who must assume, for the sake of answering these questions, these things about themselves—that is the trauma of gratuitous generalization. The frame places blacks in the position of speaking against ourselves. It forces us to accept as "truth" constructions that go to the heart of who we are.

In the Othello problem, the exam is put in a frame where to contest those subtly generalized "truths" (blacks are sexually dangerous, blacks are militaristic—would the Capulets or the Montagues ever be characterized as "militaristic"?) is not only irrelevant but costs the student points: it is, according to the model answer, *necessary* to argue that "a rough untutored Moor might understandably be deceived by the wiles of a more sophisticated European." In other words, a student who refuses to or cannot think like a racist—most people of color, I would guess—will receive a lower grade. My further guess is that everyone, including perhaps the students of color, will rationalize this result away as an inability to "think like a lawyer."

I agree to speak to the professor on behalf of K. "Just make sure he understands I'm not an activist," implores K. "This could ruin my career."

I visit Professor L. the next day and present our concerns. L.'s explanation is that this was merely his attempt to respect the minority and feminist quest to bring issues of race, class, and gender more directly into the curriculum. I say I'm concerned that he shares a deep misunderstanding of the struggle, a misunderstanding that threatens to turn the quest for empowering experiential narrative into permission for the most blatant expressions of cynical stereotypification. I cite the example of an exam given by another professor at another school, who handed out to his class a detailed and luridly violent wife-battering hypothetical in which a man knocks out his wife's teeth, urinates on the floor and throws their baby down into it, rips her blouse off, calls her a "castrating bitch," and arranges for a friend to come in and rape her. At the top of the question there is a disclaiming explanation that it only reflects "the world" where "there is a lot of violence directed at women" and that "the legal system has (often in response to organized feminist concerns) at least partly shifted its responses to situations involving that violence." I use this example to question the potential, no doubt unintended, voyeuristic repercussions of well-meaning attempts to include race and gender without also attempting to examine the *way* in which such material is included. I don't do a good job of making this point, and L. sees no comparison.

L. asks me: "Are you suggesting that race and gender issues be censored from the law-school classroom?"

I answer: The catch-22 of using terms like "black" and "white" has to do with fathoming when and why race or gender or violence or anything else is important. On the one hand, race isn't important because it isn't important; most of us devoutly wish this to be a colorblind society, in which removing the words "black" and "white" from our vocabulary would render the world, in a miraculous flash, free of all division. On the other hand, real life isn't that simple. Often we have to use the words in order to acknowledge the undeniable psychological and cultural power of racial constructions upon all our lives; we have to be able to call out against the things that trouble us, whether racism or other forms of suffering.

This is not the same, I say, as retreating to a completely race-neutral point of view for any and all circumstances. That would be like saying we should never study Shakespeare, particularly *Othello* and *The Merchant of Venice*—or, to take it to an extreme, that we should never discuss why racism is racist. (And we desperately need to get past the point of angst about whether we're guilty of guilt-tripping each other.) But it is something quite again if I were to use the authority of what this culture considers "classical" to justify every instance of violent gratuity. It simply would not be valid for me to say, "Well, these are Shakespeare's facts, not mine"—as if "Shakespeare" were some fixed object, some physically determinate piece of marble, as if I could discount all my own interpretive power and responsibility over what I render from it.

"What you are proposing," says L., "sounds like the very antithesis of academic freedom."

Over the next few weeks, I think about ways in which to clarify what I am trying to say. Word has gotten out among my students and friends that I am interested in this sort of thing, and they bring me sheaves of exams; in addition I do my own research. I end up with a stack of exams written on a variety of subjects, and given at schools around the country. I find:

> —a tax exam that asks students to calculate the tax implications for Kunta Kinte's master when the slavecatchers cut off his foot.
> —a securities-regulation exam in which the professor muses about whether white-collar defendants should go to jail, since "unlike ghetto kids" they are not equipped to fare in that environment.
> —a constitutional-law exam in which students are given the lengthy text of a hate-filled polemic entitled "How To Be a Jew-Nigger" and then told to use the first amendment to defend it.

—a description of the "typical criminal" as "a young black male with an I.Q. of 87 who is one of eight children and has always lived on welfare and who spends his time hanging out in pool halls with his best friend Slick."

—numerous criminal-law exams whose questions feature exclusively black or Hispanic or Asian criminals and exclusively white victims.

—many questions depicting gay men as the exclusive spreaders of AIDS, asking students to find the elements of murder.

—many, many questions in which women are beaten, raped, and killed in descriptions pornographically detailed (in contrast to streamlined questions, by the same professors, that do not involve female victims).

I review all these exams and ponder what to do with them, how to raise the issues in a way that can best be heard, and heard in a way that will not be taken as "censorship." Finally I decide to write a memorandum to the faculty, worded generally, without names of professors or schools, but using real exams to illustrate real issues of propriety. I write:

I have been looking at law-school exams and studying them as a genre of legal writing involving complex relations of power and influence. I am interested in opening discussion about the extent to which what we write into exams, as much as what we teach, conveys stereotypes, delimits the acceptable, and formulates ideals. I have been reviewing a collection of exams that exploit race and gender and violence in ways that I think are highly inappropriate. By "inappropriate" I mean that they use race, gender, and violence in ways that have no educational purpose, that are gratuitous and voyeuristic, and that simultaneously perpetuate inaccurate and harmful stereotypes as "truthful." This is accomplished by a variety of devices:

1. Compartmentalizing the relevant from the irrelevant is one of the primary skills law students are expected to master during their education. Frequently, professors employ red-herring facts from which the legally dispositive kernel facts must be clearly identified. But in the exams about which I am concerned, race, ethnicity, class,

and gender are irrelevant even to the process of winnowing the relevant from the irrelevant. They function as sheer gratuity. Their mention has absolutely nothing to do with the manipulation of rules necessary to resolve the fact patterns as constructed.

Furthermore, in the one or two questions in which a specified characteristic (e.g., a "gay male prostitute" being tried for murder in the spread of AIDS) is arguably important to the disposition, or reflective of some current controversy in the law, students are specifically instructed not to consider it, or to consider it only to a limited extent (e.g., that same exam contained the following instruction: "while we're all concerned about homophobia, don't consider it in answering this problem"). I found exams whose basic message was: M. is black, N. is a white racist, but you, you're colorblind. O. is battered wife, P. is her vicious spouse-battering husband, but you, you must not consider provocation if O. hits P.

It is thus that information that is quite important in real life and real courtrooms becomes unimportant for purposes of answering a law school exam. Students are left to deal with raised issues of race and gender as unframed information, as mere backdrop—in a society where large numbers of people hold powerful, if not always spoken, impressions that "most blacks are criminals" or "women can't be raped by their husbands" or "all Chicanos belong to gangs."

The message that is reinforced by such exams is that while racist, sexist stereotypes may be part of life, it's not important—or important *not*—to deal with them in the law. (And yet of course we know it is.) Or that it's not so important that it can't be severed, caged, and neatly suppressed. Actual importance is thus not legitimated.

Nevertheless, although devalued expressly or implicitly, race, gender, sexual preference are part of these problems. They're written in them by virtue of some inscrutable design. And they do have a power and a function in such questions, if beyond the answer to that question; yet that function is rendered invisible—not less powerful, just not acknowledged. They become powerful as external markers of what must be suppressed or ignored, of what must be rendered unconscious as "unsightly." These interrogatories, in so directly turning students' attention away from precisely what is most provocative and significant in these problems, reiterates exactly what is so difficult about raising these issues in any kind of social setting: the feeling of impropriety, the sheer discourtesy of talking about what has been, by our teachers at every stage of life, explicitly tabooed: it's o.k. to purvey these unchallenged images as gratuity, but not to talk about them in a way that matters, that changes outcomes.

2. These problems draw for their justification upon one of the law's best-loved inculcations: the preference for the impersonal above the personal, the "objective" above the "subjective." Most of these problems require blacks, women who have been raped, gays and lesbians, to not just re-experience their oppression, but to write *against* their personal knowledge. They actually require the assumption of an "impersonal" (but racist/sexist/homophobic) mentality in order to do well in the grading process. Consider, for example, the exam in which a white woman premeditatedly lures a 13-year-old black would-be thief to her balcony and then kills him, her actions motivated by racial hatred. In one interrogatory, students are asked to "make the best argument you can that [the white woman] ought to be exculpated entirely, ignoring arguments (say that she might be diplomatically immune or insane) grounded in general incapacity to be convicted." This requires students either to indulge the imaginative flowering of their most insidious rationalizations for racial hatred; or it requires them to suppress any sense of social conscience. It requires them to devalue their own and others' humanity for the sake of a grade. (This is also how, over time, perfectly rational and humanitarian insights and concerns are devalued, as a matter of habit rather than wisdom, as "merely experiential" and "irrelevant to the law." Law professors can thus set up irresponsibly authoritarian constructs that give permission to, and legitimize, some really warped world views. The result will be students who are cultured to hate; yet who still think of themselves as very very good people; who will be deeply offended, and *personally* hurt, if anyone tries to tell them otherwise. I think this sort of teaching, rampant throughout the educational system, is why racism and sexism remain so routine, so habitually dismissed, as to be largely invisible.)

3. While styled as hypotheticals, these collected exams set themselves up as instructional mirrors of real life. In talking to some of the professors whose exams concerned me, I was always given some version of the following explanation: "Well, (people of color)

(women) (gays) do commit crimes after all. It's naive to assume this doesn't happen in the real world." The problem with this reasoning, however, is that everything under the sun could be rationalized by the open-ended authority of "what happens," no matter how depraved, singular, or despicable.

We, as law teachers, create miniworlds of reality, by the faith that students put in our tutelage of the rules of reality. We define the boundaries of the legitimate and the illegitimate, in a more ultimately powerful way than almost anyone else in world. It is enormously important therefore to consider the process by which we include, as well as the process by which we exclude. It is thus that an exam, which includes only three problems, two of which feature black criminality and the third of which deals with gay criminality, constructs a miniworld that reinforces the widely held misperceptions that blacks commit most of the crimes, that only gays carry AIDS, or that all gays are promiscuous.

It is not that there aren't racially or sexually motivated crimes of all sorts in the world; what is problematic about casting problems (directed to a hypothetically diverse student body) repeatedly and persistently in racially or sexually stereotypical terms is that it not only perpetuates the idea, for example, that most blacks commit most crimes, but that it makes invisibie white criminality. In any event, race has nothing to do with the resolution of these problems, which for the most part are problems going beyond race and class; yet students are set up to believe that this is "what happens."

Furthermore, there is a relativistic, cynical majoritarianism in the idea that "it happens in the real world," akin to the childish excuse that "everybody does it." I am struck, for example, by the general absence of reference to white people in exams written by people who do specify race when they are referring to nonwhites. Yet we all know that there are white gangs (e.g., skinheads, the White Aryan Resistance) as well as black, Asian, and Chicano gangs. None of these exams, or any I could find, present gratuitous "white-people" problems. "White" is used only to distinguish from blacks and other nonwhites. The absence of "white" thus signals that "everyone" is white. "Blacks" therefore become distanced, different, "othered." In order to deal with such a problem on an exam, moreover, students are required to take the perspective of "everybody"; for black students this requires their taking a stance in which they objectify themselves with reference to the interrogatories. (I use the word "objectify" in the literal, grammatical sense of subject-verb-object: the removing of oneself from the subject position of power, control, and direction over the verb-action. "We," blacks, become "them.") The law becomes less than universally accessible or participatory. The point of view assumes a community of "everybody's" that is in fact exclusionary.

When my sister was in the fourth grade, she was the only black child in the class. One Valentine's Day, when the teacher went out of the room, all her white classmates ripped up the valentines she had sent them and dumped them on her desk. It was so traumatic that my sister couldn't speak again in that class, she refused to participate: so completely had they made her feel not part of that group. For a while she stopped performing altogether. Ultimately my mother convinced her that she could "show them" by outperforming them, but I think the joy of education for its own sake was seriously impaired, in both her and me (for I felt it almost as much as she did; we had made the valentines together).

Our roles repeatedly defined as "outsiders" in both cruel and unintentional ways, we were faced with a curious dilemma: we could continually try to be insiders, which would have been quite frustrating, because "insider" is not an act of will but a cooperative relation, defeated as easily as the turn of a head; or we could resign ourselves to being outsiders. A few exceptionally strong people, usually reinforced by an alternative sense of community, can just ignore it and carry on, despite the lack of that part of education which flows from full participation, perhaps thus resulting in a brand of knowledge that is more abstract than relational. But most others become driven to transform the outsider status into its own excuse, either by obsessional and abstracted overachievement, or by underachievement occasioned by the loss of relation and loss of interest. Either way the outsider status is a kind of unresolved wound, driven by pain, for after all that is the seeded prophecy contained in the word and the concept of those who are designated "outsider."

The students who have been coming to my office have been describing occurrences, in class as well as on exams, that if true are just as powerfully and complexly traumatizing. Perhaps if all we value is toughness of spirit in our interactions, then what happened to my sister was a good lesson. It's certainly not just as easy to inflict the same lesson on women and students of color, or white men for that matter, if the project is only to toughen them up. We will, in the forge of exam pressure and general humiliation, be able to produce a tough human being totally split inside. But I trust that is not the exclusive project of institutions engaged in the training of ethical servants of either private or public interest.

This brings me back to my original issue—how to distinguish the appropriate introduction of race, gender, class, social policy, into law-school classrooms. I don't think there's an easy answer or a formula that can be applied. That's why I think such discussion should be ongoing, constant, among faculties willing to hear divers points of view—as difficult as such conversations are, and as long-term and noisy as they may have to be.

Nor do I think that handling these exams should be limited to discussions of wording in specific instances, or to specific professors who may have suffered momentary lapses of consciousness or whose motives may have been misunderstood. I think that the ultimate resolution has to do with understanding relations of power. It is significant that in my sister's class everyone ripped up her valentines; it might not have been more than a few hours of hurt feelings if only one person had done it. Similarly, it is significant when not just one but many law professors feel free to propagate (if unintentionally) racism in fanciful classroom hypotheticals and in publicly disseminated exams, bound for posterity in volumes in the library. It is significant that professors feel that they *can't talk* about exams like these without interfering with the first-amendment rights or the academic freedom of their colleagues. It is significant that we are teachers and have power over our students. It is significant that significant numbers of students are desperately unhappy about what they consider the abusive exercise of that power, and yet are too afraid to speak openly of their unhappiness. It is significant because people are hired and fired and graded and held to accountability under law, based on factors about which we cannot or will not speak.

The response to my memo is not good. I am accused of being didactic, condescending, "too teacherly." I am told that I have humiliated a number of professors because, although no names were used, identities were easily divined. I have, I am told, "reduced the conversation to one of personalities and pot shots."

These accusations frighten me. I share the lawyerly resistance to the windy, risky plain of exposure that the "personal" represents. I am just as fearful of my own personality having been put into public debate as my critics are of theirs. My instinct is to retreat—the responses to my memo render the debate too subjective, complicated, messy, detailed. Somewhere inside, I know that my fear of being called didactic, condescending, and teacherly is related to K.'s fear of being called an activist.

I sit down and write my sister a long letter, including my memo. I tell her how I have fictionalized the identities of people and collapsed several conversations with different colleagues into the mouths of only a few characters. My sister responds with a phone call: she tells me I'm a coward. She thinks I should write up everything Exactly As It Happened and have it published somewhere. Otherwise, she says, I open myself up to being dismissed as merely literary; people will be able to say It Didn't Happen.

But the exams are all real, I insist, and all the events did happen, just not all in the same instant, not all in that order; it happened, just not exactly that way.

Then it's not true, she says, and you will have committed an act of bad scholarship.

But my point is not to hold individual people or institutions up for ridicule, I persist. I generalized because the power of these events is precisely their generality throughout legal education and practice. The lessons lie in the principles, not in the personalities.

The power of these events, says my sister the historian, is that they happened, and there is no one who is in a more ideal position to document them in detail than you. You are just afraid to do that.

I promise to think about what she has said, and our conversation ends. And I do think about what my sister has said, long and hard, for weeks and weeks.

In the meantime, I avoid K. whenever I see her on the other side of the student union.

I am lured, eventually, from my hibernation by two memos I receive from colleagues. The first is from Q., who inquires about the tone assumed in my memo as well as in my other writing. Q. asks whether I am not afraid that my personal style is "too much" for an academic audience; he says that it is inevitable that my words will be read as "all about me" and speculates that my writing necessarily involves the reader's passing judgment on me. Rather than risking another memo written in the first person, I take Q. to lunch and we talk.

I say: Writing for me is an act of sacrifice, not denial. (I think: I'm so glad I didn't try to write this down.) I deliberately sacrifice myself in my writing. I leave no part of myself out, for that is how much I want readers to connect with me. I want them to wonder about the things I wonder about, and to think about some of the things that trouble me.

What is "impersonal" writing but denial of self? If withholding is an ideology worth teaching, we should be clearer about that as the bottom line of the enterprise. We should also acknowledge the extent to which denial of one's authority in authorship is not the same as elimination of oneself; it is ruse, not reality. And the object of such ruse is to empower still further; to empower beyond the self, by appealing to neutral, shared, even universal understandings. In a vacuum, I suppose there's nothing wrong with that attempt to empower: it generates respect and distance and a certain obeisance to the sleekness of a product that has been skinned of its personalized complication. But in a world of real others, the cost of such exclusive forms of discourse is empowerment at the expense of one's relation to those others; empowerment without communion. And as the comfort of such false power becomes habitual, it is easy to forget that the source of one's power is quite limited, not the fiat of a heavenly mandate. It is easy to forget how much that grandiosity of power depends on the courtesy and restraint of a society of others no less equally endowed than you.

The other thing contained in assumption of neutral, impersonal writing styles is the lack of risk. It is not only a ruse, but a warm protective hole to crawl in, as if you were to throw your shoe out the front door while insisting that no one's home. I also believe that the personal is not the same as "private": the personal is often merely the highly particular. I think the personal has fallen into disrepute as sloppy because we have lost the courage and the vocabulary to describe it in the face of the enormous social pressure to "keep it to ourselves"—but this is where our most idealistic and our deadliest politics are lodged, and are revealed.

The second memo is from R. He writes:

> I can't think of anyone who claims to have liked law school. I haven't taken a poll, but I suspect most students feel like they are suffering in law school . . . I didn't go to Harvard for law school, or Yale. I had messed up the beginning of my undergraduate education. In any event I am a certified member of the class of also-rans. It is possible to generalize about us . . . Some of us, of course, are among the strongest critics of affirmative action. I never really felt that way. I guess I always believed the idea that diversity is more than just a campaign slogan, and that an all-vanilla law school is an insipid place.
>
> But there is another kind of *ressentiment* which, however irrational, I confess I do share. That directs itself not against the affirmative action candidates but rather against the pampered children of privilege who tell me how terrible it all is. It's not that they're "undeserving" per se; some of them are clearly just as brilliant as the development officers say they are. But they sure do seem unappre-

ciative. "My god!" I find myself saying. "You've got a chance I'd clean out privies for, and you're telling me it isn't worth very much? You should be wearing an MIA bracelet in my name; you should fall down on your knees and whisper prayers of thanks, just for the chance to be in that seat!"

Into my computer I write:

Dear R.: I do agree with you that most law students are indeed miserable. In the context of my concerns about exams, however, I was not concerned with ranking degrees of pain into some kind of hierarchy, although of course degree is vital to the maintenance of perspective. It is not comforting to me that "everyone," not just particular students, suffer in law school. Misery may love company, but I trust none of us particularly loves misery. It helps me not at all to know that others are unhappy; there is nothing possessive about my unhappiness. I know I am not the only one. The three (white) students who committed suicide when I was in law school may have complained less than I did, but obviously suffered more; their loss intensified my unhappiness. I do not think my life became easier by the comparison.

Rather, my personal concern is with identifying the specifics of my pain. What causes it, what sustains it, what interferes with my ability to be most fully and most productively myself. My unhappiness, whether alone or among many, makes me inefficient. It makes me hide myself.

None of this, however, should be mistaken for doubts about the value of my education. It should not be taken as a denial of the wonderful people and wonderful moments that have also characterized my schooling and my career. My complaining doesn't mean that I devalue who I am; but just because Harvard admitted me or Stanford hired me doesn't mean that they own me to the extent that I can never speak about my feelings. There would be some element of unthinking fervor in that, I think, akin to blind patriotism: love it or leave it. Not to complain about real inequities and real sources of misery in even the most powerful institutions seems only to kowtow to power rather than participate in a meaningful and great-souled manner.

I never give R. a copy of this response; I'm not sure why. Instead I look for my student K. to see if she wants to have lunch.

It is the end of a long academic year. I sit in my office reviewing my students' evaluations of me. They are awful, and I am devastated. The substantive ones say that what I teach is "not law." The nonsubstantive evaluations are about either my personality or my physical features. I am deified, reified, and vilified in all sorts of cross-directions. I am condescending, earthy, approachable, and arrogant. Things are out of control in my classroom, and I am too much the taskmaster. I am a PNCNG (Person of No Color and No Gender) as well as too absorbed with ethnicity and social victimhood. My braids are described as being swept up over my "great bald dome of a skull," and my clothes, I am relieved to hear, are "neat." I am obscure, challenging, lacking in intellectual rigor, and brilliant. I think in a disorganized fashion and insist that everyone think as I do. I appear tired all the time and talk as if I'm on speed, particularly when reading from texts. My writing on the blackboard is too small.

"The failure of this class was a group effort," writes one student. "When Professor Williams got off to a rocky start, rather than cooperating with her, the class would adopt an adversarial posture. For instance, knowing full well that Professor Williams did not look to the sides of the room very often, certain individuals would raise their hands quietly and leave them up without saying a word, thereby sending titters all through the class; this unnecessarily heightened the perception of students that the professor was in over her head."

My head hurts. In nine years of teaching I have never felt less like a law professor. Who wants to be the worst so-called law professor who ever lived anyway? I marvel, in a moment of genuine bitterness, that anonymous student evaluations speculating on dimensions of my anatomy are nevertheless counted into the statistical measurement of my teaching proficiency. I am expected to woo students even as I try to fend them off; I am supposed to control them even as I am supposed to manipulate them into loving me. Still I am aware of the paradox of my power over these students. I am aware of my role, my place in an institution that is larger than myself, whose power I wield even as I am powerless, whose shield of respectability shelters me even as I am disrespected.

I am always aware of my first years in teaching when students would come in upset that I had yelled at them on paper by virtue of red-ink exclamatory comments in their margins. These days I correct my exams in pencil, faintly, softly. Red pen was too much of a shout to students if I had anything other to say than "Great!" I never say "Wrong" in the margins, but always ask questions: "Are you sure that's the section you mean?" "Have you compared this conclusion with that in the preceding paragraph?" Any occasional imperative begins with "Try to distinguish this thought from . . ." I circle spelling errors rather than correct them.

I am always aware of the ex-pro-football player/student whom I had told in class to read the cases more carefully; he came to my office to tell me that I had humiliated him in front of everyone and he was going to "get you, lady." At that, I ordered him out of my office, whereupon he walked down to the associate dean's office and burst into tears, great heaving, football-player sobs, the tears dripping off the tip of his nose, as it was described to me later. Now I admit that of all the possible ways in which I thought he might try to get me, this was the one for which I was least prepared; but it could not have been more effective in terms of coalescing both the student body and the administration against me. I became the drill sergeant. A militant black woman who took out her rage on her students. Someone who could make a big man like him cry and cry hard.

And it is true that I did make him cry. I thought long about how a situation in which I thought I was being plucky and self-protective had turned into such a nightmare. How did my self-

assertion become so powerful as to frighten, frustrate, or humiliate this man? Part of the answer is that he indeed felt humiliated;
it is hard to be criticized in a large classroom, although I had
perceived mine to be gentle criticism. Part of it lies in the power I
wield as teacher over all my students; each of us seeks uncondi-
tional approval even from the teachers we may hate. But I'm not
sure this explains sufficiently the intensity of my student's reaction
or, even if I conclude that he was simply sensitive, the intensity of
the sympathy that rushed in this largely male institution away
from me and unto him.

Two students come to visit me in the wake of the evaluations,
my scores having been published in the student newspaper. They
think the response has to do with race and gender, and with the
perceived preposterousness of the authority that I, as the first
black woman ever to have taught at this particular institution,
symbolically and imagistically bring to bear in and out of the classroom. Breaking out of this, they say, is something we all suffer as
pawns in a hierarchy, but it is particularly aggravated in the confusing, oxymoronic hierarchic symbology of me as black female
law professor.

That, I tell them in a grateful swell of unscholarly emotionalism, feels like truth to me.

6

The Obliging Shell

(an informal essay on formal equal opportunity)

I have decided to attend a Continuing Education of the Bar course on equal-employment opportunity. Bar-style questions are handed out for general discussion. The first question reads:

> Question One: X and Y apply for the same job with firm Z. X and Y are equally qualified. Which one should get the job?

I panic. What exactly is meant by Question One? But apparently this is supposed to be a throwaway question. On the blackboard the instructor writes:

> Right Answer: Whichever one you like better.

As usual I have missed the point and am busy complicating things. In my notebook I write:

> Wrong Answer: What a clear, graspable comparison this is; it is like choosing between smooth pebbles. X, the simple crossing of two lines, the intersection of sticks; Y, the cleaned bones of a flesh-and-blood referent. There is something seductive about this stone-cool algebra of rich life stories. There is something soothing about its static neutrality, its emotionless purity. It is a choice luxuriantly free of consequence.
>
> At any rate, much of this answer probably depends on what is meant by "equal qualifications." Rarely are two people absolutely

equally qualified (they both went to Harvard, they graduated in the same class, they tied for number one, they took all the same classes, etc.) so the judgment of equality is usually pretty subjective to begin with (a degree from Yale is as good as one from Harvard, a degree in philosophy is as useful as a degree in political science, an editor of the school paper is as good as the class president) and usually overlooks or fills in a lot of information that may in fact distinguish the candidates significantly (is it the same to be number one in a small class as in a huge class; is the grading done by some absolute standard, or on a strictly enforced bell curve; did X succeed by taking only standardized tests in large lecture courses; does Y owe his success to the individualized attention received in small seminars where he could write papers on subjects no one else knew or cared about?). All such differentiations are matters of subjective preference, since all such "equality" is nothing more than assumption, the subjective willingness not to look past a certain point, or to accept the judgments of others (the admissions director of Harvard, the accuracy of the LSAT computer-grader).

The mind funnels of Harvard and Yale are called standards. Standards are concrete monuments to socially accepted subjective preference. Standards are like paths picked through fields of equanimity, worn into hard wide roads over time, used always because of collective habit, expectation, and convenience. The pleasures and perils of picking one's own path through the field are soon forgotten; the logic or illogic of the course of the road is soon rationalized by the mere fact of the road.

But let's assume that we do find two candidates who are as alike as can be. They are identical twins. They've had exactly the same training from the same teachers in a field that emphasizes mastery of technique or skill in a way that can be more easily calibrated than, say, writing a novel. Let's say it's a hypothetical school of ultraclassical ballet—the rules are clear, the vocabulary is rigid, artistry is judged in probably far too great a measure by mastery of specific placements and technical renderings of kinetic combinations. (The formal requirements of the New York City Rockettes, for example, are that a dancer must be between 5 feet 5½ inches and 5 feet 8 inches tall precisely and be able to do twenty eye-level kicks with a straight back.) I could probably hire either one, but I am left with the nagging wonder as to my own hypothetical about whether I want either one of these goody-two-shoed automatons. I wonder, indeed, if the fact that the "standard" road is good may obscure the fact that it is not the only good road. I begin to wonder, in other words, not about my two candidates, but about the tortoise-shell nature of a community of employees that has managed to successfully suppress or ignore the distinguishing variegation of being human. (Even if we were talking about an assembly line, where the standard were some monotonous minimal rather than a rarefied maximum, my concern holds that certain human characteristics are being dishonored as irrelevant—such as creativity, humor, and amiability.)

I wonder if this simple but complete suppression of the sterling quirks and idiosyncrasies of what it is that makes a person an individual is not related to the experience of oppression. I wonder if the failure to be held accountable for the degree to which such so-called neutral choices are decided on highly subjective, articulable, but mostly unarticulated factors (the twin on the left has a higher voice and I like high voices) is not related to the perpetuation of bias.

By the time I finish writing this, the teacher is well along into discussion of the next question, this time a real one:

Question Two: X and Y apply for the same job with firm Z. X and Y are equally qualified. X is black and Y is white; Z is presently an all-white firm. Which one should get the job?

It feels almost blasphemous to complicate things like this. I feel the anger in the challenge to the calm neatness of the previous comparison; it seems to me that this is a trick question, full of labyrinthian twists and illusion. Will I be strong enough to cut my way through the suggestions and shadows, the mirror tricks of dimensionality? I hold my breath as the teacher writes on the blackboard:

Right Answer: Whichever one you like better, because race is irrelevant. Our society will impose no rules grounded in preference according to race.

In my notebook I write:

> Left Answer: The black person should get the job. If the modern white man, innocently or not, is the inheritor of another's due, then it must be returned. I read a rule somewhere that said if a thief steals so that his children may live in luxury and the law returns his ill-gotten gain to its rightful owner, the children cannot complain that they have been deprived of what they did not own. Blacks have earned a place in this society; they have earned a share of its enormous wealth, with physical labor and intellectual sacrifice, as wages and as royalties. Blacks deserve their inheritance as much as family wealth passed from parent to child over the generations is a "deserved" inheritance. It is deserved as child support and alimony. It is ours because we gave birth to it and we raised it up and we fed it. It is ours because our legal system has always idealized structuring present benefit for those who forbore in the past.
>
> But, then, I'm doing what I always seem to do—mistaking the rules of fraud and contract for constitutional principles. How's this: It's important to hire the black person because the presence of blacks within, as opposed to without, the bell jar of a given community changes the dynamic forever.

As I write, a discussion has been raging in the room. One of the course participants growls: "How can you force equality down the throats of people who don't want it? You just end up depriving people of their freedom, and creating new categories of oppressed, such as white men."

I think: the great paradox of democratic freedom is that it involves some measure of enforced equality for all. The worst dictatorships in history have always given some freedom: freedom for a privileged some at the expense of the rest is usually what makes oppression so attractively cost-effective to begin with. Is freedom really such a narrowly pluralistic concept that, so long as we can find some slaves to say they're happy with the status quo, things are fine and free? Are they or the rest of the slaves less enslaved by calling enslavement freedom?

The tension voiced by the growler seems to be between notions of associative autonomy, on the one hand, and socialized valuations of worth—equality and inequality notions—whose foundations are not in view and go unquestioned. Categorizing is not the sin; the problem is the lack of desire to examine the categorizations that are made. The problem is not recognizing the ethical worth in attempting to categorize with not only individual but social goals in mind as well. The problem is in the failure to assume responsibility for examining how or where we set our boundaries.

Privatized terms so dominate the public discourse that it is difficult to see or appreciate social evil, communal wrong, states of affairs that implicate us whether we will it or not. Affirmative action challenges many people who believe in the truism that this is a free country. For people who don't believe that there is such a thing as institutional racism, statements alleging oppression sound like personal attacks, declarations of war. They seem to scrape deep from the cultural unconscious some childish feelings of wanting to belong by forever having others as extensions of oneself, of never being told of difference, of not being rent apart by the singularity of others, of the privilege of having the innocence of one's most whimsical likes respected. It is a feeling that many equate with the quintessence of freedom; this powerful fancy, the unconditionality of self-will alone. It is as if no others exist and no consequences redound; it is as if the world were like a mirror, silent and infinitely flat, rather than finite and rippled like a pool of water.

The "it's a free country" attack on affirmative action is also an argument, however, that is profoundly inconsistent with the supposed rationale for the imposition of "standards," however frequently the arguments are paired. The fundamental isolationism of individual preference as an arbiter is quite different from the "neutrality," the "blindness," and the "impersonality" used to justify the collectivized convenience of standardized preference. I wonder what a world "without preference" would look like anyway. Standards are nothing more than structured preferences. Preferential treatment isn't inherently dirty; seeing its ubiquity, within and without racial politics, is the key to the underground vaults of freedom locked up in the idea of whom one likes. The whole historical object of equal opportunity, formal or informal, is to structure preferences for rather than against—to like rather than dislike—the participation of black people. Thus affirmative action is very different from numerical quotas that actively structure society so that certain classes of people remain unpreferred. "Quotas," "preference," "reverse discrimination," "experienced," and "qualified" are con words, shiny mirror words that work to dazzle the eye with their analogic evocation of other times, other contexts, multiple histories. As a society, we have yet to look carefully beneath them to see where the seeds of prejudice are truly hidden.

If, moreover, racism is artificially relegated to a time when it was written into code, the continuing black experience of prejudice becomes a temporal shell game manipulated by whites. Such a refusal to talk about the past disguises a refusal to talk about the present. If prejudice is what's going on in the present, then aren't we, the makers and interpreters of laws, engaged in the purest form of denial? Or, if prejudice is a word that signified only what existed "back" in the past, don't we need a new word to signify what is going on in the present? Amnesia, perhaps?

We live in an era in which women and people of color compose and literally define both this society's underclass and its most underserved population. A recent study by the Urban League reports:

> The difference in the percentage of blacks and whites holding managerial and professional jobs is unlikely to narrow significantly before the year 2039. Currently, white men are twice as likely as black men to hold sales, managerial or professional positions.
> With the wages of white men averaging $450 a week in 1987 as

against $326 a week for black men, income parity between the two groups will not be achieved before 2058.

Black children are completing high school at a slower rate than whites. But the paper said that the percentage of blacks finishing high school rose from 55 percent of the white graduation rate in 1967 to 79 percent in 1985, and it estimated that equal percentages of blacks and whites will graduate in 2001.[1]

This last statistic is complicated by the fact that "between 1976 and 1985, the college-going rate of black high school graduates fell from 34 to 26 percent, despite the fact that the percentage of black high school graduates rose from 67 to 75 percent."[2] This decrease was largely due to the Reagan Administration's cuts in federal financial aid to students.[3]

Remedying this, therefore, must be society's most pressing area of representational responsibility; not only in terms of fairly privatized issues such as "more pro bono" or more lawyers taking on more cases of particular sorts, but in closely examining the ways in which the law operates to omit women and people of color at all levels including the most subtle—to omit them from the literature of the law, from the ranks of lawyers, and from the numbers of those served by its interests.

One week after the end of the equal-opportunity course, the Supreme Court came down with its opinion in *City of Richmond v. J. A. Croson Co.* That case presented a challenge, as well as its own model of resistance, to the pursuit of "proper findings . . . necessary to define both the scope of the injury [in race and gender cases] and the extent of the remedy."[4]

Croson involved a minority set-aside program in the awarding of municipal contracts. Richmond, Virginia, with a black population of just over 50 percent had set a 30 percent goal in the awarding of city construction contracts, based on its findings that local, state, and national patterns of discrimination had resulted in all but complete lack of access for minority-owned businesses. The Supreme Court stated:

> We, therefore, hold that the city has failed to demonstrate a *compelling* interest in apportioning public contracting opportunities on the basis of race. To accept Richmond's claim that past societal discrimination alone can serve as the basis for rigid racial preferences would be to open the door to competing claims for "remedial relief" for *every* disadvantaged group. The dream of a Nation of equal citizens in a society where race is irrelevant to personal opportunity and achievement would be lost in a mosaic of shifting preferences based on *inherently unmeasurable* claims of past wrongs. [Citing *Bakke:*] Courts would be asked to evaluate the extent of the prejudice and consequent harm suffered by various minority groups. Those whose societal injury *is thought* to exceed some *arbitrary* level of tolerability then would be entitled to preferential classification. We think such a result would be contrary to both the letter and the spirit of a constitutional provision whose central command is equality.[5]

What strikes me most about this holding are the rhetorical devices the court employs to justify its outcome:

(a) It sets up a "slippery slope" at the bottom of which lie hordes-in-waiting of warring barbarians: an "open door" through which would flood the "competing claims" of "every disadvantaged group." It problematizes by conjuring mythic dangers.

(b) It describes situations for which there are clear, hard statistical data as "inherently unmeasurable." It puts in the diminutive that which is not; it makes infinite what in fact is limited.

(c) It puts itself in passive relation to the purported "arbitrariness" of others' perceptions of the intolerability of their circumstances ("those whose societal injury is thought to . . .").

These themes are reiterated throughout the opinion: Societal discrimination is "too amorphous"; racial goals are labeled "unyielding"; goals are labeled "quotas"; statistics are rendered "generalizations"; testimony becomes mere "recitation"; legislative purpose and action become "mere legislative assurances of good intention"; and lower-court opinion is just "blind judicial deference." This adjectival dismissiveness alone is sufficient to hypnotize the reader into believing that the "assumption that white prime contractors simply will not hire minority persons is completely unsupported."[6]

And as I think about the *Croson* opinion, I cannot but marvel at how, against a backdrop of richly textured facts and proof on both local and national scales, in a city where more than half the population is black and in which fewer than 1 percent of contracts are awarded to minorities or minority-owned businesses, interpretative artifice alone allowed this narrow vision that not just that 30 percent was too great a set-aside, but that there was no proof of discrimination. Moreover, the rhetorical devices that accomplished this astonishing holding are comprehensible less from the perspective of traditionally conceived constitutional standards—whether rational relation or strict scrutiny—than by turning to interpretive standards found in private law. The process by which the court consistently diminished the importance of real facts and figures is paralleled only by the process of rendering "extrinsic" otherwise probative evidence under the parol evidence rule.[7] In particular, I am struck by the court's use of the word "equality" in the last line of its holding. It seems an extraordinarily narrow use of equality, when it excludes from consideration so much clear inequality. Again it resembles the process by which the parol evidence rule limits the meaning of documents or words by placing beyond the bounds of reference anything that is inconsistent with or even supplementary to the written agreement.

A few months after the *Croson* decision, the Supreme Court followed up with a string of famous cases that effectively gutted enforcement of the whole Civil Rights Act, to say nothing of affirmative action. After the first of these, *Martin v. Wilks*,[8] in which consent decrees setting goals for the hiring of black firefighters in Birmingham, Alabama, were permitted to be challenged collaterally by white firefighters, Reagan's Assistant Attorney General Charles J. Cooper was reported in the *Washington Post* as having said that the case was "a home run for white men." Two days later the *Post* printed a clarification saying that Cooper's remarks had been "incorrectly characterized": "Cooper felt that the ruling was a 'home run' for the proposition that people injured by affirmative action plans should be allowed to challenge them."[9] In the *New York Times* David Watkins, a lawyer for the city of Birmingham, hailed reverse discrimination cases as "the wave of the future": "I think whites have correctly perceived the new attitude of the U.S. Supreme Court, which seems to be giving encouragement to white citizens to challenge black gains in virtually every aspect of social and economic life."[10]

A quick review of the parol evidence rule: Before I went into teaching, I practiced consumer protection. I remember one trial in particular, a suit against a sausage manufacturer for selling impure and contaminated products. The manufacturer insisted that the word "sausage" meant "pig meat and lots of impurities." Here is part of my final argument to the jury:

> You have this thing called a sausage-making machine. You put pork and spices in at the top and crank it up, and because it is a sausage-making machine, what comes out the other end is a sausage. Over time, everyone knows that anything that comes out of the sausage-making machine is known as a sausage. In fact, there is law passed that says it is indisputably sausage.
>
> One day, we throw in a few small rodents of questionable pedigree and a teddy bear and a chicken. We crank the machine up and wait to see what comes out the other end. (1) Do we prove the validity of the machine if we call the product a sausage? (2) Or do we enlarge and enhance the meaning of "sausage" if we call the product a sausage? (3) Or do we have any success in breaking out of the bind if we call it something different from "sausage"?
>
> In fact, I'm not sure it makes any difference whether we call it sausage or if we scramble the letters of the alphabet over this thing that comes out, full of sawdust and tiny claws. What will make a

difference, however, is a recognition of our shifting relation to the word "sausage," by:

(1) enlarging the authority of sausage makers and enhancing the awesome, cruel inevitability of the workings of sausage machines—that is, everything they touch turns to sausage or else it doesn't exist; or by

(2) expanding the definition of sausage itself to encompass a wealth of variation: chicken, rodent, or teddy-bear sausage; or, finally, by

(3) challenging our own comprehension of what it is we really mean by sausage—that is, by making clear the consensual limits of sausage and reacquainting ourselves with the sources of its authority and legitimation.

Realizing that there are at least three different ways to relate to the facts of this case, to this product, this thing, is to define and acknowledge your role as jury and as trier of fact; is to acknowledge your own participation in the creation of reality.

At this point there was an objection, overruled, from the sausage maker's lawyer, based on too much critical theory in the courtroom. I continued:

This suit is an attempt to devour the meaning of justice in much the same way that this machine has devoured the last shred of common-sense meaning from sausage itself. But the ultimate interpretive choice is yours: will you allow the machine such great transformative power that everything which goes into it is robbed of its inherency, so that nonconformity ceases to exist? Or will you choose the second alternative, to allow the product to be so powerful that "sausage" becomes all-encompassing, so engorged with alternative meaning as to fill a purposeful machine with ambiguity and undecidability? Or will you wave that so-called sausage, sawdust and tiny claws spilling from both ends, in the face of that machine and shout: this is not Justice! For now is the time to revolt against the tyranny of definition-machines and insist on your right to name what your senses well know, to describe what you perceive to be the limits of sausage-justice, and the beyond of which is this *thing*, this clear injustice.

There was a spattering of applause from the gallery as I thanked the ladies and gentlemen of the jury and returned to my seat at counsel table.

Since that time, I have used sausages to illustrate a whole range of problems: I just substitute "constitution" or "equality" or "black" or "freedom of speech" instead of "sausage." It helps me to think about word entanglements on theoretical as well as prosaic levels. For one thing, the three levels of meaning correspond to

(1) a positivist mode of interpretation, in which the literal meaning of words is given great authority;

(2) a legal-realist, as well as mainstream feminist and civil-rights, mode of interpretation (squeezing room into meaning for "me too"); and

(3) what is often attributed to a "nihilistic" interpretive stance ("I don't know what it is, but I do know what it isn't"). A better way of describing this last category may be as interpretive discourse that explores the limits of meaning, gives meaning by knowing its bounds. (I think, by the way, that an accurate understanding of critical theory requires recognition of the way in which the concept of indeterminacy questions the authority of definitional cages; it is not "nihilism" but a challenge to contextualize, because it empowers community standards and the democratization of interpretation.)

This model also corresponds to the three levels of "integration" of contracts under the parol evidence rule: (1) Written contracts that are found by a judge to be "totally integrated" are limited to their "plain meaning," just as the dominant social contract as understood by the Reagan court is limited in its meaning and will not suffer any variation of interpretation from evidence of prior or contemporaneous circumstances, events, or sources of meaning. (2) Contracts that are found to be only "partially integrated" allow for multiplicities of meaning and may have their terms supplemented by additional or "extrinsic" evidence. (3) And contracts that are found "not integrated" may be altogether undone by a range of possible meaning that includes the wholly inconsistent.[11]

Law and life are all about the constant assessment of where on the scale one's words are meant—and by which level of the scale one evaluates the words of others. But I think the game is more complicated than choosing a single level on which to settle for all time. That truth exists on all three levels is the underlying truth I want to pursue here.

Situational sausage-machine analysis is a way of reexamining what is lost by narrow interpretative ideologies, and of rediscovering those injuries made invisible by the bounds of legal discourse. Affirmative-action programs, of which minority set-asides are but one example, were designed to remedy a segregationist view of equality in which positivistic categories of race reigned supreme. "White" had an ironclad definition that was the equivalent of "good" or "deserving". "Black" had an ironclad definition that was the equivalent of "bad" or unworthy of inclusion.

Although the most virulent examples of such narrow human and linguistic interpretations have been removed from the code books, much of this unconsciously filtered vision remains with us in subtler form. An example may be found in the so-called Ujaama House incidents that took place on Stanford University's campus in the fall of 1988. (Ujaama House is one of several "theme" houses set up with the idea of exposing students to a variety of live-in cultural and racial exchanges. There is a Hispanic theme house, a Japanese theme house; Ujaama is the African-American theme house.)

On the night of September 29, 1988, a white student identified only as "Fred" and a black student called "Q.C." had an argument about whether the composer Beethoven had black blood.

Q.C. insisted that he did; Fred thought the very idea "preposterous."

> The following night, the white students said that they got drunk and decided to color a poster of Beethoven to represent a black stereotype. They posted it outside the room of Q.C., the black student who had originally made the claim about Beethoven's race.
>
> Later, on October 14, after the defacing but before the culprits had been identified, a black fraternity's poster hanging in the dorm was emblazoned with the word "niggers." No one has admitted to that act, which prompted an emergency house staff meeting that eventually led to the identification [of Fred as one] of the students who had defaced the Beethoven poster.[12]

In subsequent months there was an exhaustive study conducted by the university, which issued a report of its findings on January 18, 1989. There were three things about Fred's explanation that I found particularly interesting in the report:

(1) Fred said he was upset by "all this emphasis on race, on blackness. Why can't we just all be human—I think it denies one's humanity to be 'racial.'" I was struck by the word boxes in which "race", "blackness," and "humanity" were structured as inconsistent concepts.

(2) Fred is a descendant of German Jews and was schooled in England. He described incidents that he called "teasing"—I would call them humiliation, even torture—by his schoolmates about his being Jewish. They called him miserly, and his being a Jew was referred to as a weakness. Fred said that he learned not to mind it and indicated that the poster defacement at Ujaama House had been in the spirit of this teaching. He wondered why the black students couldn't respond to it in the spirit in which it was meant: "nothing serious," just "humor as a release." It was a little message, he said, to stop all this divisive black stuff and be human. Fred appeared to me to be someone who was humiliated into conformity and then, in the spirit of the callousness and dis-

placed pain that humiliation ultimately engenders, was passing it on.

(3) Fred found the assertion that Beethoven was black not just annoying but "preposterous." In the wake of the defacement, he was assigned to do some reading on the subject and found that indeed Beethoven was a mulatto. This discovery upset him, so deeply in fact that his entire relation to the music changed: he said he heard it differently.[13]

Ultimately, Stanford's disciplinary board found no injury to Q.C. and recommended no disciplining of Fred because they felt that would victimize him, depriving him of his first-amendment rights. As to this remedy, I was struck by the following issues:

(1) The privatization of remedy to Q.C. alone.

(2) The invisibility of any injury to anyone, whether to Q.C. or to the Stanford community, whether to whites or to blacks.

(3) The paradoxical pitting of the first amendment against speaking about other forms of injury—so that the specter of legal censorship actually blocks further discussion of moral censure. This is always a hard point to make: I am not arguing against the first amendment; what I am insisting upon is some appreciation for the power of words—and for the other forms of power abuses that may lurk behind the "defense" of free speech.

As in *Croson*'s definition of equality, I think that the resolution of the Ujaama House incident rested on a definition of harm that was so circumscribed in scope as to conceal from any considera-tion—legal or otherwise—a range of serious but "extrinsic" harms felt by the decisionmakers to be either inconsistent with the first amendment or beside the point ("additional to," according to the parol evidence rule). In limiting the investigation and remedy to Fred and Q.C. exclusively, the group harm (to the collective of the dorm, to the Stanford community generally, to the group identity of blacks) was avoided. To illustrate this point, I will try to re-count my own sense of the Beethoven injury.

Even though the remark was not made to me or even in my

presence, I respond to it personally and also as a member of the group derogated; I respond personally but as part of an intergenerational collective. I am the "first black female" in many circumstances. I am a first black pioneer just for speaking my mind. The only problem is that every generation of my family has been a first black something or other, an experimental black, a "different" black—a hope, a candle, a credit to our race. Most of my black friends' families are full of generations of pioneers and exceptions to the rule. (How else would we have grown up to such rarefied heights of professionalism? Nothing is ever really done in one generation, or done alone.) It is not that we are all that rare in time—it is that over time our accomplishments have been coopted and have disappeared; the issue is when we can stop being perceived as "firsts." I wonder when I and the millions of other people of color who have done great and noble things or small and courageous things or creative and scientific things— when our achievements will become generalizations about our race and seen as contributions to the larger culture, rather than exceptions to the rule, isolated abnormalities. ("If only there were more of you!" I hear a lot. The truth is, there are lots more of me, and better of me, and always have been.)

The most deeply offending part of the Beethoven injury is its message that if I ever manage to create something as monumental as Beethoven's music, or the literature of the mulatto Alexandre Dumas or the mulatto Alexander Pushkin, then the best reward to which I can aspire is that I will be remembered as white. Perhaps my tribe will hold a candle in honor of my black heart over the generations—for blacks have been teaching white people that Beethoven was a mulatto for over a hundred years now—and they will be mocked when they try to make some claim to me. If they do press their point, the best they can hope for is that their tormenters will be absolved because it was a reasonable mistake to assume I was white: they just didn't know. But the issue is precisely the appropriation of knowledge, the authority of creating a canon, revising memory, declaring a boundary beyond which lies the "extrinsic" and beyond which ignorance is reasonably suffered. It is not only the individual and isolating fact of that ignorance; it is the violence of claiming in a way that denies theories of group rights and empowerment, of creating property that fragments collectivity and dehumanizes.[14]

This should not be understood as a claim that Beethoven's music is exclusively black music or that white people have no claim to its history or enjoyment; it is not really about Beethoven at all. It is about the ability of black and brown and red and yellow people to name their rightful contributions to the universe of music or any other field. It is the right to claim that we are, after all, part of Western Civilization.

The determination that Beethoven was not black is an unspoken determination that he was German and therefore could not be black. To acknowledge the possibility of his mulatto ancestry is to undo the supposed purity of the Germanic empire. It challenges the sanctification of cultural symbols rooted in notions of racial purity. One of the most difficult parts of the idea that Beethoven was not pure white has to do with the implication this has for the purity of all western civilization: if Beethoven, that most western musical warlord, is not really white, if the word 'German" also means "mulatto," then some of the most powerfully uplifting, inspiring, and unifying of what we call "western" moments come crashing down to the aesthetic of vaudevillian blackface. The student who defaced the poster said that before he "knew Beethoven was black he had a certain image of Beethoven and hearing he was black changed his perception of Beethoven and made him see Beethoven as the person he drew in the picture."

All of this is precisely the reasoning that leads so many to assume that the introduction of African-American or South American or feminist literature into Stanford's curriculum is a threat to the very concepts of what is meant by "western" or "civilization." It is indeed a threat. The most frightening discovery of all will be the eventual realization of the degree to which people of color have always been part of western civilization.

When Fred's whole relationship to the music changed once he discovered that Beethoven was black, it made me think of how much my students' relationship to me is engineered by my being black; how much I am marginalized based on a hierarchy of perception, by my relation to definitional canons that exercise superhuman power in my life. When Beethoven is no longer übermensch, but real and really black, he falls to a place beneath contempt, for there is no racial midpoint between the polarities of adoration and aversion. When some first-year law students walk in and see that I am their contracts teacher, I have been told, their whole perception of law school changes. The failure of Stanford to acknowledge this level of harm in the Ujaama House incident allows students to deface me. In the margins of their notebooks, or unconsciously perhaps, they deface me; to them, I "look like a stereotype of a black person" (as Fred described it), not an academic. They see my brown face and they draw lines enlarging the lips and coloring in "black frizzy hair." They add "red eyes, to give . . . a demonic look."[15] In the margins of their notebooks, I am obliterated.

The Beethoven controversy is an example of an analytic paradigm in which "white equals good, and black equals bad." Although that paradigm operated for many years as a construct in United States law, it cannot be said to exist as a formal legal matter today. Rather, an interpretative shift has occurred, as if our collective social reference has been enlarged somewhat, by slipping from what I described above as the first level of sausage analysis to the second: by going from a totally segregated system to a partially integrated one. In this brave new world, "white" still retains its ironclad (or paradigmatic) definition of "good," but a bit of word stretching is allowed to include a few additional others: blacks, whom we all now know can be good too, must therefore be "white." Blacks who refuse the protective shell of white goodness and insist that they are black are inconsistent with the paradigm of goodness, and therefore they are bad. As silly as this sounds as a bare-bones schematic, I think it is powerfully hypostatized in our present laws and in Supreme Court holdings: this absurd type of twisted thinking, racism in drag, is propounded not just as a theory of "equality" but as a standard of "neutrality." (This schematic is also why equality and neutrality have become such constant and necessary companions, two sides of the same coin: "equal . . ." has as its unspoken referent ". . . to whites"; "neutral . . ." has as it hidden subtext ". . . to concerns of color.")

Consider, for example, the case of the Rockettes. In October 1987 the Radio City Music Hall Rockettes hired the first black dancer in the history of that troupe. Her position was "to be on call for vacancies." (Who could have thought of a more quintessentially postmodern paradox of omission within the discourse of omission?) As of December 16, 1987, she had not yet performed but, it was hoped, "she may soon do so." Failure to include blacks before this was attributed not to racism but to the desire to maintain an aesthetic of uniformity and precision. As recently as five years ago, the director of the Rockettes, Violet Holmes, defended the all-white line on artistic grounds. She said that the dancers were supposed to be "mirror images" of one another and added: "One or two black girls in the line would definitely distract. You would lose the whole look of precision, which is the hallmark of the Rockettes." I read this and saw allegory—all of society pictured in that one statement.

Mere symmetry, of course, could be achieved by hiring all black dancers. It could be achieved by hiring light-skinned black dancers, in the tradition of the Cotton Club's grand heyday of condescension. It could be achieved by hiring an even number of black dancers and then placing them like little black anchors at either end or like hubcaps at the center, or by speckling them throughout the lineup at even intervals, for a nice checkerboard, melting-pot effect. It could be achieved by letting all the white dancers brown themselves in the sun a bit, to match the black dancers—something they were forbidden to do for many years, because the owner of the Rockettes didn't want them to look "like colored girls."

There are many ways to get a racially mixed lineup to look like a mirror image of itself. Hiring one black, however, is not the way to do it. Hiring one and placing her third to the left is a sure way to make her stick out, like a large freckle, and the imprecision of the whole line will devolve upon her. Hiring one black dancer and pretending that her color is invisible is the physical embodiment of the sort of emptiness and failure of imagination that more abstract forms of so-called neutral or colorblind remedies represent. As a spokeswoman for the company said: "[Race] is not an issue for the Rockettes—we're an equal opportunity employer."[16]

An issue that is far more difficult to deal with than the simple omission of those words that signify racism in law and society is the underlying yet dominant emotion of racism—the very perception that introducing blacks to a lineup will make it ugly ("unaesthetic"), imbalanced ("nonuniform"), and sloppy ("imprecise"). The ghostly power of this perception will limit everything the sole black dancer does—it will not matter how precise she is in feet and fact, since her presence alone will be construed as imprecise; it is her inherency that is unpleasant, conspicuous, unbalancing.

The example of the Rockettes is a lesson in why the limitation of original intent as a standard of constitutional review is problematic, particularly where the social text is an "aesthetic of uniformity"—as it appears to be in a formalized, strictly scrutinized but colorblind liberal society. Uniformity nullifies or at best penalizes the individual. Noninterpretive devices, extrinsic sources, and intuitive means of reading may be the only ways to include the reality of the unwritten, unnamed, nontext of race.

In *Croson* the Supreme Court responded to a version of this last point by proclaiming that the social text, no matter how uniform and exclusive, could not be called exclusionary in the absence of proof that people of color even *want* to be recipients of municipal contracts, or aspire to be Rockettes, or desire to work in ths or that profession. But the nature of desire and aspiration as well as the intent to discriminate are far more complicated than that, regulated as they are by the hidden and perpetuated injuries of racist words. The black-power movement notwithstanding, I think many people of color still find it extremely difficult to admit, much less prove, our desire to be included in alien and hostile organizations and institutions, even where those institutions also represent economic opportunity. I think, moreover, that even where the desire to be included is acknowledged, the schematic leads to a simultaneous act of race abdication and self-denial.

In January 1988, for example, on the day after Martin Luther King's birthday, the *New York Times* featured a story that illustrates as well as anything the paradoxical, self-perpetuating logic of this form of subordination and so-called neutrality. In Hackensack, New Jersey, African-American residents resisted efforts to rename their street after King because it would signal to "anyone who read the phone book" that it was a black neighborhood. It was feared that no white person would ever want to live there and property values would drop: "It stigmatizes an area."[17]

The Hackensack story struck a familiar chord. I grew up amidst a clutter of such opinions, just such uprisings of voices, riotous, enraged, middle-class, picky, testy, and brash. Our house was in Boston on the border of the predominantly black section of Roxbury. For years the people on my street argued about whether they were really in Roxbury or whether they were close enough to be considered part of the (then) predominantly white neighborhood of Jamaica Plain.

An even more complicated example occurred in North Baltimore. Two white men, one of them legally blind, heaved a six-pound brick and a two-pound stone through the front window of a black couple's house. They did so, according to the U.S. attorney, "because they felt blacks should not be living in their neighborhood and wanted to harrass the couple because of their race." The two men pleaded guilty to interfering with the couple's housing rights. The couple, on the other hand, criticized the prosecutor's office for bringing the indictment at all. "Describing himself as Moorish-American, [the husband] said he does not consider himself black and does not believe in civil rights. 'I'm tired of civil rights, I hate civil rights,' Mr. Boyce-Bey, a carpenter's apprentice, said. Moorish-Americans associate civil rights with racism and slavery." [18] Subsequently, the couple moved out of the house.

It seems to me that the stigma of "Dr. Martin Luther King Boulevard" or "Roxbury" is reflective of a deep personal discomfort among blacks, a wordless and tabooed sense of self that is identical to the discomfort shared by both blacks and whites in even mentioning words like "black" and "race" in mixed company. Neutrality is from this perspective a suppression, an institutionalization of psychic taboos as much as segregation was the institutionalization of physical boundaries. What the middle-class, propertied, upwardly mobile black striver must do, to accommodate a race-neutral world view, is to become an invisible black, a phantom black, by avoiding the label "black" (it's all right to be black in this reconfigured world if you keep quiet about it). The words of race are like windows into the most private vulnerable parts of the self; the world looks in and the world will know, by the awesome, horrific revelation of a name.

I remember with great clarity the moment I discovered that I was "colored." I was three and already knew that I was a "Negro"; my parents had told me to be proud of that. But "colored" was something else; it was the totemic evil I had heard my little white friends talking about for several weeks before I finally realized that I was one of *them*. I still remember the crash of that devastating moment of union, the union of my joyful body and the terrible power of that devouring symbol of negritude. I have spent the rest of my life recovering from the degradation of being divided against myself; I am still trying to overcome the polarity of my own vulnerability.

Into this breach of the division-within-ourselves falls the helplessness of our fragile humanity. Unfortunately, the degree to which it is easier in the short run to climb out of the pit by denying the mountain labeled "colored" than it is to tackle the sheer cliff that is our scorned mortality is the degree to which blacks internalize the mountain labeled colored. It is the degree to which blacks remain divided along all sorts of categories of blackness, including class, and turn the speech of helplessness upon ourselves like a firehose. We should do something with ourselves, say the mothers to the daughters and the sons to the fathers, we should do something. So we rub ointments on our skin and pull at our hair and wrap our bodies in silk and gold. We remake and redo and we sing and pray that the ugliness will be hidden and our beauty will shine through and be accepted. And we work and we work and we work at ourselves. Against ourselves, in spite of ourselves, and in subordination of ourselves.

We resent those of us who do not do the same. We resent those who are not well-groomed and well-masked and have not reined in the grubbiness of their anger, who have not sought the shelter of the most decorous assimilation possible. So confusing are the "colored" labels, so easily do they masquerade as real people, that we frequently mistake the words for ourselves.

My dispute is perhaps not with formal equal opportunity. So-called formal equal opportunity has done a lot but misses the heart of the problem: it put the vampire back in its coffin, but it was no silver stake. The rules may be colorblind, but people are not. The question remains, therefore, whether the law can truly exist apart from the color-conscious society in which it exists, as a skeleton devoid of flesh; or whether law is the embodiment of society, the reflection of a particular citizenry's arranged complexity of relations.

All this is to say that I strongly believe not just in programs like affirmative action, but in affirmative action as a socially and professionally pervasive concept. This should not be understood as an attempt to replace an ideology controlled by "white men" with one controlled by "black women"—or whomever. The real issue is precisely the canonized status of any one group's control. Black individuality is subsumed in a social circumstance—an idea, a stereotype—that pins us to the underside of this society and keeps us there, out of sight/out of mind, out of the knowledge of mind which is law. Blacks and women are the objects of a constitutional omission that has been incorporated into a theory of neutrality. It is thus that omission becomes a form of expression, as oxymoronic as that sounds: racial omission is a literal part of original intent; it is the fixed, reiterated prophesy of the Founding Fathers. It is thus that affirmative action is an affirmation; the affirmative act of hiring—or hearing—blacks is a recognition of individuality that includes blacks as a social presence, that is profoundly linked to the fate of blacks and whites and women and men either as subgroups or as one group. Justice is a continual balancing of competing visions, plural viewpoints, shifting histories, interests, and allegiances. To acknowledge that level of complexity is to require, to seek, and to value a multiplicity of knowledge systems, in pursuit of a more complete sense of the world in which we all live. Affirmative action in this sense is as mystical and beyond-the-self as an initiation ceremony. It is an act of verification and vision, an act of social as well as professional responsibility.

In the last ten or fifteen years, there has been increasing effort to expand racial paradigms. A standard allowing increased differentiation, and celebrating "difference," is more frequently touted as a desirable social norm. This is, I think, very much like yet another shift in the sausage-machine analogy, from the second level of partial integration to the third level, where whole new worlds of meaning are allowed to coexist and to contradict one another. In that happily cacophonous universe, white is white and white is good, and black is good and black is really black.

This paradigm is what has given us all the instructional and cultural experiments, in academia and elsewhere, such as Stanford's theme houses. Soul-food nights, salsa dances. Or, at one institution with which I was associated, a Real White Men's Day, celebrated on the occasion of the first blizzard of the season. (Real White Men in their shirtsleeves would go out to the parking lot, set up grilles, and barbecue Real Red Meat. We, the rest of the community, would be there rooting them on from the warmth of the cafeteria, always ready to acknowledge anyone's difference but most particularly theirs.) All this is good, with the possible problem that, in such exclusive celebrations, difference becomes a property launching us back into a complicated version of the first level of parol-evidence-sausage, so that: if white is good and black is good and white and black are different, then goodness must be different for each—or goodness becomes a limited property that is the subject of intense competition, as if it were a physical thing, a commodity or object whose possession can know only one location.

Let me give you an example, shifting from race to gender, of how this third-level "difference" can get complicated and overlap with first-level exclusion of the "extrinsic." When I was living in California I had a student, S., who was very unhappy being a man and informed me of his intention to become a woman. He said he wanted to talk to me before anyone else at the school because I was black and might be more understanding. I had never thought about transsexuality at all and found myself lost for words.[19]

After the sex-change operation, S. began to use the ladies' room. There was an enormous outcry from women students of all political persuasions, who "felt raped," in addition to the more academic assertions of some who "feared rape." In a complicated storm of homophobia, the men of the student body let it be known that they too "feared rape" and vowed to chase her out of any and all men's rooms. The oppositional forces of men and women reached a compromise: S. should use the dean's bathroom. Alas, in the dean's bathroom no resolution was to be found, for the suggestion had not been an honest one but merely an integration of the fears of each side. Then, in his turn the dean, circumspection having gotten him this far in life, expressed polite, well-modulated fears about the appearance of impropriety in having students visit his inner sanctum, and many other things most likely related to his fear of a real compromise of hierarchy.

I remember thinking how peculiar and revealing were the scripts that people shook in the face of poor S. Gender as property. Gender as privilege. Hierarchy as sexualized oppression. "I am not a homosexual," I remember S. crying out at one point in the middle of all that mess. Those words echo in me still. She was not homosexual first and foremost as to her best friend, a man with whom she was in love and for whom she had gone through the operation. She was not homosexual as to the women, whose outcry she took for fear of lesbianism. She was not homosexual as to the men, for this would have been an ultimate betrayal of her bitter, hard-won love. She was not homosexual as to the dean, as if this bit of clarity would save him from some embarrassment or reassure him that his status would not be lowered by the ambivalence of her identity.

At the vortex of this torment, S. as human being who needed to go to the bathroom was lost. Devoured by others, she carved and shaped herself to be definitionally acceptable. She aspired to a notion of women set like jewels in grammatical mountings, fragile and display-cased. She had not learned what society's tricksters and dark fringes have had to learn in order to survive: to invert, to stretch, meaning rather than oneself. She to whom words meant so much was not given the room to appropriate them. S. as "transsexual", S. as "not homosexual," thus became a mere floating signifier, a deconstructive polymorph par excellence.

In retrospect, I see clearly the connection between S.'s fate and my being black, her coming to me because I was black. S.'s experience was a sort of Jim Crow mentality applied to gender. Many men, women, blacks, and certainly anyone who identifies with the term "white" are caught up in the perpetuation and invisible privilege of this game; for "black," "female," "male," and "white" are every bit as much properties as the buses, private clubs, neighborhoods, and schools that provide the extracorporeal battlegrounds of their expression. S.'s experience, indeed, was a reminder of the extent to which property is nothing more than the mind's enhancement of the body's limitation. This is true to some extent in all cultures, I think, but particularly in ours, where possessions become the description of who we are and the reflection of our worth; and where land usually is referred to not by its use but by the name of its owner (Queens, Victoria, Washington, Pennsylvania)—as if the greater the expanse of an estate, the greater in personhood will its master become.

Another dimension of this encounter was that the property of my blackness was all about my struggle to define myself as "somebody." Into the middle of that struggle, S. was coming to me both because I was black and because others had defined her as "nobody." Initially it felt as if she were seeking in me the comfort of another nobody; I was a bit put off by the implication that my distinctive somebody-ness was being ignored—I was being used, rendered invisible through her refusal to see all of me. Very quickly, however, I realized that a literal designation of "black" in my self-definition was probably not appropriate in this situation. Though all of the above may be true, I realized that another truth existed also: a discursive property of black somebody-ness was to be part of a community of souls who had experienced being permanently invisible nobodies; "black" was a designation for those who had no place else to go; we were both nobody and somebody at the same time, if for different purposes.

This is not an easy concept. I am not saying that my blackness is unimportant or not different. In other circumstances it might be presumptuous for S. to "become black" or for me to feel obligated to stretch the definition to include her. What I am saying is that my difference was in some ways the same as hers, that simultaneously her difference was in some ways very different from mine, and that simultaneously we were in all ways the same.

Not long ago, a white acquaintance of mine described her boyfriend as "having a bit of the Jewish in him." She meant that he was stingy with money. I said, "Don't talk like that! I know you didn't mean it, but there are harmful implications in thinking like that." She responded with profuse apologies, phone calls, tears, then anger. She said repeatedly that she had no wish to offend me or anyone: that it was just a cultural reality, there was no offense in it, she had heard Jewish people say the same thing, it was just the way things were, nothing personal. There was an odd moment at which I thought we were in agreement, when she said she was sorry and it was "just a cultural reality": I thought she was referring to racism's being so deeply imbedded in culture that it was unconscious—but what she meant was that stinginess was a Jewish "thing."

As we argued, words like "overly sensitive," "academic privilege," and "touchy" began to creep into her description of me. She accused me of building walls, of being unrealistic, of not being able to loosen up and just be with people. She didn't use the word "righteous," but I know that's what she meant. I tried to reassure her that I didn't mean to put her on the defensive, that I had not meant to attack or upset her, and that I deeply valued her friendship. But I could not back down. I felt our friendship being broken apart. She would be consoled with nothing less than a retraction of my opinion, an admission that I was wrong. She didn't want me to understand merely that she meant no harm, but wanted me to confess that there was no harm. Around this time, my sister sent me an article about the difficulties of blacks and whites in discussing racial issues in social settings. It included the warning of Shelby Steele, a black professor of English at San Jose State University ("If you are honest and frank, you may come to be seen as belligerent, arrogant, a troublemaker"), and the advice of Harvard professor Alvin Poussaint ("Defuse the situation; devise a way of getting out of it quickly. Develop some humorous responses . . . and take charge by steering the conversation in another direction").[20]

Not long after that, I went shopping for a sweatshirt in the emptiness of nearly closing time at Au Coton, a clothing store near my home. The three young salespeople told me that a waffle-weave sweater would make me look "really fly." I said I was too old to be fly. One of them persisted: "Well, all the really fly people are wearing waffle weave." As I continued to shop, I could hear them laughing among themselves. When I came closer to the counter, I heard that they were joking about Jews. They mentioned "princesses" and imitated "Jewish" accents—New Yorkers imitating other New Yorkers. To an outsider like me, it sounded as if they were imitating themselves.

"Speak of the devil," said one of them as four other young people came into the store. I don't know why the salespeople had decided that the newcomers were Jews—again, it was as if they were pointing fingers at themselves. They all wore waffle-weave tops; denim jackets with the collars turned up; their hair in little moussed spikes and lacquered ringlets; colorful kerchiefs knotted at their throats.

"Tell that girl to get a job," murmured one of the salesgirls. There was both playfulness and scorn in her voice. Her friends tittered. The designated Jews wandered around the store, held clothes on hangers up to their chins, generally looked as youthfully fly as could be. One of the salesgirls said, "Can I help you guys?" Her voice was high-pitched and eager. Then she turned her head and winked at her friends.

I didn't say anything. I wanted to say something and, since

I'm usually outspoken about these things, I was surprised when no words came out. It is embarrassing but worthwhile nonetheless, I think, to run through all the mundane, even quite petty, components of the self-consciousness that resulted in my silence. Such silence is too common, too institutionalized, and too destructive not to examine it in the most nuanced way possible.

My self-consciousness was a powerful paralyzer. I was self-conscious about being so much older than they. I was afraid of sounding so maternally querulous that they would dismiss my words. I was self-conscious too about shopping in a store with posters that said "As advertised in *Seventeen Magazine*." As old as I was, I felt very young again, in a sticky, tongue-tied awful adolescent way. In some odd way that is extremely hard to admit in print, I wanted their approval. I was on the edge of their group, the odd person out (as I always was as a teenager, that time in one's life when attitudes about everything social—including race—are most powerfully reinforced). I didn't want to be part of them, but I didn't want to be the object of their derision either. The whole room was filled with adolescent vanity, social pressure, and a yearning to belong. The room was ablaze with the crossfire of self-assertive groupings. The four who wandered in, preening and posing and posturing, pretending self-confidence. The three who worked there, lounging and diffident, pretending they owned the place. For those brief, childish, powerful moments, I wasn't sure I could survive being on the wrong side.

I was also caught short because they were so *open* about their antisemitism. They smiled at me and commented on the clothing I was looking at; they smiled and commented on the clothing being looked at by the others. Their antisemitism was smiling, open, casually jocular, and only slightly conspiritorial or secretive. They were such nice young people—how could they possibly mean any harm? This little piece of cognitive dissonance was aided and abetted by my blackness, the fact that I am black: I grew up in a neighborhood where blacks were the designated Jews. I can think of few instances in which I have ever directly heard the heart, the uncensored, undramatic day-to-day core of it—heard it as people think it and heard it from the position of an "insider." And it was irresistible, forbidden, almost thrilling to be on the inside. I was "privileged" to hear what these people thought, earmarked as someone who would not reveal them; I was designated safe. I was also designated as someone who didn't matter.

What they had constructed around me was the architecture of trust. As strange as it sounds, I realized that breaking the bond of my silence was like breaking the bond of *our* silence. At the same time, I realized that their faith in me was oppressively insulting. I became an antisemite by the stunning audacity of their assumption that I would remain silent. If I was "safe," I was also "easy" in my desire for the illusion of inclusion, in my capitulation to the vanity of mattering enough even to be included. It did not occur to me that I was simply being ignored. I could have been Jewish, as much as the four random souls who wandered into the store; but by their designation of me as "not Jewish" they made property of me, as they made wilderness of the others. I became colonized as their others were made enemies.

I left a small piece of myself on the outside, beyond the rim of their circle, with those others on the other side of the store; as they made fun of the others, they also made light of me; I was watching myself be made fun of. In this way I transformed myself into the third person; I undermined the security of my most precious property, I. I gave much power to the wilderness of strangers, some few of whom I would feel as reflections of my lost property by being able to snare them in the strong beartraps of my own familiarizing labels.

I have thought a lot about this incident. Part of my reaction was premised on the peculiarities of my own history. Although I was quite young, I remember the Woolworth sit-ins; I remember my father walking trepidatiously into stores in Savannah, Georgia, shortly after desegregation, cautiously disbelieving of his right to be there, disproportionately grateful for the allowance just to be. Very much my father's daughter, I am always grateful when store-keepers are polite to me; I don't expect courtesy, I value it in a way that resembles love and trust and shelter. I value it in a way that is frequently misleading, for it is neither love nor trust nor shelter.

I know that this valuing is a form of fear. I am afraid of being alien and suspect, of being thrown out at any moment; I am relieved when I am not. At the same time, I am enraged by the possibility of this subsurface drama-waiting-to-happen. My rage feels dangerous, full of physical violence, like something that will get me arrested. And also at the same time I am embarrassed by all these feelings, ashamed to reveal in them the truth of my insignificance. All this impermissible danger floats around in me, boiling, exhausting. I can't kill and I can't teach everyone. I can't pretend it doesn't bother me; it eats me alive. So I protect myself. I don't venture into the market very often. I don't deal with other people if I can help it. I don't risk exposing myself to the rage that will get me arrested. The dilemma—and the distance between the "I" on this side of the store and the me that is "them" on the other side of the store—is marked by an emptiness in myself. Frequently such emptiness is reiterated by a hole in language, a gap in the law, or a chasm of fear.

I think that the hard work of a nonracist sensibility is the boundary crossing, from safe circle into wilderness: the testing of boundary, the consecration of sacrilege. It is the willingness to spoil a good party and break an encompassing circle, to travel from the safe to the unsafe. The transgression is dizzyingly intense, a reminder of what it is to be alive. It is a sinful pleasure, this willing transgression of a line, which takes one into new awareness, a secret, lonely, and tabooed world—to survive the transgression is terrifying and addictive. To know that everything has changed and yet that nothing has changed; and in leaping the chasm of this impossible division of self, a discovery of the self surviving, still well, still strong, and, as a curious consequence, renewed.

But as I said earlier, the perspective we need to acquire is one beyond those three boxes that have been set up. It is a perspective that exists on all three levels and eighty-five more besides—simultaneously. It is this perspective, the ambivalent, multivalent way of seeing, that is at the core of what is called critical theory, feminist theory, and much of the minority critique of law. It has to do with a fluid positioning that sees back and forth across boundary, which acknowledges that I can be black and good and black and bad, and that I can also be black and white, male and female, yin and yang, love and hate.

Nothing is simple. Each day is a new labor.

Ursula Le Guin, in her novel *The Lathe of Heaven*, writes that making love is like baking bread: each time it must be done with care and from the beginning.

Each day is a new labor.

III

Ladder to the Light

A Series of Hinged Turning Points

Fire and Ice

(some thoughts on property, appearance,
and the language of lawmakers)

Last January I went to a gingerbread-man-making party. Lots of children, popcorn, eggnog, and cookie cutting. The party was in a neighborhood that used to be the Lower East Side but is now struggling for the separate identity of a gentler (and more gentrified) name. It reaches for inspiration to the other side of Broadway, to Soho and the Village, where I was living then. After the party I wandered home, along the Bowery, up Lafayette. It was no temperature at all, zero degrees. I decided to stop in at the dance studio where I took classes and get the latest schedule. It's located in an old warehouse that used to be an informal home for the homeless, an abandoned-factory refuge from the cold. In the old days I would make my way through the littered hallways, the slumped bodies in the foyer, dispensing change upon request, praying for divine protection, both for them and for me. My car was broken into occasionally, but for the most part it was safe for all of us, because so well-trafficked. We were each other's guardians. Then one day all that "empty space" in the building was converted into loft-condominiums, and the old familiar bodies from inside began to be seen slumped on the sidewalk outside the old warehouse.

At any rate there I was, late on a frozen Sunday afternoon,

walking through a border-line Bowery neighborhood, toward the factory-condominium that was also my dance studio. As I opened the heavy iron door, I met three angry people stalking down the hallway. The procession was led by a child of about eight who flounced through the door I held open for her, without lifting her eyes from the ground. Her younger sister, about six, followed through the door I continued to hold open, looked me coldly in the eye, and did not say thank you. Their mother followed, a deep furrow between her eyes; as she drew abreast of me, she turned and sharply asked if I were going upstairs to the dance studio. When I said yes, she shouted at me, with the unique intensity of a neurotic New Yorker: "Well, tell them to call the police! There are BUMS in the lobby again!" Then she pushed past, after her little girls.

I let myself cautiously in and walked through the hallway to the staircase. There was one old, bent, toothless black woman huddled under a yellow blanket with holes in it. She was sucking on a cigarette with one hand and pulling at her skirt with the other. She wore black round-toed sneakers with white rubber rims and gray argyle kneesocks. I gave her $1.25 when she asked for spare change; then I went upstairs to get a copy of the dance schedule. No one molested me and I called no police.

Back out on the sidewalk a few minutes later, I saw the angry woman and her two children across the street, waiting to get their car from a garage. In what was clearly the most spontaneous action of my well-ordered day, I jaywalked over to her and said, simply, that if she wanted to call the police for that old woman, she would have to take on the responsibility herself. If I had taken the few seconds that indignation eclipsed, I would have been prepared for her anger. She jumped in her car, locked the doors, and through her window (rolled down two inches) yelled at me about how she was spending "too much goddamned money" to live in that building, how she had been shot at, how she had been mugged, how maybe one woman wasn't dangerous but, where there's one woman, the men will follow and "those men" are dangerous. "Those men" are dangerous, she said over and over again.

I wanted to say more, I wanted to ask her to observe that the warmth of something as simple as fire is no longer free in this city, that the dismantling of the welfare state means people will steal to survive. I wanted to tell her that when people are too tired to be angry, when they lose the will to survive, that only then will the war exit their bodies. When they become sunken, spiritless, haunted by the living, pursued by death, abandoned by all but pathos—then graphic artists will flock to their grave, sad images and proclaim them indominable human spirits, pietàs, survivors. Then, at last, they will be sympathetic. I wanted to say all of that, but she kept shouting and shouting at me about all the goddamned money she was spending to keep "those people" out of her life and off "her" streets.

Her two young children sat in the back seat through all this, frightened puppies hovering in their mother's shadow—frightened by their mother's fury, frightened by me, who deeply did not wish this confrontation. They stared at me in round-eyed, innocent terror. I hated them for their terror of me more than I hated their mother for her protective rage. When they finally drove off, in a back-wheeled spray of salt and slush, I cried. Unexpectedly I felt exiled, intensely alien, cold and alone, despite the fact that I was only two blocks from home.

Over a year has passed. The neighborhood has continued to change. Japanese restaurants and oriental rug marts abound. There's a security guard in the foyer of the building now; they hired an old black man in a blue suit with a badge, to keep out other old tired black people. The guard smiles and nods benevolently at me when I come and go. I nod back at him. He says I make his day worthwhile; he is paternal, flirtatious. We both enjoy the fantasy that he is protecting me. I walk out into the cold dark winter of New York. I look back through the moist glass doors and see his blackened shape, pot-bellied and alone; a plastic chair;

his transistor radio, its tiny antenna raised into the empty space of the stairwell. He is brilliantly backlit, like the wick of a candle. He stays in my mind like that, a burning marker, a flaming signifier.

On October 29, 1984, Eleanor Bumpurs, a 270-pound, arthritic sixty-seven-year-old woman, was shot to death while resisting eviction from her apartment in the Bronx. She was $96.85, or one month, behind in her rent. Mayor Ed Koch and Police Commissioner Benjamin Ward described the struggle that preceded her demise as involving two officers with large plastic shields, one with a restraining hook, one with a shotgun, and at least one other who was supervising. All of these officers also carried service revolvers. During the course of the attempted eviction, Mrs. Bumpurs wielded a knife that Commissioner Ward says was "bent" on one of the plastic shields and escaped the constraint of the restraining hook twice. At some point, Stephen Sullivan, the officer positioned farthest away from her and the one with the shotgun, took aim and fired at her. He missed (mostly—it is alleged that this blast removed half of the hand that held the knife and, according to the Bronx district attorney's office, "it was anatomically impossible for her to hold the knife"), pumped his gun, and shot again, making his mark the second time around.[1]

What has not been made clear in discussion relating to this case is that Mrs. Bumpurs was evicted on a default judgment of possession and warrant of eviction issued without any hearing of any kind. She was never personally served because, allegedly, she was not at home on the two occasions the process server says he called. Since Mrs. Bumpurs did not appear in court to answer the petition for her eviction, the default judgment for possession and warrant for her eviction were signed by the Civil Court judge solely on the papers submitted. From what we know now . . . there is serious doubt about the validity of those papers.

Only last year, in announcing the indictments of five process servers, the Attorney General and the New York City Departments of

Consumer Affairs and Investigation issued a report on service of process in Civil Court, finding that at least one-third of all default judgments were based on perjurious affidavits.[2]

The case against Officer Sullivan was not brought to trial until January 1987. Initially a grand jury indicted him for reckless manslaughter. Two lower courts rejected the indictment, but in 1986 the New York Court of Appeals reversed and ordered a trial regarding the second shot.

In the two-and-a-half-year interval between the incident and the trial, controversy billowed and swirled around the poles of whether Mrs. Bumpurs ought to have brandished a knife or whether the officer ought to have used his gun. In February 1987 a New York Supreme Court justice found Officer Sullivan innocent of manslaughter charges. The case centered on a very narrow use of language pitted against circumstance. District Attorney Mario Merola described the case as follows: "*Obviously* [emphasis added], one shot would have been justified. But if that shot took off part of her hand and rendered her defenseless, whether there was any need for a second shot, which killed her, that's the whole issue of whether you have reasonable force or excessive force.' "[3] My intention in this chapter is to analyze the task facing judges and lawyers in undoing institutional descriptions of what is "obvious" and what is not; and in resisting the general predigestion of evidence for jury consumption.

Shortly after Merola's statement, Sullivan's attorney expressed eagerness to get the case before a jury. Then, after the heavily publicized attack in Howard Beach, the same attorney decided that a nonjury trial might be better after all. " 'I think a judge will be much more likely than a jury to understand the defense that the shooting was justified,' said Officer Sullivan's lawyer, Bruce A. Smiry, when asked why he had requested a nonjury trial. 'The average lay person might find it difficult to understand why the police were there in the first place, and why a shotgun was employed . . . Because of the climate now in the city, I don't want people perceiving this as a racial case.' "[4]

Since 1984 Mayor Koch, Commissioner Ward, and a host of other city officials have repeatedly termed the shooting of Eleanor Bumpers as completely legal.[5] At the same time, Ward admitted publicly that Mrs. Bumpurs should not have died. Koch admitted that her death had been the result of "a chain of mistakes and circumstances that came together in the worst possible way, with the worst possible consequences."[6] The officers could have waited until she calmed down, or they could have used tear gas or mace, Ward said. But, according to Ward, all that is hindsight (prompting one to wonder how often this term is used as a euphemism for short-circuited foresight). As to whether this white officer's shooting of a black woman had racial overtones, Ward said he had "no evidence of racism." (Against this, it is interesting to note that in New York City, where blacks and Latinos account for close to half the population, "86.8% of police officers are white; 8.6% are black; 4.5% Latino; and 0.1% Asian or American Indian."[7]) The commissioner pointed out that he is sworn to uphold the law, which is "inconsistent with treating blacks differently," and that the shooting was legal because it was "within the code of police ethics."[8] Finally, city officials resisted criticism of the police department's handling of the incident by accusing "outsiders" of not knowing all the facts and not understanding the pressure under which officers labor.

The word *legal* has as its root the Latin *lex*, which meant law in a fairly concrete sense, law as we understand it when we refer to written law, codes, systems of obedience. The word *lex* did not include the more abstract, ethical dimension of law which includes not merely consideration of rules but their purposes and effective implementation. The larger meaning was contained in the Latin *jus* from which we derive the word *justice*. This is not an insignificant semantic distinction: the word of law, whether statutory or judge-made, is a subcategory of the underlying social motives and beliefs from which it is born. It is the technical embodiment of attempts to order society according to a consensus of ideals. When a society loses sight of those ideals and grants obeisance to words alone, law becomes sterile and formalistic; lex is applied without jus and is therefore unjust. A sort of punitive literalism ensues that leads to a high degree of thoughtless conformity; for literalism has, as one of its primary underlying values, order (the ultimate goal may be justice, but it is the ordering of behavior that is deemed the immediate end). Living solely according to the letter of the law means that we live without spirit, that one can do anything one wants to as long as it complies in a technical sense. The cynicism or rebelliousness that infects one's spirit, the enthusiasm or dissatisfaction with which one technically conforms, is unimportant. It implies furthermore that such compliance is in some ways arbitrary, that is to say, inconsistent with the will of the compliant. The law becomes a battleground of wills. But the extent to which technical legalisms are used to obfuscate the human motivations that generate our justice system is the real extent to which we as human beings are disenfranchised.

Cultural needs and ideals change with the momentum of time; the need to redefine our laws in keeping with the spirit of cultural flux is what keeps a society alive and humane. In instances like the Bumpurs case, the words of the law called for nonlethal alternatives to be applied first, but allowed for a degree of police discretion in determining which situations were so immediately life-endangering as to require the use of deadly force. It was this discretionary area that presumably was the basis upon which the claim was founded that Officer Sullivan acted legally. Yet the purpose of the law as written was to prevent unnecessary deaths; it is ironic that a public mandate so unambiguous about its concern and, in this instance, relatively unambiguous about the limits of its application should be used as the justification for this shooting. The law as written permitted shooting in general and therefore, by extension of the city's reasoning, it would be impossible for a police officer ever to shoot someone in a specifically objectionable way.

If our laws are thus piano-wired on the exclusive validity of literalism, if they are picked clean of their spirit, then society risks heightened irresponsibility for the consequence of abominable actions. Jonathan Swift's description of lawyers in *Gulliver's Travels* (part 4, chapter 5) comes weirdly and ironically alive: "there was a society of men among us, bred up from their youth in the art of proving by words multiplied for the purpose, that white is black, and black is white, according as they are paid. To this society all the rest of the people are slaves." We risk as well subjecting ourselves to such absurdly empty rhetoric as Commissioner Ward's comments that Mrs. Bumpurs' death was "unfortunate, but the law says . . ." or that racism is "unfortunate, but the law says . . ." What's worse, this sort of apologizing is the softened inverse of something akin to fascism. Ward's sentiments may as well read: "The law says . . . and therefore the death was unfortunate but irremedial; the law says . . . and therefore there is little that can be done about racism." The law becomes a shield behind which to avoid responsibility for the human repercussions of either governmental or publicly harmful private activity.

A related issue is the degree to which much of the criticism of the police department's handling of this case was devalued as "noisy" or excessively emotional. It is as though passionate protest were a separate crime, a rudeness of such dimension as to defeat altogether any legitimacy of content. As lawyers, we are taught from the moment we enter law school to temper our emotionalism, quash our idealism. Most of us were taught that our heartfelt instincts would subvert the law and defeat the security of a well-ordered civilization; but faithful adherence to the word of law, to *stare decisis* and clearly stated authority, would lead as a matter of course to a bright clear world in which those heartfelt instincts would, like the Wizard of Oz, be waiting. Form was exalted over substance, and cool rationales over heated feelings. Yet being ruled by the cool formality of language is surely as bad as being ruled solely by one's emotions.

But undue literalism is only one brand of sleight of tongue in the attainment of meaningless dialogue. The defense in the Bumpurs case used overgeneralization as an effective linguistic complement to their aversion of the issues; it is an old game, Enlargement of the Stakes, and an ancient tactic of irresponsibility. Allegations that the killing was illegal, unnecessary, and should be prosecuted were met with responses like: "The laws permit police officers to shoot people." "As long as police officers have guns, there will be unfortunate deaths." "The conviction rate in cases like this is very low." (This was part of the basis on which two lower courts had vacated the 1985 grand-jury indictment of Officer Sullivan, before it was finally reinstated in November 1986, and the basis on which the Police Benevolent Association staged a continuing protest against Sullivan's being tried for anything.) The observation that tear gas would have been an effective alternative to shooting drew the dismissive reply that "there were lots of things they could have done."[9]

Privatization of Response as a Justification for Public Irresponsibility is a version of the same game. This method holds up the private self as indistinguishable from the public-duty-self. Public and media commentary is responded to by officials as if it were meant specifically to hurt private, vulnerable feelings; and trying to hold a public official accountable while not hurting his feelings is a skill the acquisition of which could consume time better spent on almost any conceivable issue. Thus, when Commissioner Ward was asked if the internal review board planned to discipline Officer Sullivan, many seemed conditioned to accept as responsive his saying that, while he was personally very sorry she had died, he couldn't understand why the media were focusing so closely on him. "How many other police commissioners," he asked repeatedly, "have gotten as much attention as I have?" (Not that there wasn't truth to that. Ward was the first black commissioner in the history of the New York Police Department; the excessive scrutiny to which he was subjected in the public's search for irony, as opposed to other responsible officials, was glaring.)

Finally, a most cruel form of semantic slipperiness infused Mrs. Bumpurs' death from the beginning: Victim Responsibility. It is the least responsive form of dialogue, yet apparently the easiest to buy into (were we hardened to its fallacy during our helpless, finger-pointing, guilt-ridden childhoods?). The following examples can be found in the answers, from various public officials and law-enforcement personnel, to questions posed by television reporter Gil Noble on the program "Like It Is":

> —*Don't you think this officer was motivated by racism?* "She was psychotic; she said that she saw Reagan coming through her walls."
> —*Wasn't the discharge of the shotgun illegal?* "She waved a kinfe."
> —*Wasn't shooting her unnecessary?* "She made the officers fear for their lives."
> —*Couldn't the officers have used tear gas?* "Couldn't her children have paid her rent and taken care of her?" (The hypothesized failure of Mrs. Bumpurs' children to look after her actually became a major point in Officer Sullivan's defense attorney's opening and closing statements. Ironically, "a former employee of the Housing Authority said that, three weeks before Mrs. Bumpurs's death . . . her relatives tried to make a payment of about . . . half of the rent she owed . . . But the former Authority employee, Joan Alfredson . . . who was a bookkeeper, said she turned down the payment because she was forbidden to accept partial payment without the written consent of a supervisor."[10])

All these words, from the commissioner, from the mayor, from the media and the public generally, have rumbled and resounded with the sounds of discourse; we want to believe that their symmetrical, pleasing structure adds up to discourse; and if we are not careful, we will hypnotize ourselves into believing that it is discourse. When the whole world gets to that point, I know that I, for one, will see Ronald Reagan, clear and sprightly, coming through my walls as Mrs. Bumpurs alleged he did in her last hours. And I have not yet been able to settle within myself whether that would be the product of psychosis.

The night after the Bumpurs story became public, I dreamed about a black woman who was denied entry to a restaurant because of her color. In response she climbed over the building. The next time she found a building in her way, she climbed over it, and the next time and the next and the next. She became famous, as she roamed the world, traveling in determined straight lines, wordlessly scaling whatever lay in her path, including skyscrapers. Well-meaning white people came to marvel at her and gathered in crowds to watch and applaud. But she never acknowledged their presence and went about her business in unsmiling silence. The white people were annoyed, angry that she did not appreciate their praise and seemed ungrateful for their gift of her fame; they condemned her. I stood somewhere on the periphery of this dream and wondered what unspoken rule, what deadened curiosity, it was that kept anyone from ever asking why.

I have tried to ask myself a progression of questions about the Bumpurs death: my life experiences prepared me to comprehend the animating force behind the outraged, dispossessed knife wielding of Eleanor Bumpurs. I know few blacks who have not had some encounter with police intimidation. My earliest memory of such an instance was when I was about nine, my sister seven. My family was driving to Georgia to see my father's relatives. Two highway patrolmen stopped our car on a deserted stretch of highway in South Carolina. They were attracted by the Massachusetts license plates; they wanted to know what "y'all" were doing in those parts; they asked about the weather in Boston, they fondled with great curiosity my father's driver's license, they admired the lines of the car. They were extremely polite, their conversation a model of southern hospitality and propriety. Throughout the entire fifteen or twenty minutes of our detention, one officer questioned my mother and father in soothing, honeyed tones; the other held a double-barreled shotgun through the rear window, pointed at my sister and me. If he had "accidently" shot us both, our deaths would have been, like that of Eleanor Bumpurs, entirely legal in the state of South Carolina.

What I found more difficult to focus on was the "why," the animus that inspired such fear and impatient contempt in a police officer that the presence of six other well-armed men could not allay his need to kill a sick old lady fighting off hallucinations with a knife. It seemed to me a fear embellished by something beyond Mrs. Bumpurs herself; something about her that filled the void between her physical, limited presence and the "immediate threat and endangerment to life" in the beholding eyes of the officer. Why was the sight of a knife-wielding woman so fearful to a shotgun-wielding policeman that he had to blow her to pieces as the only recourse, the only way to preserve his physical integrity? What offensive spirit of his past experience raised her presence to the level of a physical menace beyond what it in fact was; what spirit of prejudgment, of prejudice, provided him such a powerful hallucinogen?

However slippery these questions may be on a legal or conscious level, unresponsiveness does not make them go away. Failure to resolve the dilemma of racial violence merely displaces its power. The legacy of killing finds its way into cultural expectations, archetypes, and isms. The echos of both dead and deadly others acquire an hallucinatory quality; their voices speak of an unwanted past, but also reflect images of the future. Today's world condemns those voices as superstitious, paranoid; neglected, they speak from the shadows of such inattention in garbles and growls, in the tongues of the damned and the insane. The superstitious listen, and perhaps in the silence of their attention they hear and understand. So-called enlightened others who fail to listen to these voices of demonic selves, made invisibly uncivilized, simply make them larger, more barbarously enraged, until the nearsightedness of looking-glass existence is smashed in by the terrible dispossession of dreams too long deferred.

8

The Pain of Word Bondage

(a tale with two stories)

Some time ago, Peter Gabel and I taught a contracts class together. (He was one of the first to bring critical theory to legal analysis and so is considered a "founder" of Critical Legal Studies.) Both recent transplants from California to New York, each of us hunted for apartments in between preparing for class. Inevitably, I suppose, we got into a discussion of trust and distrust as factors in bargain relations. It turned out that Peter had handed over a $900 deposit in cash, with no lease, no exchange of keys, and no receipt, to strangers with whom he had no ties other than a few moments of pleasant conversation. He said he didn't need to sign a lease because it imposed too much formality. The handshake and the good vibes were for him indicators of trust more binding than a form contract. At the time I told Peter he was mad, but his faith paid off. His sublessors showed up at the appointed time, keys in hand, to welcome him in. There was absolutely nothing in my experience to prepare me for such a happy ending. (In fact I remain convinced that, even if I were of a mind to trust a lessor with this degree of informality, things would not have worked out so successfully for me: many Manhattan lessors would not have trusted a black person enough to let me in the door in the first place, paperwork, references, and credit check notwith-standing.)

I, meanwhile, had friends who found me an apartment in a building they owned. In my rush to show good faith and trust-worthiness, I signed a detailed, lengthily negotiated, finely printed lease firmly establishing me as the ideal arm's-length transactor.

As Peter and I discussed our experiences, I was struck by the similarity of what each of us was seeking, yet with such polar ap-proaches. We both wanted to establish enduring relationships with the people in whose houses we would be living; we both wanted to enhance trust of ourselves and to allow whatever close-ness was possible. This similarity of desire, however, could not reconcile our very different relations to the tonalities of law. Peter, for example, appeared to be extremely self-conscious of his power potential (either real or imagistic) as white or male or lawyer authority figure. He therefore seemed to go to some lengths to overcome the wall that image might impose. The logical ways of establishing some measure of trust between strangers were an avoidance of power and a preference for informal processes gen-erally.[1]

On the other hand, I was raised to be acutely conscious of the likelihood that no matter what degree of professional I am, people will greet and dismiss my black femaleness as unreliable, untrust-worthy, hostile, angry, powerless, irrational, and probably desti-tute.[2] Futility and despair are very real parts of my response. So it helps me to clarify boundary; to show that I can speak the lan-guage of lease is my way of enhancing trust of me in my business affairs. As black, I have been given by this society a strong sense of myself as already too familiar, personal, subordinate to white people. I am still evolving from being treated as three-fifths of a human, a subpart of the white estate. I grew up in a neighborhood where landlords would not sign leases with their poor black ten-ants, and demanded that rent be paid in cash; although superficially resembling Peter's transaction, such informality in most white-on-black situations signals distrust, not trust. Unlike Peter, I am still engaged in a struggle to set up transactions at arm's length, as legitimately commercial, and to portray myself as a bargainer of separate worth, distinct power, sufficient *rights* to manipulate commerce.

Peter, I speculate, would say that a lease or any other formal mechanism would introduce distrust into his relationships and he would suffer alienation, leading to the commodification of his being and the degradation of his person to property.[3] For me, in contrast, the lack of formal relation to the other would leave me estranged. It would risk a figurative isolation from that creative commerce by which I may be recognized as whole, by which I may feed and clothe and shelter myself, by which I may be seen as equal—even if I am stranger. For me, stranger-stranger relations are better than stranger-chattel.

The unifying theme of Peter's and my discussions is that one's sense of empowerment defines one's relation to the law, in terms of trust/distrust, formality/informality, or rights/no-rights ("needs"). In saying this I am acknowledging points that are central in most CLS literature—that rights may be unstable and indeterminate. Despite this recognition, however, and despite a mutual struggle to reconcile freedom with alienation, and solidarity with oppression, Peter and I found the expression of our social disillusionment lodged on opposite sides of the rights/needs dichotomy.

On a semantic level, Peter's language of circumstantially defined need, of informality, solidarity, overcoming distance, sounded dangerously like the language of oppression to someone like me who was looking for freedom through the establishment of identity, the formulation of an autonomous social self. To Peter, I am sure, my insistence on the protective distance that rights provide seemed abstract and alienated.

Similarly, while the goals of CLS and of the direct victims of racism may be much the same, what is too often missing is acknowledgment that our experiences of the same circumstances may be very different; the same symbol may mean different things to each of us. At this level, the insistence of certain scholars that the "needs" of the oppressed should be emphasized rather than their "rights" amounts to no more than a word game. The choice has merely been made to put needs in the mouth of a rights discourse—thus transforming need into a new form of right. "Need" then joins "right" in the pantheon of reified representations of what it is that you, I, and we want from ourselves and society.

Although rights may not be ends in themselves, rights rhetoric has been and continues to be an effective form of discourse for blacks. The vocabulary of rights speaks to an establishment that values the guise of stability, and from whom social change for the better must come (whether it is given, taken, or smuggled). Change argued for in the sheep's clothing of stability ("rights") can be effective, even as it destabilizes certain other establishment values (segregation). The subtlety of rights' real instability thus does not render unusable their persona of stability.

What is needed, therefore, is not the abandonment of rights language for all purposes, but an attempt to become multilingual in the semantics of evaluating rights. One summer when I was about six, my family drove to Maine. The highway was straight and hot and shimmered darkly in the sun. My sister and I sat in the back seat of the Studebaker and argued about what color the road was. I said black, she said purple. After I had harangued her into admitting that it was indeed black, my father gently pointed out that my sister still saw it as purple. I was unimpressed with the relevance of that at the time; but with the passage of years, and much more observation, I have come to see endless overheated highways as slightly more purple than black. My sister and I will probably argue about the hue of life's roads forever. But the lesson I learned from listening to her wild perceptions is that it really is possible to see things—even the most concrete things—simultaneously yet differently; and that seeing simultaneously yet differently is more easily done by two people than one, but that one person can get the hang of it with time and effort.

In addition to our different word usage, Peter and I had qualitatively different experiences of rights. For me to understand fully the color my sister saw when she looked at a road involved more than my simply knowing that her "purple" meant my "black." It required as well a certain slippage of perception that came from my finally experiencing how much her purple felt like my black:

> Wittgenstein's experiments in some of the passages of his *Zettel* teach us about multiple perception, ellipsis and hinging, as well as about seeing and saying. He speaks of "entering the picture" . . . and indeed his tricks try out our picture as our thought . . . Ambivalence is assumed. It is as if the imagination were suddenly to be stretched: "Suppose someone were to say: 'Imagine this butterfly exactly as it is, but ugly instead of beautiful'?! . . . The transfer we are called upon to make includes a . . . stretching not just of the imagination, but of the transfer point . . . "It is as if I were told: here is a chair. Can you see it clearly?—Good—now translate it into French!"[4]

In Peter's and my case, such a complete transliteration of each other's experience is considerably harder to achieve. If it took years for me to understand my own sister, probably the best that Peter and I can do—as friends and colleagues, but very different people—is to listen intently to each other so that maybe our children can bridge the experiential distance. Bridging such gaps requires listening at a very deep level, to the uncensored voices of others. To me, therefore, one of the most troubling positions advanced by some in CLS is that of rights' *disutility* in political advancement. The CLS disutility argument is premised on the assumption that rights' rigid systematizing may keep one at a permanent distance from situations that could profit from closeness and informality: "It is not just that rights-talk does not do much good. In the contemporary United States it is positively harmful."[5] Furthermore, any marginal utility to be derived from rights discourse is perceived as being had at the expense of larger issues, rights being pitted against, rather than asserted on behalf of, agendas of social reform. This line of reasoning underlies much of the rationale for CLS' abandonment of rights discourse and for its preference for informality—for restyling, for example, arguments about rights to shelter for the homeless into arguments about the needs of the homeless.[6]

Such statements, however, about the relative utility of needs over rights discourse overlook that blacks have been describing their needs for generations. They overlook a long history of legislation *against* the self-described needs of black people. While it is no longer against the law to teach black people to read, there is still within the national psyche a deep, self-replicating strain of denial of the urgent need for a literate black population. (*"They're* not intellectual," *"They* can't . . .") In housing, in employment, in public and private life, it is the same story: the undesired needs of black people transform them into those-without-desire. (*"They're* lazy," *"They* don't want to . . .")

For blacks, describing needs has been a dismal failure as political activity. It has succeeded only as a literary achievement. The history of our need is certainly moving enough to have been called poetry, oratory, epic entertainment—but it has never been treated by white institutions as the statement of a political priority. (I don't mean to undervalue the liberating power for blacks of such poetry, oratory, and epic; my concern is the degree to which it has been compartmentalized by the larger culture as something other than political expression.[7]) Some of our greatest politicians have been forced to become ministers or blues singers. Even white descriptions of "the blues" tend to remove the daily hunger and hurt

151

from need and abstract it into a mood. And whoever would legislate against depression? Particularly something as rich, soulful, and sonorously productive as black depression.

It may be different when someone white is describing need. Shorn of the hypnotic rhythmicity that blacks are said to bring to their woe, white statements of black needs suddenly acquire the sort of stark statistical authority that lawmakers can listen to and politicians hear. But from blacks, stark statistical statements of need are heard as strident, discordant, and unharmonious. Heard not as political but only against the backdrop of their erstwhile musicality, they are again abstracted to mood and angry sounds. (Mythologically speaking, black anger inspires white fear and fear is the one mood to which legislators have responded, but that story has nothing to do with black need.)

For blacks, then, the battle is not deconstructing rights, in a world of no rights; nor of constructing statements of need, in a world of abundantly apparent need. Rather the goal is to find a political mechanism that can confront the *denial* of need. The argument that rights are disutile, even harmful, trivializes this aspect of black experience specifically, as well as that of any person or group whose vulnerability has been truly protected by rights.

This difference of experience from whites is not, I think, solely attributable to such divisions as positive/negative, bourgeois/proletariat; given our history, it is a difference rooted in race and in the unconsciousness of racism. It is only in acknowledging this difference, however, that one can fully appreciate the underlying common ground of the radical left and the historically oppressed: the desire to heal a profound existential disillusionment. Wholesale rejection of rights does not allow for the expression of such difference.

The white left is perhaps in the position of King Lear, when he discovered in himself a "poor, bare, forked animal" who *needed* no silks, furs, or retinue, only food, water, and straw to sleep on.

The insight of this experience also freed him to see the weight, the constrictions, that his due as king had imposed on him. Similarly, the white left may feel that words and rights "have only the meaning that power wishes them to have." In this context, relationships of trust (which require neither speech nor rights) are replaced by the kind of "sufferance with which force condescends to weakness."[8] From this perspective, the Olympus of rights discourse may indeed be an appropriate height from which those on the resourced end of inequality, those already rights-empowered, may wish to jump.

Blacks, however, may symbolize that King Lear who was pushed to the point of madness: who did not find his essential humanity while retaining some reference point to an identity as social being temporarily lost in the wilderness—and who ultimately lost everything including a sense of self. The black slave experience was that of lost languages, cultures, tribal ties, kinship bonds, even of the power to procreate in the image of oneself and not that of an alien master. That sort of confrontation with the utter powerlessness of status which is the true and full condition of the wilderness is what ultimately drove Lear from insight into madness. Reduced to the basic provisions of food, water, and a straw pallet, kings may gain new insight into those needs they share with all humankind. For others, however—slaves, sharecroppers, prisoners, mental patients—the experience of poverty and need is fraught with the terrible realization that they are dependent "on the uncertain and fitful protection of a world conscience,"[9] which has forgotten them as individuals. For the historically disempowered, the conferring of rights is symbolic of all the denied aspects of their humanity: rights imply a respect that places one in the referential range of self and others, that elevates one's status from human body to social being. For blacks, then, the attainment of rights signifies the respectful behavior, the collective responsibility, properly owed by a society to one of its own.

Another way of describing the dissonance between blacks and CLS is in terms of the degree of moral utopianism with which blacks regard rights. For blacks, the prospect of attaining full rights under law has been a fiercely motivational, almost religious, source of hope ever since arrival on these shores. It is an oversimplification to describe that hope as merely a "compensation for . . . feelings of loss," rights being a way to "conceal those feelings."[10] Black loss is not of the sort that can be compensated for or concealed by rights assertion. It must be remembered that *from the experiential perspective of blacks,* there was no such thing as "slave law."[11] The legal system did not provide blacks, even freed blacks, with structured expectations, promises, or reasonable reliances of any sort. If one views rights as emanating from either slave "legal" history or from that of modern bourgeois legal structures, then of course rights would mean nothing because blacks have had virtually nothing under either. And if one envisions rights as economic advantages over others, one might well conclude that "because this sense of illegitimacy [of incomplete social relations] is always threatening to erupt into awareness, there is a need for 'the law.'"[12]

But where one's experience is rooted not just in a sense of illegitimacy but in *being* illegitimate, in being raped, and in the fear of being murdered, then the black adherence to a scheme of both positive and negative rights—to the self, to the sanctity of one's own personal boundaries—makes sense.[13]

The individual unifying cultural memory of black people is the helplessness of living under slavery or in its shadow. I grew up living in the past: the future, some versions of which had only the vaguest possibility of happening, was treated with the respect of the already-happened, seen through the prismatic lenses of what had already occurred. Thus, when I decided to go to law school, my mother told me that "the Millers were lawyers so you have it in your blood." (Of course Mother did not mean that law was literally part of my genetic makeup; she meant that law was an intimate part of the socially constructed reality into which I had been born. She meant that dealing with law and lawyers was something with which my ancestors were all too familiar.) Now the Millers were the slaveholders of my maternal grandmother's clan. The Millers were also my great-great-grandparents and great-aunts and who knows what else. My great-great-grandfather Austin Miller, a thirty-five-year-old lawyer, impregnated my eleven-year-old great-great-grandmother Sophie, making her the mother of Mary, my great-grandmother, by the time she was twelve.

In ironic, perverse obeisance to the rationalizations of this bitter ancestral mix, the image of this self-centered child molester became the fuel for my survival in the dispossessed limbo of my years at Harvard, the *Bakke* years, when everyone was running around telling black people that they were very happy to have us there but, after all, they did have to lower the standards and readjust the grading system. (I do not mean this as a criticism of affirmative action, but of those who tried to devalue the presence and contributions of us, the affirmatively active.) And it worked. I got through law school, quietly driven by the false idol of white-man-within-me, and absorbed much of the knowledge and values that had enslaved my foremothers.

I learned about images of power in the strong, sure-footed arm's-length transactor. I learned about unique power-enhancing lands called Whiteacre and Blackacre, and the mystical fairy rings encircling them, called restrictive covenants. I learned that excessive power overlaps generously with what is seen as successful, good, efficient, and desirable in our society.

I learned to undo images of power with images of powerlessness; to clothe the victims of excessive power in utter, bereft, naiveté; to cast them as defenseless supplicants pleading defenses of duress, undue influence, and fraud. A quick review of almost any contracts text will show that most successful defenses feature women, particularly if they are old and widowed; illiterates; blacks and other minorities; the abjectly poor; and the old and infirm. A white male student of mine once remarked that he couldn't imagine "reconfiguring his manhood" to live up to the "publicly craven defenselessness" of defenses like duress and undue influence.[14]

I learned that the best way to give voice to those whose voice had been suppressed was to argue that they had no voice.[15]

Some time ago, I taught a property class in which we studied the old case of *Pierson v. Post:*

> Post, being in possession of certain dogs and hounds under his command, did, "upon a certain wild and uninhabited, unpossessed and waste land, called the beach, find and start one of those noxious beasts called a fox," and whilst there hunting, chasing and pursuing the same with his dogs and hounds, and when in view thereof, Pierson, well knowing the fox was so hunted and pursued, did, in the sight of Post, to prevent his catching the same, kill and carry it off.[16]

One day a student gave me a version of the case as reinterpreted by her six-year-old, written from the perspective of the wild fox. In some ways it resembled Peter Rabbit with an unhappy ending; most important, it was a tale retold from the doomed prey's point of view, the hunted reviewing the hunter. It was about this time that I began studying something that may have been the contract of sale of my great-great-grandmother as well as a census accounting that does list her, along with other, inanimate evidence of wealth, as the "personal property" of Austin Miller.

In reviewing those powerfully impersonal documents, I realized that both she and the fox shared a common lot, were either owned or unowned, never the owner. And whether owned or unowned, rights over them never filtered down to them; rights to their persons were never vested in them. When owned, issues of physical, mental, and emotional abuse or cruelty were assigned by the law to the private tolerance, whimsy, or insanity of an external master. And when unowned—free, freed, or escaped—again their situation was uncontrollably precarious, for as objects *to be* owned, they and the game of their conquest were seen only as potential enhancements to some other self. (In *Pierson*, for example, the dissent described the contest as between the "gentleman" in pursuit and the "saucy intruder." The majority acknowledged that Pierson's behavior was "uncourteous" and "unkind" but decided the case according to broader principles of "peace and order" in sportsmanship.) They were fair game from the perspective of those who had rights; but from their own point of view, they were objects of a murderous hunt.

This finding of something that could have been the contract of sale of my great-great-grandmother irretrievably personalized my analysis of the law of her exchange. Repeatedly since then, I have tried to analyze and undo her situation employing the tools of adequacy of valuable consideration—how much value, I wonder. Just how did the value break down? Did they haggle? Was it a poker game, a trade, a promissory note? How much was she *worth?* The New York Public Library's Shomberg Center has in its archives a contract in which a young woman was sold for a dollar. In contrast, a review of the literature on the slave trade from Africa shows that the death of one fourth to two thirds of every cargo ship's population still provided "a good return on their investment." With what literalism must my philosophizing be alloyed: "There's something in me which might have been great, but due to the unfavorable market, I'm only worth a little."[17]

I have tried to rationalize and rescue her fate using defenses to formation, grounds for discharge and remedies (for whom?). That this was a dead-end undertaking is obvious, but it was interesting to see how the other part of my heritage, Austin Miller the lawyer and his confreres, had constructed their world so as to nip quests like mine in the bud.

The very best I could do for her was to throw myself upon the mercy of an imaginary, patriarchal court and appeal for an exercise of its extraordinary powers of conscionability and "humanitarianism." I found that it helped to appeal to the court's humanity, not to stress the fullness of hers. I found that the best way to get anything for her, whose needs for rights were so overwhelmingly manifest, was to argue that she, poor thing, had no rights.[18] It is this experience of having, for survival, to argue for our own invisibility in the passive, unthreatening rhetoric of "no-rights" which, juxtaposed with the CLS abandonment of rights theory, is both paradoxical and difficult for minorities to accept.

My discussion may prompt the argument that this last paradox is the direct product of rights discourse itself. So, in addition, I tried arguing my great-great-grandmother's fate in terms more direct, informal, descriptive, and substantive. I begged, pleaded, "acted out," and cried. I prayed loudly enough for all to hear, and became superstitious. But I didn't get any relief for Sophie's condition; my most silver-tongued informality got her nothing at all.

The problem, as I came to see it, is not really one of choosing rhetoric, of formal over informal, of structure and certainty over context, of right over need.[19] Rather it is a problem of appropriately choosing signs within any system of rhetoric. From the object-property's point of view (that of my great-great grandmother and the nameless fox), the rhetoric of certainty (of rights, formal rules, and fixed entitlements) has been enforced at best as if it were the rhetoric of context (of fluidity, informal rules, and unpredictability). Yet the fullness of context, the trust that enhances the use of more fluid systems, is lost in the lawless influence of cultural insensitivity and taboo. So while it appears to jurisdictionally recognized and invested parties that rights designate outcomes with a clarity akin to wisdom, for the object-property the effect is one of existing in a morass of unbounded irresponsibility.

But this failure of rights discourse, much noted in CLS scholarship, does not logically mean that informal systems will lead to better outcomes. Some structures are the products of social forces and people who wanted them that way. If one assumes, as blacks must, not that the larger world wants to overcome alienation but that many heartily embrace it, driven not just by fear but by hatred and taboo, then informal systems as well as formal systems will be run principally by unconscious or irrational forces: "Human nature has an invincible dread of becoming more conscious of itself."[20] (By this I do not mean to suggest a Hobbesian state of nature, but a crust of cultural habit and perception whose power shelters as it blinds.)

This underscores my sense of the importance of rights: rights are to law what conscious commitments are to the psyche. This country's worst historical moments have not been attributable to rights *assertion* but to a failure of rights commitment. From this perspective, the problem with rights discourse is not that the discourse is itself constricting but that it exists in a constricted referential universe. The body of private laws epitomized by contract, including slave contract, is problematic because it denies the object of contract any rights at all.

The quintessential rule of contract interpretation, the parol evidence rule, illustrates the mechanics by which such constriction is achieved. It says: "Terms with respect to which the confirmatory memoranda of the parties agree . . . may not be contradicted [by extrinsic evidence] . . . but may be explained or supplemented . . . by evidence of consistent additional terms."[21] If this rule is understood as a form of social construction, the words could as well read: "Terms with respect to which the constructed reality (or governing narrative) of a given power structure agree, may not be contradicted, but only supplemented or explained."

Such a social construction applied to rights mythology suggests the way in which rights assertion has been limited by delimiting certain others as "extrinsic" to rights entitlement: "Europe during the Discovery era refused to recognize legal status or rights for indigenous tribal peoples because 'heathens' and 'infidels' were legally presumed to lack the rational capacity necessary to assume an equal status or exercise equal rights under the European's medievally-derived legal world-view."[22] The possibility of a broader referential range of considered types of rights may be found by at least adding to, even contradicting, traditional categories of rights recipients.

Imagine, for example, a world in which a broader range of inanimate objects (other than corporations) were given rights—as in cases of the looting of American Indian religious objects: spurred by a booming international art market and virtually no fear of prosecution, raiders have taken "ceremonial objects and ancient tools [as well as] the mummified remains of Anasazi children . . . the asking price for quality specimens starts at $5000. The best of these are said to have been preserved by casting them into acrylic blocks, an expensive, high-tech procedure . . . 'To us,' says Marcus Sekayouma, a Hopi employee of the Bureau of Indian Affairs, 'the removal of any old object from the ground is the equivalent of a sacrilege." [23]

Such expanded reference—first made controversial by Christopher Stone's famous article "Should Trees Have Standing?"—is premised on the degree to which rights do empower and make visible:

> We are inclined to suppose the rightlessness of rightless "things" to be a decree of Nature, not a legal convention acting in support of some status quo. It is thus that we defer considering the choices involved in all their moral, social and economic dimensions . . . The fact is that each time there is a movement to confer rights onto some new "entity," the proposal is bound to sound odd or frightening or laughable. This is partly because until the rightless thing receives its rights, we cannot see it as anything but a thing for the use of "us"—those who are holding rights at the time. [24]

One consequence of this broader reconfiguration of rights is to give voice to those people or things that, by virtue of their object relation to a contract, historically have had no voice. Allowing this sort of empowering opens up the *egoisme à deux* of traditional contract and increases the limited bipolarity of relationship that characterizes so much of western civilization. [25] Listening to and looking for interests beyond the narrowest boundaries of linear, dualistically reciprocal encounters is characteristic of gift relationships, networks of encompassing expectation and support. As my colleague Dinesh Khosla describes it, "In the circularity of gift, the wealth of a community never loses its momentum. It passes from one hand to another; it does not gather in isolated pools. So all have it, even though they do not possess it and even though they do not own it."[26]

Such an expanded frame of rights reference underlies a philosophy of more generously extending rights to all one's fellow creatures, whether human or beast. Think how differently might have been the outcome in the Tuskegee syphilis experiment, in which illiterate black men were deliberately allowed to go untreated from 1932 until 1972, observed by doctors from the U.S. Public Health Service. Approximately four hundred diseased men with two hundred more as controls were allowed to degenerate and die; doctors told them only that they had "bad blood."[27]

Similarly, every year one reads in the newspapers about millions of cattle who are periodically destroyed for no other purpose than to drive up the price of milk or beef. One also reads about the few bleeding hearts who wage a mostly losing war to save the lives of the hapless animals. Yet before the Reformation, the bleeding heart was the Christian symbol of one who could "feel the spirit move inside all property. Everything on earth is a gift and God is the vessel. Our small bodies may be expanded; we need not confine the blood." Today, on the other hand, the "bleeding heart' is . . . the man of dubious mettle with an embarrassing inability to limit his compassion."[28]

One lesson I never learned in school was the degree to which black history in this nation is that of fiercely interwoven patterns of family, as conceived by white men. Folklore notwithstanding, slaves were not treated "as though" they were part of the family (for that implies a drawing near, an overcoming of market-placed distance); too often the unspoken power of white masters over slaves was the covert cohesion *of* family.[29] Those who were, in fact or for all purposes, family were held at a distance as strangers and commodities: strangers in the sense that they were excluded from the family circle at the hearth and in the heart, and commodities in the sense that they could be sold down the river with no more consideration than the bales of cotton they accompanied.

In the thicket of those relations, the insignificance of family connection was consistently achieved through the suppression of any image of blacks as capable either of being part of the family of white men or of having family of their own: in 1857 the Supreme Court decided the seminal case of *Dred Scott v. Sandford* in which blacks were adjudged "altogether unfit to associate with the white race, either in social or political relations; and so far inferior, that they had no rights which the white man was bound to respect; and that the negro might justly and lawfully be reduced to slavery for his benefit."[30] A popular contemporary pamphlet likened blacks to "ourang outangs" and determined them to be the descendants of Canaan. (In the Bible, Noah condemns his son's son Canaan to be a "servant of servants.")

Moreover, "Since slaves, as chattels, could not make contracts, marriages between them were not legally binding . . . Their condition was compatible only with a form of concubinage, voluntary on the part of the slaves, and permissive on that of the master. In law there was no such thing as fornication or adultery between slaves; nor was there bastardy, for, as a Kentucky judge noted, the father of a slave was 'unknown' to the law. No state legislature ever seriously entertained the thought of encroaching upon the master's rights by legalizing slave marriages."[31] Antimiscegenation laws also kept blacks outside the family of those favored with rights; and laws restricting the ability of slaveholders to will property or freedom to blacks suspended them in eternal illegitimacy.

The recognition of such a threshold is the key to understanding slavery as a structure of denial—a denial of the generative independence of black people. A substitution occurred: instead of black motherhood as the generative source for black people, master-cloaked white manhood became the generative source for black people. Although the "bad black mother" is even today a stereotypical way of describing what ails the black race, the historical reality is that of careless white fatherhood. Blacks are thus, in full culturally imagistic terms, not merely unmothered but badly fathered, abused and disowned by whites. Certainly the companion myths to this woeful epic are to be found in brutalized archetypes of black males (so indiscriminately generative as to require repression by castration) and of white females (so discriminatingly virginal as to wither in idealized asexuality).[32]

To say that blacks never fully believed in rights is true. Yet it is also true that blacks believed in them so much and so hard that we gave them life where there was none before; we held onto them, put the hope of them into our wombs, mothered them and not the notion of them. And this was not the dry process of reification, from which life is drained and reality fades as the cement of conceptual determinism hardens round—but its opposite. This was the resurrection of life from ashes four hundred years old.[33] The making of something out of nothing took immense alchemical fire—the fusion of a whole nation and the kindling of several generations. The illusion became real for only a few of us; it is still elusive for most. But if it took this long to breathe life into a form whose shape had already been forged by society, and which is therefore idealistically if not ideologically accessible, imagine how long the struggle would be without even that sense of definition, without the power of that familiar vision. What hope would there be if the assignment were to pour hope into a timeless, formless futurism? The desperate psychological and physical oppression suffered by black people in this society makes such a prospect either unrealistic (experienced as unattainable) or other-worldly (as in the false hopes held out by many religions of the oppressed.)

It is true that the constitutional foreground of rights was shaped by whites, parceled out to blacks in pieces, ordained from on high in small favors, random insulting gratuities. Perhaps the predominance of that imbalance obscures the fact that the recursive insistence of those rights is also defined by black desire for them—desire fueled not by the sop of minor enforcement of major statutory schemes like the Civil Rights Act, but by knowledge of, and generations of existing in, a world without any meaningful boundaries—and 'without boundary' for blacks has meant not untrammeled vistas of possibility but the crushing weight of total—bodily and spiritual—*intrusion*. "Rights" feels new in the mouths of most black people. It is still deliciously empowering to say. It is the magic wand of visibility and invisibility, of inclusion and exclusion, of power and no power. The concept of rights, both positive and negative, is the marker of our citizenship, our relation to others.

In many mythologies, the mask of the sorcerer is also the source of power. To unmask the sorcerer is to depower.[34] So CLS's unmasking of rights mythology in liberal America is to reveal the source of much powerlessness masquerading as strength; it reveals a universalism of need and oppression among whites as well as blacks. In those ancient mythologies, however, unmasking the sorcerer was only part of the job. It was impossible to destroy the mask without destroying the balance of things, without destroying empowerment itself. The mask had to be donned by the acquiring shaman and put to good ends.

The task for Critical Legal Studies, then, is not to discard rights but to see through or past them so that they reflect a larger definition of privacy and property: so that privacy is turned from exclusion based on self-regard into regard for another's fragile, mysterious autonomy; and so that property regains its ancient connotation of being a reflection of the universal self.[35] The task is to expand private property rights into a conception of civil rights, into the right to expect civility from others. In discarding rights altogether, one discards a symbol too deeply enmeshed in the psyche of the oppressed to lose without trauma and much resistance. Instead, society must *give* them away. Unlock them from reification by giving them to slaves. Give them to trees. Give them to cows. Give them to history. Give them to rivers and rocks. Give to all of society's objects and untouchables the rights of privacy, integrity, and self-assertion; give them distance and respect. Flood them with the animating spirit that rights mythology fires in this country's most oppressed psyches, and wash away the shrouds of inanimate-object status, so that we may say not that we own gold but that a luminous golden spirit owns us.

Mirrors and Windows

(an essay on empty signs, pregnant meanings,
and women's power)

At a faculty meeting once, I raised several issues: racism among my students, my difficulty in dealing with it by myself, and my need for the support of colleagues. I was told by a white professor that "we" should be able to "break the anxiety by just laughing about it." Another nodded in agreement and added that "the key is not to take this sort of thing too seriously."

Sometime after that, the *New York Times* ran a story about the arrest of one hundred parole violators who had been lured to a brunch with promises of free tickets to a Washington Redskins–Cincinnati Bengals football game: "The suspects reported to the Washington Convention Center after receiving a letter saying they had won the tickets from a cable television company, which had been set up as part of the police operation."[1] That evening, the televised news accounts of this story were infinitely more graphic. They showed one hundred black men entering a hall dressed for a party, some in tuxedos, some with fresh shiny perms, some with flowers in their lapels, some clearly hungry and there for the promised food, some dressed in the outfits of anticipatory football spectators, in raccoon coats and duckbill hats that said "Redskins." One hundred black men rolling up the escalators to the convention hall were greeted by smiling white (undercover) masters of ceremony, popping flashbulbs, lots of cameras, and pretty white women in skimpy costumes. Everyone smiled and laughed, like children at a birthday party. Everyone looked as though they were about the business of having a good time together. We saw the one hundred black men being rounded up by a swarm of white men, white women (also undercover agents) dressed as cheerleaders bouncing up and down on the side, a policeman dressed as a chicken with an automatic hidden in the lining, a SWAT team dressed in guerrilla-warfare green bursting in with weapons drawn.

My faculty colleagues have urged me not to give the voices of racism "so much power." Laughter is the way to disempower the forces of evil, I am told. But is it the racism I am disempowering if I laugh? Wouldn't this betray the deadly seriousness of it all? Laughing purposefully at what is hurtful seems somehow related to a first lesson in the skill of staged humiliation. Racism will thus be reduced to fantasy, a slapstick vaunting of good over evil— except that it is real. The cultural image of favored step-siblings laughing and pointing at such stupidity, at the sheer disingenuousness of bad children falling for the promise that they will get gifts, of even daring to imagine that they will get wonderful gifts too . . . if I laugh, don't I risk becoming that or, worse, a caricature of that image, that glossy marketing of despair?

Those who compose the fringe of society have always been the acceptable scapegoats, the butt of jokes, and the favored whipping boys. It resembles the pattern within psychotic families where one child is set up as "sick" and absorbs the whole family's destructiveness. The child may indeed be sick in unsociably visible and dramatically destructive ways, but the family is unhealthy in its conspiracy not to see in themselves the emanation of such sickness. The child becomes the public mirror of quietly enacted personality slaughter. Resistance to seeing the full reality is played out in the heaving of blame and, most cowardly of all, in disempowering others and ourselves by making fun of serious issues. The alternative (and infinitely more difficult) course is to face the interconnectedness, the enmeshed pattern of public dismissiveness and private humiliation, of private crimes and publicly righteous wrongs, of individual disappointments and national tragedies.

In sum, I see the problem at hand not as one of *my* giving racism too much power, but of how we may all give more power to the voices that racism suppresses.

I am attending a conference called The Sounds of Silence. The topic of the day is the social construction of race and gender and oppression. People hurl heavy names at one another: Hegel, Foucault, Adorno. The discussion is interesting, but the undercurrent is dialectical war; there are lots of authority-bullets whizzing through the air.

I think: my raciality is socially constructed, and I experience it as such. I feel my blackself as an eddy of conflicted meanings—and meaninglessness—in which my self can get lost, in which agency and consent are tumbled in constant motion. This sense of motion, the constant windy sound of manipulation whistling in my ears, is a reminder of society's constant construction of my blackness.

Somewhere at the center, my heart gets lost. I transfigure the undesirability of my racial ambiguity into the necessity of deference, the accommodation of condescension. It is very painful when I permit myself to see all this. I shield myself from it wherever possible. Indeed, at the conference it feels too dangerous to say any of this aloud, so I continue to muse to myself, pretending to doze. I am awakened suddenly to a still and deadly serious room: someone has asked me to comment on the rape of black women and the death of our children.

Caught with my guard down, I finesse the question with statistics and forgotten words. What actually comes to my mind, however, is a tragically powerful embodiment of my ambiguous, tenuous, social positioning: the case of Tawana Brawley, a fifteen-year-old black girl from Wappinger Falls, New York. In late November 1987, after a four-day disappearance, she was found in a vacant lot, clothed only in a shirt and a plastic garbage bag into which she had apparently crawled; she was in a dazed state, not responding to noise, cold, or ammonia; there was urine-soaked cotton stuffed in her nose and ears; her hair had been chopped off; there were cigarette burns over a third of her body; "KKK" and "Nigger" had been inscribed on her torso; her body was smeared with dog feces.[2] This much is certain, "certain" because there were objective third persons to testify as to her condition in that foundling state (and independent "objective" testimony is apparently what is required before experience gets to be labeled truth) although even this much certainty was persistently recast as nothing-at-all in the subsequent months. By September the *New York Times* was reporting that "her ears and nose were *protected* by cotton wads"; that it was not her *own* hair that was cut, but hair extensions "woven into her own short hair" that had either been torn or cut out; that only her clothes and not her body had been burned; that, from the moment she was found, "*seemingly* dazed and degraded, [she] assumed the mantle of victim"; and that her dazed condition was "ephemeral" because, in the emergency room, after resisting efforts to pull open her eyes, "Dr. Pena concluded that Tawana was not unconscious and was aware of what was going on around her . . . In a moment of quiet drama, Dr. Pena confronted Miss Brawley: 'I know you can hear me so open your eyes,' she commanded. Tawana opened her eyes and was able to move them in all directions by following Pena's finger."[3]

This much is certainly worth the conviction that Tawana Brawley has been the victim of some unspeakable crime. No matter how she got there. No matter who did it to her—and even if she did it to herself. Her condition was clearly the expression of some crime against her, some tremendous violence, some great violation that challenges comprehension. And it is this much that I grieve about. The rest of the story is lost, or irrelevant in the worst of all possible ways.

But there is a second version of the story. On July 14, 1988, New York State Attorney General Robert Adams stated that "there may not have been any crime committed here."[4] A local television call-in poll showed that the vast majority of New Yorkers—the vast majority of any potential jury pool, in other words—agreed with him. Most people felt either that if she were raped it was "consensual" (as cruel an oxymoron that ever was) or that she "did it to herself" (as if self-mutilation and attempted suicide are free-enterprise, private matters of no social consequence with reference to which the concern of others is an invasion of privacy). It was a surprise to no one, therefore, when a New York grand jury concluded that Tawana Brawley had made the whole thing up.[5]

When Tawana Brawley was finally able to tell her story—she remained curled in fetal position for several days after she was found—she indicated that she had been kidnapped and raped by six white men:

> Nodding or shaking her head to questions . . . Miss Brawley gave contradictory answers. She indicated that she had been subjected to acts of oral sex, and after first indicating she had not been raped, she suggested she had been assaulted by three white men . . . Asked who assaulted her, she grabbed the silver badge on his uniform but did not respond when he asked if the badge she saw was like this. He then gave her his notebook and she wrote "white cop." Asked where, she wrote "woods." He then asked her if she had been raped, and she wrote: "a lot" and drew an arrow to "white cop" . . . This response was the closest Miss Brawley ever came to asserting to authorities that she had been raped; her family and advisers, however, asserted many times that she was raped, sodomized and subjected to other abuse.[6]

The white men she implicated included the district attorney of Wappinger Falls, a highway patrolman, and a local police officer. This accusation was not only the first but also the last public statement Tawana Brawley ever made. (One may well question why she, a minor and a rape victim, was ever put in the position of making public statements at all. One might also inquire why the Child Protective Services Agency, which is supposed to intervene in such cases, did not.[7])

What replaced Tawana's story was a thunderous amount of media brouhaha, public offerings of a thousand and one other stories, fables, legends, and myths. A sampling of these enticing distractions includes:

—Tawana's mother, Glenda Brawley, who fled to the sanctuary of a church to avoid arrest for failing to testify before a grand jury and to protest the failure of the same grand jury to subpoena the men named by her daughter.

—Tawana's stepfather, from whom she had allegedly run away on prior occasions; by whom she had allegedly been beaten many times before—once even in a police station, in the presence of officers before they had a chance to intervene; and who served seven years for manslaughter in the death of his first wife, whom he stabbed fourteen times and, while awaiting trial for that much, then shot and killed.

—Tawana's boyfriend, who was serving time on drug charges in an upstate facility and whom she had gone to visit shortly before her disappearance.

—Tawana's lawyers, civil-rights activists Alton Maddox and C. Vernon Mason, who advised their client not to cooperate with investigating authorities until an independent prosecutor was appointed to handle the case.

—Tawana's spiritual counselor, the Reverend Al Sharpton, described variously as a "minister without a congregation" ("Mr. Sharpton, who is still a member of the Washington Temple Church of God in Christ, does not serve as the pastor of any church. 'My total time is civil rights,' he said. 'It's kind of hard to do both.' "[8])

and as an informer for the FBI ("The Rev. Al Sharpton, a Brooklyn minister who has organized civil disobedience demonstrations and has frequently criticized the city's predominantly white political leadership, assisted law-enforcement officials in at least one recent criminal investigation of black community groups, Government sources said. He also allowed investigators to wiretap a telephone in his home, the sources said."[9]). Al Sharpton, a man who had a long and well-publicized history of involvement in the wiretapping of civil rights leaders, yet *mirabile dictu* a sudden but "trusted adviser" to the Brawley family. Al Sharpton, tumbling off the stage in a bout of fisticuffs with Roy Innis on the Morton Downey television show, brought to you Live! from the Apollo Theater.[10] Al Sharpton, railing against the court order holding Glenda Brawley in contempt, saying to the television cameras, "Their arms are too short to box with God."

It was Al Sharpton who proceeded to weave the story where Tawana left off. It was he who proceeded, on the Phil Donahue show, to implicate the Irish Republican Army, a man with a missing finger, and the Mafia. And it was he who spirited Tawana Brawley off into hiding, shortly after the police officer she had implicated in her rape committed suicide.

More hiding. As if it were a reenactment of her kidnap, a re-reenactment of her disappearing into the middle of her own case. It was like watching the Pied Piper of Harlem, this slowly replayed television spectacle of her being led off by the hand, put in a car, and driven to "a secret location"; a dance into thin air that could be accounted for by nothing less than sheer enchantment. I had a terrible premonition, as I watched, that Tawana Brawley would never be heard from again.

She has not been heard from again. From time to time there are missives from her advisers to the world: Tawana is adjusting well to her new school; Tawana wants to be a model; Tawana approves of the actions of her advisers; and, most poignantly, Tawana is "depressed," so her advisers are throwing her a party.

But the stories in the newspapers are no longer about Tawana anyway. They are all about black manhood and white justice; a contest of wills between her attorneys, the black community, and the New York state prosecutor's office. Since Tawana's statement implicated a prosecutor, one issue was the propriety of her case's being handled through the usual channels, rather than setting up a special unit to handle this and other allegations of racial violence. But even this issue was not able to hold center stage with all the thunder and smoke of raucous male outcry, curdling warrior accusations, the flash of political swords and shields—typified by Governor Cuomo's gratuitous offer to talk to Tawana personally; by Al Sharpton's particularly gratuitous statement that Tawana might show up at her mother's contempt hearing because "most children want to be in court to say good-bye to their mothers before they go to jail"[11]; by Phil Donahue's interview with Glenda Brawley, which he began with "No one wants to jump on your bones and suggest that you are not an honorable person but . . ."; by the enlistment of the support of Louis Farrakhan and a good deal of antisemitic insinuation; by the mishandling and loss of key evidence by investigating authorities; by the commissioning of a so-called Black Army to encircle Glenda Brawley on the courthouse steps; by the refusal of the New York attorney general's office to take seriously the request for an independent prosecutor; and by the testimony of an associate of Sharpton's, a former police officer named Perry McKinnon, that Mason, Maddox, and Sharpton did not believe Tawana's story. (On television I hear this story reported in at least three different forms: McKinnon says Tawana lied; McKinnon says Sharpton lied about believing Tawana's story; McKinnon says that Mason and Maddox made up the whole thing in order to advance their own political careers. Like a contest, or a lottery with some drunken, solomonic gameshow host at the helm, the truth gets sorted out by a call-in poll. Channel 7, the local ABC affiliate, puts the issue to its viewers: Do you believe Sharpton? Or do you believe McKinnon? I forgot to listen to the eleven o'clock news, when the winner and the weather were to have been announced.)

To me, the most ironic thing about this whole bad business—as well as the thread of wisdom that runs at the heart of the decision not to have Tawana Brawley testify—is that were she to have come out of hiding and pursued trial in the conventional manner, she would no doubt have undergone exactly what she did undergo, in the courts and in the media. Without her, the script unfolded at a particularly abstract and fantastical level, but the story would be the same: wild black girl who loves to lie, who is no innocent (in New York television newscasters inadvertently, but repeatedly, referred to her as the "defendant") and whose wiles are the downfall of innocent, jaded, desperate white men; this whore-lette, the symbolic consort of rapacious, saber-rattling, buffoonish black men asserting their manhood, whether her jail-bird boyfriend, her smooth-headed FBI drugbuster informant of a spiritual adviser, or her grandstanding, unethically boisterous so-called lawyers who have yet to establish "a *single* cognizable legal claim."[12]

Tawana's terrible story has every black woman's worst fears and experiences wrapped into it. Few will believe a black woman who has been raped by a white man. In one of the more appallingly straightforward statements to this effect, Pete Hamill, while excoriating the "racist hustlers" Sharpton, Mason, and Maddox for talking "about 'whites' as if they were a monolith," asked: "After Tawana Brawley, who will believe the next black woman who says she was raped by white men? Or the one after her?"[13] A slightly more highbrow version of the same sentiment was put forth in a *New York Times* editorial: "How can anyone know the depths of cynicism and distrust engendered by an escapade like this? Ask the next black person who is truly victimized—and meets skepticism and disbelief. Ask the next skeptic, white or black."[14]

174

If anyone believes that some white man even wanted her, no one will believe that she is not a whore. (White women are prostitutes; black women are whores. White women sell themselves, in implied Dickensian fashion, because they are jaded and desperate; black women *whore* as a way of being, as an innateness of sootiness and contamination, as a sticky-sweet inherency of black womanhood persistently imaged as overripe fruit—so they whore, according to this fantasy-script, as easily as they will cut your throat or slit open said deep sweet fruit, spitting out afterwards a predictable stream of blood and seeds and casual curses.) Black women whore because it is sensual and lazy and vengeful. How can such a one be raped? Or so the story goes.

It is no easier when a black woman is raped by a black man (many of the newspapers have spun eager nets of suspicion around Tawana's stepfather[15] or a boyfriend). Black-on-black rape is not merely the violation of one woman by one man; it is a sociological event, a circus of stereotypification.[16] It is a contest between the universalized black man and the lusty black female. The intimacy of rape becomes a public display, full of passion, pain and gutsy blues.

Tawana Brawley herself remains absent from all this. She is a shape, a hollow, an emptiness at the center. Joy Kogawa's "white sound":

> There is a silence that cannot speak.
> There is a silence that will not speak.
> Beneath the grass the speaking dreams and beneath the dreams is a sensate sea. The speech that frees comes forth from that amniotic deep. To attend its voice, I can hear it say, is to embrace its absence. But I fail the task. The word is stone.[17]

There is no respect or wonder for her silence. The world that created her oppression now literally countenances it, filling the void of her suffering with sacrilegious noise, clashing color, serial tableaux of lurid possibility. Truth, like a fad, takes on life of its own, independent of action and limited only by the imagination of self-proclaimed visionaries; untruth becomes truth through belief, and disbelief untruths the truth. The world turns upsidedown; the quiet, terrible, nearly invisible story of her suffering may never emerge from the clamor that overtook the quest for "what happened" and polarized it into the bizarre and undecideable litigation of "something happened" versus "nothing happened."

In the face of all this, there is some part of me that wanted this child to stay in hiding, some part of me that understands the instinct to bury her rather than expound. Exposure is the equivalent of metarape, as hiding with Al Sharpton is the equivalent of metakidnap. It feels as if there are no other options than hiding or exposing. There is danger everywhere for her, no shelter, no protection. There is no medicine circle for her, no healing society, no stable place to testify and be heard, in the unburdening of one heart.

There are three enduring pictures I have of Tawana Brawley. The first is drawn from the images that both signaled and sensationalized the public controversy: the "television cameras invading the Brawley home to zoom in for a close-up of Tawana lying on a couch, looking brutalized, disoriented, almost comatose." And the pictures that were either leaked or "escaped" from the attorney general's office, the "police-evidence photographs showing Tawana Brawley as she looked when she was first brought by ambulance to a hospital following her rape: unconscious, dirty, half-naked, a 'censorship band' on the pictures covering only the nipples on her otherwise exposed breasts."[18] Her body so open and public; her eyes closed, her face shuttered, her head turned always away from the cameras.

The second image I carry of her is the widely circulated picture of her standing just behind Al Sharpton as he spoke for her. It is an image retained from innumerable photographs, taken from every angle and published over and over again, for months, everywhere: Al Sharpton with his mouth open, the perpetually open mouth. Tawana standing in his shadow clothed in silence, obedient and attentive, patient, wide-eyed, and unremittingly passive.

The third image is one described by a student of mine. At the height of the controversy, Tawana attended a comedy show at the Apollo Theater in Harlem. One of the comedians called attention to her presence in the audience and, in a parody of the federal antisex and antidrug campaigns, advised her to "just say no next time." As the audience roared with merriment and the spotlight played on her, Tawana threw back her head and laughed along with the crowd. She opened her mouth and laughed, in false witness of this cruel joke. It is the only image I have of Tawana with her mouth open—caught in a position of compromise, of satisfying the pleasure and expectations of others, trapped in the pornography of living out other people's fantasy.

I also take away three images of the men in whose shadow Tawana always stood. The first, and just plain weirdest, is that of Al Sharpton boxing with Roy Innis on the ultraconservative and ultrapsychotic Morton Downey show:

> Conservative black leader Roy Innis toppled Tawana Brawley adviser Al Sharpton while taping a TV program on black leadership, and the two civil rights gadflies vowed yesterday to settle their dispute in a boxing ring . . . "He tried to 'Bogart' me in the middle of my statement," said Innis . . . "I said no dice . . . We stood up and the body language was not good. So I acted to protect myself. I pushed him and he went down" . . . As the rotund preacher tumbled backward, Downey and several bodyguards jumped between the pair. Neither man was hurt . . . Sharpton said he hoped boxing promoter Don King would help organize a Sharpton-Innis charity boxing match . . . but said he would promote it himself if necessary . . . "The best part is that we will be giving a very positive lesson to young black people in this city about conflicting resolution—but not on the street with guns and knives," Innis said. "It will be an honest, clean and honorable contest."[19]

The second image I have is of heavyweight champion Mike Tyson, whose own tumultuous home life was momentarily overshadowed when, with a great deal of public ceremony, he presented Tawana with a gold Rolex watch and ringside tickets for his next match. Yet there was an odd intersection in the Brawley and Tyson stories: in the contemporaneous coverage of the marital spats between Tyson and his wife, actress Robin Givens—and in the face of uncontested allegations that Tyson used his lethal million-dollar fists to beat her up—it was somehow Givens and her mother, like Tawana and hers, who became everyone's favorite despised object in supermarket-checkout conversation.[20] Tyson's image as a big harmless puppy whose uncontrolled paws were only a feature of his exuberant lovability found ultimate and ironic expression, as cultured in the media, with his visit and gifts to the Brawley family.

The last image is one I saw in the newspaper shortly after the grand-jury report had been published, of Louis Farrakhan, unkindly captured with his mouth wide open. The story says that Tawana Brawley has surfaced from her long silence and

> expressed a desire to become a Muslim and will receive a new Muslim name . . . Mr. Farrakhan [leader of the Nation of Islam] . . . told an audience of 10,000 on Sunday that he . . . rejected the grand jury's findings, and he vowed vengeance on those who, he said, had attacked the girl. "You raped my daughter and I will kill you and dismember your body and feed it to the fowl of the air."[21]

The photo also shows Tawana, standing just behind Farrakhan. She is wrapped and turbanned in white, the image of chastity, of rigid propriety, of womanhood's submission to rule and ritual in a world where obedience is an unendingly complicated affair. There is a prayerful expression on her face. Her eyes are unreadable, and her mouth is closed.

IV

The Incorruptible Simplicity of Being

A String of Crystalline Parables

10

Owning the Self in a Disowned World

(a menagerie of nightmares and hallucinations)

Dr. Temple Grandin of the University of Illinois has shown that pigs like toys that dangle and people that are solicitous. In a five-week experiment, pigs with rubber hoses hanging in their pens were found to be less excitable . . . The pigs did not get fatter any faster, but they were easier to handle. They went through a narrow chute more willingly, which is useful at the slaughterhouse. Pigs in a panic can get bruised, and stress affects the texture and appearance of their meat.

Visits also pacify the pigs. In the same experiment, pigs that had been visited by a handler for only five minutes each week were less excitable and easier to handle than those that had been left alone. For the visit to count, a handler had to enter the pen; saying hello from an aisle was not enough. But such fraternizing can be overdone. One student spent so much time with her pigs that they refused to go through the chute to oblivion.[1]

It is early on a weekday afternoon. I sit at home watching a PBS children's program called "3–2–1 Contact." A woman with a smarmy talking-down-for-children voice is conducting an interview of Frank Perdue at his chicken farm. The camera is panning the "plant room" where 250,000 chicks have hatched, all only a few hours old. They are placed on a long assembly line, packed on so that the black conveyor belt is yellow with densely piled chicks;

human hands reach out at high speed and innoculate each fuzzy yellow chick by slamming it against an innoculator and throwing it back on the line. At the end of that line is a chute—and a shot of chicks scrambling for footing as they are dumped from a height onto yet another assembly line. Cute, catchy, upbeat music accompanies their tumbling, a children's song for the hurtling chicks.

"We deliver the little baby chicks in schoolbuses to the farms," says the voice of Frank Perdue. The interviewer laughs. "So it's like they're going off to kindergarten?" She holds a chick in her hand and strokes it like a pet. "You take really good care of them, don't you?" she says softly, as though to the chick. "We have to," says Frank Perdue. "It's our business." Fade to the farm: here they feed a million chicks a week. The farm is actually a huge factory building. The chickens never go outside. They are kept indoors all their lives, it is explained, because otherwise it would be "too unsanitary."

I switch channels. A soap-opera actress is the guest on some talk show. Her character has recently died on the soap opera, and the host shows a still photograph of that demise to the audience. The photo shows her body, crumpled in a twisted heap, bruised, abandoned in an alley, a trickle of blood seeping from her mouth. The talk host says in a hearty voice to the live studio audience, as well as to those of us viewers at home in the afterworld, "Remember that scene, guys? So how about a nice hand for the lovely . . ." and the audience applauds warmly.

I'm at home watching television in the middle of the afternoon because I don't feel well. I have a headache and think I'm going crazy. The world is filled with rumor and suspicion: Elvis has been reborn. I see the news in the *Midnight Sun* or the *Noonday Star,* some paper with a heavenly body in the name. Elsewhere there is a sighting of a whole tribe of Elvises, reborn in the Amazonian rain forest. They have been singing "Hound Dog" and beating on drums for an estimated five thousand years. The most amazing reincarnation of all, however, occurs on the Oprah Winfrey show, manifested in the body of a young black rap singer named L. D. Shore, rising to fame as "the Black Elvis." It is divinely parodic: Elvis, the white black man of a generation ago, reborn in a black man imitating Elvis.

I wonder, in my disintegration into senselessness, in whom I shall be reborn. What would "the white Pat Williams" look like? Have I yet given birth to myself as "the black Pat Williams"? I wonder about children, how I might be split in order to give life; I wonder how to go about inventing a child.

Recently, in Massachusetts, a woman who suffered a miscarriage in a drunk-driving accident was charged with vehicular homicide when the fetus was delivered stillborn.[2] I suppose this makes sense from the perspective of some litigation model in which mother "versus" fetus is the order of the day, in which the shell of a woman's body is assumed to be at cross-purposes with the heart within. It makes no sense from the perspective of a model in which woman and fetus are one, and in which the home of the body is also the site of sheer torment; it makes no sense from the sad seductive wisdom of self-destruction.

I edit myself as I sit before the television. I hold myself tightly and never spill into the world that hates brown spills. I'm afraid that everything I am will pour out onto the ground and be absorbed without a word. I may disappear. So I hold onto myself because I still have much left to say. I am brown by own invention, a crazy island, a suspicious hooded secret. One day I will give birth to myself, lonely but possessed. I organize my dreams in anticipation, combing out the frustration, ironing the pleats of my complications: soft empty complicated soft lonely. Dreaming all the time.

On TV, in between the chickens and the Amazon, there is a news snippet about a pregnant inmate in a Missouri prison who is suing the state on behalf of her unborn fetus, claiming that the thirteenth amendment prevents imprisonment of the fetus because it has not been tried, charged, and sentenced. The suit is premised on a Missouri antiabortion statute declaring that life begins at conception; the inmate is arguing that such a statute affords a fetus all the rights of personhood. "The fetus should not serve a sentence for the mother," says Michael Box, the Kansas City attorney representing the inmate.[3] Hearing about this case makes my head throb even harder, and my craziness advances several notches. Somewhere at the back of my head I remember having gone crazy before, only a few months ago, over a story about another pregnant woman, this one in Washington D.C., who was put into prison by a judge to keep her off the streets and out of drug-temptation's way, ostensibly in order to *protect* her fetus.[4] In the litigation that followed, the underlying issue turned out to be similar to the one in the Missouri case: the living conditions for prisoners, whether pregnant or not, but epitomized by the lack of exercise, health care, and nutrition so necessary for prenatal nurture.

My head is throbbing because these cases don't make sense to me. I don't believe that a fetus is a separate person from the moment of conception; how could it be? It is interconnected, flesh-and-blood-bonded, completely a part of a woman's body. Why try to carve one from the other? Why is there no state interest in not simply providing for but improving the circumstances of the woman, whether pregnant or not? I'm not sure I believe that a child who has left the womb is really a separate person until sometime after the age of two. The entire life force is a social one, a process of grafting onto our surroundings and then growing apart and then grafting again, all in our own time and in all kinds of ways that defy biological timetables alone. (But I have been called extreme in this, and by my own mother, from whom I have not even yet moved fully apart.)

In both of these cases, it seems to me, the Idea of the child (the fetus) becomes more important than the actual Child (who will be reclassified as an adult in the flick of an eye in order to send him back to prison on his own terms), or the actual condition of the woman of whose body the real fetus is a part. In both cases the idea of the child is pitted against the woman; her body, and its need for decent health care, is suppressed in favor of a conceptual entity that is innocent, ideal, and all potential.

It seems only logical, I think while applying a cold compress to my brow, that in the face of a statute like Missouri's, pregnant women would try to assert themselves through their fetuses; that they would attempt to rejoin what has been conceptually pulled asunder. They would of course attempt to assert their own interests through the part of themselves that overlaps with some architecture of the state's interest, in order to recreate a bit of the habitable world within the womb of their protective-destructive prisons.

In bargaining this way, however, pregnant women trade in interests larger than the world of prisoners' rights. In having the fetus declared an other person, in allowing the separation in order to benefit the real mutuality, they enslave themselves to the state. They become partialized, moreover, in the commodification of that bargain, as a prostitute becomes seen only as a "cunt" and as pigs dressed for slaughter become only "hoof," "head," or "hide." Pregnant women become only their fetuses; they disguise and sacrifice the rest of themselves and their interests in deference to the state's willingness to see only a small part of their need. The fetus thus becomes an incorporation of the woman, a business fiction, an uncomfortable tapestry woven from rights-assertion-given-personhood. It is an odd, semiprivate, semipublic undertaking, in which an adversarial relationship is assumed between the public and the private.

What a cycle of absurdity, I think as the melting ice drips down my nose: protecting the fetus from the woman by putting her in jail, then protecting the fetus from jail by asserting the lack of due process accorded the fetus in placing it there. The state's paternalism in these cases is very like the nightmare of another woman I read about, named Melody Baldwin, who injected her baby with her own toxic antidepressant medication in order to protect the infant from the toxin of life's despair: it was a madperson's metaphor of maternalism.[5]

It's all enough to drive a person legally insane (but then of course the person would get thorazine).

After a while I turn off the television and pick up the newspaper. I think to find solace there, but the world gets weirder and weirder all the time. This particular day there's a story about a couple who deposited the husband's sperm in a bank and then some time later the wife came back to be artificially inseminated. In due time she gave birth to a child "whom she describes as black." (Did I forget to mention that the couple is white?) Though officials of the fertility clinic insist with the unflappable certitude of biological imperative and scientific imperialism that "the sperm that impregnated the woman and which resulted in the birth of her child did not come from this sperm bank," the woman charges the clinic with negligence and medical malpractice. She says that "her insemination 'became a tragedy and her life a nightmare.'" While stating that the child's "color has nothing to do with her anguish," the woman sued when the "racial taunting of her child became unbearable":

> [Her lawyer] said that she "loves her 3-year-old daughter very much."
>
> But he said the child was the repeated target of "racial teasing and embarrassment" and "she is determined that what happened to her and her daughter doesn't happen to any other couple."
>
> By contending that her daughter is a victim of prejudice, the woman is building a case for monetary damages.[6]

I ponder this case about the nightmare of giving birth to a black child who is tormented so that her mother gets to claim damages for emotional distress. I think about whether my mother shouldn't bring such a suit, both of us having endured at least the pain of my maturation in the racism of the Boston public school system. Do black mothers get to sue for such an outcome, or is it just white mothers? I wonder if this child can get damages of her own, for having been born to a litigation-happy white mother. I think about whether this might not be a nifty way of collecting reparations, this suit for racial deviance as breach of birthright, a broken warranty of merchantability in the forum of marketed actors.

I think about suing. This is not, mind you, the usual case of "wrongful life." In those cases a woman who thought she had been sterilized, for example, gives birth to triplets. The family sues for the cost of raising said children. Typically, at least an argument can be made, as one case put it, that

> the parents' suit for recovery of the child rearing costs is in no reasonable sense a signal to the child that the parents consider the child an unwanted burden. They obviously want to keep the child. The love, affection, and emotional support any child needs they are prepared to give. But these things do not bring with them the economic means that are also necessary to feed, clothe, educate, and otherwise raise the child. That is what this suit is about, and we trust the child in the future will be well able to distinguish the two. Relieving the family of the economic costs of raising the child may well add to the emotional well-being of the entire family, including this child.[7]

Instead, this mother's is a suit for the emotional tragedy of a child's having been born into the pinnacle of her own unlove.

I try to concoct a suit out of my own life's circumstances. What mistake can I blame for having been born into an intolerant world? Whom can I charge with the damage that will not be healed for many generations?

On the bulletin board just outside my office, there hangs a notice from the department of obstetrics and gynecology of the University of Wisconsin. It offers fifty dollars for every semen specimen "we are able to use" in an artificial-insemination program. Donors must be under thirty-five years old and have a college degree. I wonder every time I enter my office at this market of selling sperm to women of the world desperately desiring to reproduce tall blond Nobel Prizewinners or, in the unavailability of that, then tall probably-blond college graduates.

And I think, in a technological age, guerrilla warfare must be redefined. I dream of the New Age manifesto: We must all unite, perhaps with the help of white male college graduates who are willing to smuggle small hermetically sealed vials of black sperm into the vaulted banks of unborn golden people; we must integrate this world from the inside out. We must smuggle not the biological code alone, but the cultural experience. We must shake up biological normativity; bring our cause down to particulars, to the real terms of what is at stake in the debate. We must be able to assert the battle from within, and in the most intimate terms conceivable. (Of course this won't work. We will end up with yet another generation of abandoned children, damaged in the manufacture, returned to the supplier, and sued for in the effort to undo their existence by the translation of the disaster of them into compensatory dollars and cents.)

I suggest guerrilla insemination to challenge the notion of choice, to complicate it in other contexts: the likelihood that white women would choose black characteristics if offered the supermarket array of options of blond hair, blue-green eyes, and narrow upturned noses. What happens if it is no longer white male seed that has the prerogative of dropping noiselessly and invisibly into black wombs, swelling ranks and complexifying identity? Instead it will be disembodied black seed that will swell white bellies; the symbolically sacred vessel of the white womb will bring the complication home to the guarded intimacy of white families, and into the madonna worship of the larger culture.

I suppose I'd better disclaim this as a serious exhortation, lest people start actually doing it and I get arrested in this brave new world for inciting reproductive riot. But it is interesting to examine the image it evokes, the vision of white mothers rushing to remedy the depreciation of their offspring in suits about the lost property of their children's bodies—this is the gut of why such a prospect would be terrifying to so many women, why such a child would be hard to love, even when one's very own. How profound the hatred, how deep the bigotry that lives beneath the skin, that wakens in this image of black life blooming within white. It becomes an image not of encompassment but of parasitism. It is an image that squeezes racism out from the pores of people who deny they are racist, or who say it's not racism that makes them fear blacks but the high crime rate or some such.

I am overwhelmed by this image: the vault of sperm banks. The clean container of white wombs. The swift messenger, the hermetic fire of white phallic power. The materia principia of semen, sperm, paternity. From dross into capital. The daughter's born blackness as accident, as awful, as "fault" that must be rehabilitated and deterred by adequate compensation (although the mother in this case rather coyly refused to reveal exactly how much she was seeking in damages).

In Missouri a man named Steven Goodwin is an inmate in a federal prison. He and his wife are suing to allow him to father a child by artificial insemination. "The Federal Bureau of Prisons has refused this request, saying the process involved would interfere with orderly operation of the correction system." The case is now before the U.S. Court of Appeals for the Seventh Circuit. The Goodwins' attorney contends: "There is a body of law that says no matter who you are, you are allowed to have children . . . The prison comes along and says they have a right to prevent conjugal visits. But we aren't questioning that. All we are asking for is a clean container and a swift messenger."[8]

There are 650,000 young black men in the U.S. penal system today, or approximately 23 percent of all black men between the ages of twenty and twenty-nine.[9] The increasing majority of them are there for drug-related offenses. Only 450,000 young black men are enrolled in U.S. colleges today; all the rest, we must conclude, are thus ineligible to deposit their sperm in the elite vaults of the University of Wisconsin's department of obstetrics and gynecology.

Instinct and extinction. The markers between life and death, black and white, male and female, sense and sensibility. The boundary between jail and the wide open plain. The threshold of childbearing, the lost generation. Old age, if it ever comes.

I think back to the black child whose white mother is suing over the breach of such divisions—what will happen if the mother wins this suit? What will she buy with the money? Into what exactly will this compensation be transformed? What will be the manifestation of pecuniary healing, the remedial token to mend the mirage of belonging? In some central way, this child is the icon of our entire civilization. The pure child, the philosopher's child, the impossible union of elements, forged in a crucible of torment, rattling the bars of her model prison, to wit, the schoolyards and the quiet streets of small "safe" white American towns; the black daughter's very integration at the heart of her duality. Trapped in racial circumstance; a little Frankenstein of ingredients, intolerably fearsome even to her creator, this monster child's racial hermaphrodism, the unpropertied guerrilla birth of herself, like a condensation, a rain of isolated social confrontations, like a prayer without answer.

It is the next day and I have more or less put myself back together. I am at a reading group on race/gender/class and critical legal thought. The topic is Harvard Law School professor Derrick Bell's new book *And We Are Not Saved* (1987). The chapter being discussed is called "The Race-Charged Relationship of Black Men and Black Women." The chapter deals generally with the social construction of antimiscegenation laws; forced sterilization and castration; the structure of the black family; teenage pregnancy; and the disproportionate number of black men in U.S. prisons.

But the precise subject within the chapter that has caught everyone's attention is a surprising parable, "The Chronicle of the Twenty-Seventh-Year Syndrome." The Chronicle is structured as an interiorized dream had by Bell; he then tells it to an exteriorized dream-vision-anima figure named Geneva Crenshaw. In the dream, Twenty-Seventh-Year Syndrome is an affliction affecting only young black professional women: if they are not married to, or have not yet received a marriage proposal from, a black man by their twenty-seventh year, they fall into a deep coma from which they awaken only after several weeks, physically intact but having lost all their professional skills.

This story has scared everyone in the room, including me, to death. The conversation is very, very anxious and abstract. Big words rush through the air, careening dangerously close to my head. Defining feminism. Undefining feminism. Women/men. Black/white. Biology/social construction. Male creation/control of sexuality. Challenge/structure. Post-legal-realist feminist/feminist. Identify/define/understand. Privilege of white womanhood/self-flagellation. Problematic/useful. Critique of patriarchy/pervasive abstracted universal wholeness. Actual/historical pathways to possibility/perversion. And the cabbagehead of hegemony.

Sitting quietly in the vortex, I try to recall the last time I heard such definitional embattlement. Suddenly a sharp voice cuts through all the rest and states: "But look, we have One right here—a single black female over the age of twenty-seven, from whom we haven't heard anything—let's give her a chance to speak!" A hush falls over the room. I look up from my musings to find every head in the room turned toward me.

The world is full of black women who have never really been heard from. Take Maxine Thomas, for example. According to one version, Los Angeles Municipal Court Judge Maxine Thomas' nervous breakdown was inexplicable. ("'I thought Maxine was a lady of unlimited potential.' said Reginald Dunn, of the Los Angeles City Attorney's office."[10]) She was as strong a black woman

191

as ever conjured—a celebrated, savvy judge who presided over hundreds of mostly white male judges. Yet one day she just snapped and had to be carted from her chambers, helpless as a baby. ("Clerk Richard Haines found Thomas—the first black woman to head the Municipal Court and a role model for young blacks in Los Angeles—slumped in her leather chair. The 40-year-old judge's head was bowed, and she wept uncontrollably.")

Another version has it that Judge Thomas was overcommitted. She had bitten off more than she could chew; she had too many irons in the fire; and she just wasn't competent or skillful enough to handle it all. ("'She's a small, frail person,' said Johnnie L. Cochran Jr., a prominent attorney and longtime Thomas friend. 'A human being breaks . . . All these things turned in on her.'")

Some said that she was manic-depressive and that her endless politicking was nothing less than shamelessly irresponsible self-promotion, clearly the sign of an unbalanced black woman. ("Pampered, emotionally immature and unforgiving on one hand, she could also be seductively charming, selflessly kind. In public, she could inspire children with her speeches on how to succeed. In private, faced with disappointment or dissension, she could resort to temper tantrums.")

Others said she was a woman who, like many women, thought of herself through other people. A woman who drained others in search of herself. A woman who criticized others into conformity; who used others as substitutes for herself, as self-extenders, screens, crutches, and statements. A woman who was nothing without others. ("'I think that all along there was a perception of her by a not unsubstantial group of people that there was more form than substance, that there was a lot of razzle-dazzle and not a lot to back it up,' said one of [her] critics. Like several others, this judge asked not to be identified to avoid further rancor on the court.")

A woman who had forgotten her roots. ("The only child of a

192

janitor and a sometime domestic worker, Thomas grew up in the heart of South-Central Los Angeles in a nondescript frame house . . . She was adored as a child, coddled as an adult . . . 'Maxine never had to do anything. She wasn't the type of girl who ever had to clean up her room,' said actress Shirley Washington, Thomas' closest friend and confidante for the past 16 years.")

A woman who exploited her blackness. ("Attorney Cochran, who now represents Thomas, characterizes her as having 'reached almost heroine status in the black community' . . . 'She was a very friendly young lawyer with a great future,' said Atty. Gen. John K. Van de Kamp, who first met Thomas in the early 1970's. 'It was a time for strong and able black women.'")

A women who was too individualistic. ("'I think she thought the job carried a certain power it just doesn't carry,' said retired Municipal Judge Xenophon Lang Sr. 'You're certainly not the boss of other judges . . . You're not a king of anything or queen of anything.'")

A woman who couldn't think for herself. ("'She wasn't able to function very well,' said Justice Joan Dempsey Klein, who reviewed Thomas' performance.")

A woman who had the perfect marriage. ("Her career in chaos, Thomas focused on her private life and a new romantic interest. He was Donald Ware, a never-married cardiologist who admired her 'fighting spirit.' It seemed the perfect match, and after only a few months, Ware bought her a 4-carat diamond engagement ring.")

A woman who had no marriage at all. ("There was only one glitch in the fairy tale scenario. The wedding wasn't legal. The couple weren't married. They had no valid marriage license, and for that Ware blames Thomas. Thomas blames Ware.")

A woman who overpowered her men and assaulted their manhood. ("In all, the honeymoon trip lasted three weeks, the volcanic 'marriage' about four . . . 'The girl wanted everything, my money and my income,' Ware said afterward. 'Our personal life has been a tragedy. She's got a lot of problems and wanted to give me problems.' ")

A woman who was too emotional. (" 'She wasn't professional,' said one judge who observed Thomas at work. 'I remember her clapping her hands when there was a settlement . . . The way she would exclaim her glee was not very judgelike.' ")

A woman who needed to loosen up. (" 'People were afraid, truly afraid to confront her . . . because of a reputation, right or wrong, of vindictiveness . . . ,' one judge said. 'She probably came on the court with more political power than probably any of the other judges.' ")

A woman who took her profession too seriously. (" 'Here's a girl who was basically a straight-A student all her life, who never knew what rejection was, never knew what failure was until she decided to run for Superior Court,' Washington said. '. . . After the election, I went over there and had to pull her out of bed. All she was saying, 'It isn't fair; it's not fair.' ")

A woman who didn't take her profession seriously enough. ("She launched a night version of small claims court and then joined her judicial colleague Richard Adler in promoting a program to process short civil cases at night and in opening a special small claims court for visitors to the 1984 Olympics. Thomas was written up in the newspapers, not part of the routine for most Municipal Court judges. There was rumbling among some of the judges, and in private the more critical of them began deriding her, questioning where she was trying to go with her splashy programs and complaining that she was neglecting the nitty-gritty work of the court.")

My mother's most consistent message to me, growing up, was that I must become a professional woman. My only alternative, as she presented it, was to "die in the gutter." There was no in-between. My mother was a gritty realist, a chess player always on the verge of checkmate, cagey, wary, protective. And so I became a professional woman.

194

According to the best statistics available, I am the perfect average black professional woman. Single, never married—"For black career women single at age 30, the chances of marriage are only 8 percent. By age 35 it has dropped to 2.4 percent and by age 40, 0.7 percent."[11]—having bred a statistically negligible number of children. I supposed I should be miserable, but it's not the end of the world. The very existence of such a statistical category is against all the odds, is company enough for me. I feel no inclination to marry myself off just because I'm single. I like being single. (Yet, as a social statistic, sometimes I feel less like I'm single than socially widowed. Sometimes when I walk down the street and see some poor black man lying over a heating vent, I feel as if I'm looking into the face of my companion social statistic, my lost mate—so passionate, original, creative, fine-boned, greedy, and glorious—lying in the gutter, as my mother envisioned, lost, tired, drunk, howling.) Nor do I feel the obligation to have children just because engineering social statisticians say I am "better able" to parent than the vast majority of black women who, being lower-class, are purportedly "least able" to parent.[12] (Yet sometimes I wonder what denial of the death all around me, what insistence on the holy grail of a certain promised form of life, keeps me from taking into my arms the companions to my sorrow—real orphans, black and brown children who languish in institutional abandon, children born of desperate caring, unions of explosive love, with lives complicated at a more intimate level than I can know by guttered hopes and homelessness.)

It is early morning, the day after the seminar on race, gender, and class. In the next room my mother, who is visiting me, rises and prepares to greet the day. She makes several little trips to the bathroom, in developing stages of undress and dress. Back and forth, from bedroom to bath, seeking and delivering small things: washcloth, eyeliner, stockings, lipstick. The last trip to the bathroom is always the longest because it is then that she does her face and hair. Next door I can hear the anxiety of her preparations: the creaking of the floorboards as she stands closer than farther from the mirror; the lifting and replacing of infinite bottles and jars on the shelves; the click of her closing a compact of blush; the running of water over her hairbrush; an anonymous fidgety frequency of sounds. She is in a constancy of small motions, clatters, soft rattles and bumps. When she leaves the bathroom at last, she makes one final trip to the bedroom, then goes downstairs, completely composed, with quick brave steps.

When I get up in the morning I stare in the mirror and stick on my roles: I brush my teeth, as a responsibility to my community. I buff my nails, paving the way for my race. I comb my hair in the spirit of pulling myself up by the bootstraps. I dab astringent on my pores that I might be a role model upon whom all may gaze with pride. I mascara my eyelashes that I may be "different" from all the rest. I glaze my lips with the commitment to deny pain and "rise above" racism.

I gaze in the mirror and realize that I'm very close to being Maxine. When I am fully dressed, my face is hung with contradictions; I try not to wear all my contradictions at the same time. I pick and choose among them; like jewelry, I hunt for this set of expectations that will go best with that obligation. I am just this close.

Judge Maxine Thomas' job as black female judge was to wear all the contradictions at the same time, to wear them well and reconcile them. She swallowed all the stories, all the roles, opening wide to all the expectations. Standing in the mirror, I understand the logic of her wild despair, the rationality of her unbounded rage. I understand the break she made as necessary and immediate. Her impatient self-protection was the incantation of an ancient and incomprehensible restlessness. Knowing she was to be devoured by life, she made herself inedible, full of thorns and sharp edges.

She split at the seams and returned to the womb. She lay

huddled in a wilderness of meaning, lost, a speechless child again, her accommodative language heard as babble, the legacy of KKK and Nigger spilling from her heart, words and explanations seeping from her. Giving birth to a thousand possibilities, she exploded into fragments of intelligence and scattered wisdom. Her clerk found her curled into fetal position, crying in her chambers. She was singing her small songs, magic words, soothsayings of comfort and the inky juice of cuttlefish. She was singing the songs of meadow saffron and of arbor vitae, of eel serum and marking nut, snowberry, rue-bitterwort, and yew. She had—without knowing, yet feeling the way of power—invoked sea onion, shepherd's purse, red clover. In her desperation, she had called upon divinations larger than herself: pinkroot, aquilegia, jambol seeds, thornapple, and hedge-hyssop.

Her bailiff turned her in. (He, the taskmaster of the threshold world, the marker of the order of things. The tall protector of the way that things must be, a fierce border guard, bulldog-tough in his guarding of the gate, whose reward was not the scrap of salary but the satisfaction, the deep, solid warmth that comes from making-safe. How betrayed he must have felt when this warm-brown woman rose over her needled rim and rebuked him; told him, in her golden madness, above all to mix, mix it all up. Such conscientious, sacrilegious mockery of protective manhood.)

Once over the edge, once into the threshold world, another sober archangel, her attorney and spokesperson, announced to the public that not only was it unlikely she would ever be able to rejoin the ranks of the judiciary, but she would probably never be able to rejoin the ranks of practicing lawyers. Needing so much to be loved, and lacking the professionalism to intercede on behalf of those less fortunate than she, it is unlikely she will ever be heard from again.

It is two days after the seminar, and I am finally able to think directly about Derrick Bell's Chronicle of the Twenty-Seventh-

Year Syndrome—this thorn of a story, a remarkable gauntlet cast into sadness and confusion.

Here, finally, are my thoughts on the matter. Giving it every benefit of the doubt, Bell's story is about gender relations as a political issue. The issue in the twenty-seventh year is not only the behavior or lack of political black mates; the issue is also the hidden, unmentionable secret between us—the historic white master–mate. Romantic love is the fantasy bridge across this silent chasm. The wider the chasm, the more desperately passionate the structuring of our compensatory vision.

The deep sleep into which the women of the twenty-seventh year fall is an intellectual castration—they are cut off from black community as well as from all their knowledge and talent and training. The acquisition of professionalism is sexualized: its assertion masculinizes as well as whitens. Professionalism, according to this construction, is one of several ways to get marooned in an uncomprehending white and patriarchal society; thus it sets women up to be cut off and then lost in the profundity of that world's misunderstanding and shortcoming.

The blackness of black people in this society has always represented the blemish, the uncleanliness, the barrier separating individual and society. Castration from blackness becomes the initiatory tunnel, the portal through which black people must pass if they are not to fall on their faces in the presence of society, paternity, and hierarchy. Once castrated they have shed their horrid mortality, the rapacious lust of lower manhood, the raucous, mother-witted passion of lower womanhood, and opened themselves up to participation in the pseudo-celestial white community. Intellectual castration is for blacks a sign of suffering for the Larger Society's love; and a sign to others, as in the Chronicle of the Twenty-Seventh-Year Syndrome, of membership in the tribe of those who need to be loved best.

For most blacks, however, this passage from closure to openness turns out not to be a passage from mortality to divine revelation—but openness in the opposite direction: openness as profane revelation. Not communion, but exposure, vulnerability, the collapse of boundary in the most assaultive way. White society takes the place of the blinding glory of Abraham's God: Pharaoh, not Yahweh.

Another thought I have about this Chronicle is Bell's use of the imaginary Geneva Crenshaw: throughout *And We Are Not Saved* Geneva Crenshaw, this witchy, dream-filled wishing-woman, is his instrument by which to attack the monolithism of white patriarchal legal discourse. She is an anti-Founding Father, wandering across time to the Constitutional Convention and back again, a source of aboriginal wisdom and intent. She is the word creation by which he legitimizes his own critique, as he delegitimizes the limits of the larger body of law's literature. She is the fiction who speaks from across the threshold to the powerful unfiction of the legal order; he argues with her, but he owns her, this destroyer of the rational order. Yet the Chronicle of the Twenty-Seventh Year is the only one of all the Chronicles in *And We Are Not Saved* that is not of her telling, that Bell owns by himself. In a reversal of roles, she receives *his* story and critiques it; from this "outside position," it is easy to forget that Geneva Crenshaw is not a real, objective third person, but part of the author. She is an extension of Bell, no less than the doctrines of precedent and of narrow constructionism are extensions of the judges who employ them. She is an opinion, no less than any judge's opinion, an invention of her author; an outgrowth of the text; a phantom.

I remember that my father used to use my sister and me in this way. He would write poems of extraordinary beauty and interest; he wanted to publish them but did not. He gave them to us instead. That way he could resolve his need for audience in safety; with his daughters as judges, he was assured a kind and gloating reception. Fears of failure or success or exposure motivated him, I suppose; but it placed my sister and me—or me, in any event—in a remarkably authoritative position. I was powerful. I knew what I was expected to say and I did my duty. The fact that I meant it didn't matter. What I did was a lie, no matter how much I believed or not in the talent of his poetry. My power was in living the lie that I was all audiences. My power was in the temptation to dissemble, either out of love or disaffection. This is blacks' and women's power, I used to think, the power to lie while existing in the realm of someone else's fantasy. It is the power to refrain from exerting the real, to shift illusion, while serving as someone else's weaponry, nemesis, or language club.

After meeting my new sisters, these inventions of Derrick Bell's mind, I began to wonder what would happen if I told my father the truth. What would happen if I were to cut through the fantasy and really let him know that I am not an extension of his pen; what if I were to tell him that I like his writing (or not), but in my own words and on my own terms?

By the same token, what would happen if the victims of Twenty-Seventh-Year Syndrome were to awaken from their coma, no longer merely derivative of the black or white male experience but sharper-tongued than ever? Whose legitimacy would be at risk? Theirs? Bell's? Geneva Crenshaw's? The twenty-seven-year-olds who can't shake the sleep from their eyes?

Or is there any risk at all?

[An undated entry from my computer files written sometime after the seminar:

A dream. I am in an amphitheater, creeping around the back wall. I am not supposed to be there—it is after hours, the theater is not open to the general public. On the stage, dead center, surrounded by a circle of friends, spotlighted in the quiet dark of the theater, is a vision, a version of myself. I am wearing my hair in an exaggerated beehive (a style I affected only once, fresh from an application of the hotcomb, at the age of twelve) and a sequined low-cut red dress (a dress I actually wore, once again, at the liberated age of twenty-three). There I am with that hair and that ridiculous cowgirl dress: it is an eye scorcher of a sparkling evening gown, my small breasts stuffed into it and uplifted in a way that resembles cleavage.

The me-that-is-on-stage is laughing loudly and long. She is extremely vivacious, the center of attention. She is, just as I have always dreamed of being, fascinating: showy yet deeply intelligent. She is not beautiful in any traditional sense, as I am not in real life—her mouth and teeth are very large, her nose very long, like a claymation model of myself—but her features are riveting. And she is radiantly, splendidly good-natured. She is lovely in the oddest possible combination of ways. I sit down in the small circle of friends-around-myself, to watch myself, this sparkling homely woman, dressed like a moment lost in time. I hear myself speaking: *Voices lost in the chasm speak from the slow eloquent fact of the chasm. They speak and speak and speak, like flowing water.*

From this dream, into a complicated world, a propagation of me's awakens, strong, single-hearted, and completely refreshed.]

Arm's-Length Intimacies

(a diary of imagined property)

Two polar bears who have become psychotic from the boredom of a lifetime in captivity are to receive psychotherapy at their zoo in Bristol, England. Micha, 20, and Nina, 30, have taken to napping long hours and to walking the same three steps forward and backward over and over again. Dr. Roger Mugford, an animal psychologist, has designed a treatment to save the bears from madness: he plans to vary their menus and to give them unbreakable toys.[1]

It is a rainy Wednesday evening. I am in my office preparing materials for a class, Colonialism, Conformity, and the Civic Self, to which I have been invited to speak as a guest lecturer. Intricate analyses of cases about property rights in whales and slaves and foxes and wives. Deep contemplation about the meaning of "wilderness" and "Indians" and fences and the unconscious. When my eyes can no longer focus, I decide it's time to take a break, go to my African dance class, and seek communion with some other notion of transcendent self. At eight o'clock, I walk out of my office, downstairs, and into the December night. It is cold and raining hard. The streetlamps glimmer, pale moons in the misty winter solitude. I walk six yards. Suddenly, from behind the darkness of a pillar in the ivy-covered archway, leap two of my former contracts students.

"Professor Williams," they say in unison. "We have a question that was never answered from last semester and we've been fighting about it ever since: if you pay us fifty dollars to come to your funeral, is that an enforceable promise?"

(At the back of my head, there arises a clamoring of polar bears. Why, they ask me with their heads tilted inquisitively, are these two inquiring about my funeral? Go away, I say impatiently; this question is a Famous Contracts Hypothetical.)

"Well," I hear myself saying aloud, "according to the First Restatement . . ."

(But the bears in my head are raging: who would pay whom for this profit of another's demise? They smell poachers in the innocent intellectual affectations of these two young hunters. Outside I hear myself prattling dangerously on about the Second Restatement. Lie down, I snap, and try to concentrate.)

"So the answer is yes," I hear myself saying.

(Inside, the bears and I panic. Yes, what? Yes, the offer is terminable upon my death? Yes, the offer is a unilateral one looking to your performance but may be made bilateral by your agreement and enforceable upon my demise as against my estate? Yes, you have an expectation interest in seeing me dead? Yes indeed, what will the bar examiners have to say? Or yes, I should have just said the answer is no.)

I am home for Christmas. My sister and I sit at our parents' kitchen table. I tell her about having contemplated my demise through the eyes of my students. She tells me about an advertisement she has seen offering a "new funeral option for those in a rush": drive-through funeral parlors. In Chicago, she says, you can drive up to a canopied video screen, punch a button, and the monitor displays the beloved for three seconds. Then you sign the register and pass on. (Or you can push the button over and over for longer viewings—until, I suppose, the cars behind you start to honk.)

It seems to me, I tell her, that this is the ultimate in terrifyingly commodified disembodiment. My sister informs me that it is billed as a convenience for people who have no time to go home and change out of their work clothes in order to pay their respects.

"For people who have no time?" I ask, confused and uncomprehending.

"They mean the living," she assures me quickly.

I persist: "But it seems so voyeuristic! The purpose of a wake is not simply to look at the body, is it? I thought it was a ceremony of communion with those left behind."

"No problem," says my sister, and quotes the words of one enthusiastic mourner, who drove through on a bus loaded with mourners: "It was like watching a good picture on television."[2]

I sit thinking in silence for a long moment after that. There is one cat on my lap, another at my feet. My parents' presence fragile and heavy in my heart. My sister at the table with me, a bright enigma. My pleasant crouched animals. The dark immediacy of my family connection. The small circle of people who describe my life, who allow me to live in dream time, beyond time, with whom such powerful bonds exist that our quarrels are symphonies, with whom there are no others and nothing ever changes. The quiet solitude of home. The cycle of giving. The blazing intimate noise of home. The complicated affections of animals. The magnificent tendrils of the loves of a lifetime.

Death, I think, marks a stoppage of time. It marks the shifting cycle of consciousness, a moment after which nothing is ever the same. It seems important to mark the cessation of motion—what else is meaning but the need to mark the irretrievable loss of beginnings and endings?

"Sometimes I worry that I'm crazy," I say finally. After two days at home, it is my mother's voice that comes out of my mouth. "Did you hear that?" I ask my sister. I have become our mother; the merging is startling, intimate, terrifying. As I continue to speak in her voice, I look down at my hands, the fingers spread in an anxious web on the table, and I see that my hands have also become her hands.

My sister understands that I am drowning; I hear her speaking to me in measured tones, with words that belong to my father. I hang onto her words like a lifeline: "Consider the operation of the parol evidence rule," she advises. "Draw circles around yourself. Imagine that you are a fully integrated, unmerged individual. Know that all prior and contemporaneous voices are extrinsic to yourself. Cultivate the ability to seize the moment, without which ability the moment will be past and you will find yourself extrinsic. By demarcating clearly the boundaries between you and extrinction, so will you find yourself on the path to autonomy."

(*Extrinction?* I ask, turning inside to the bears for explication. Yes, says an old bear quietly; we are closer to extinction every day. No, no, I protest. Not extinct—extrinct! But the old bear was already fading fast . . .)

It is two days after Christmas. I am in New Orleans, holed up in a hotel, attending conferences. I am here for ten days, time stretched between the annual meetings of the Modern Language Association at one end and the Association of American Law Schools at the other. With satisfaction I notice that, in this gap between disciplines, the comforting specter of polar bears begins to rise before me once more.

I spend the day arguing with my colleague U., also a law-and-literature type. We argue about the meaning of things we have seen. We go shopping—there is a samba party on New Year's Day to which we have been invited, and we are hunting for suitable costumes in which to dance. We go to the biggest department store in town to see what there is to see.

A fashion show is in progress when we get there. Champagne, fruit, little chocolate things, a runway glittering with designs for spring. Models prance and sway, thrusting their hips out in front of their heads in time to the beat of Brazilian liberation songs about freedom, South Africa, and Afghanistan. Tales of torture and cultural demise blare at very high volume, in Portuguese. Two blonds, followed by two redheads, then two blacks, sashay down the runway where they swirl for the photographers, then mix themselves up in chic interracial combinations. "Soood-Afriquaaa!" the tape shouts, and a rep wearing a button that says she is sponsored by *Glamour* magazine is moved to glow aloud about the "Great Gatsby-esque" flare of the lines.

I am befuddled by this perfectly balanced incongruity of eyes and ears. The impurity of its substance is at the same time the purity of its symbolism. It is, I tell U., as corrupted a vision of the oppressed as it is the clear reverberation of the oppressor who does not listen. Like dolls, the models are dressed up to fit a free-dom (if not fighter) image: red, white, and blue tennis knits, breezy camouflage beachwear. They pose; they raise their eye-brows at the audience in coy questioning. U. turns to me and asks if I don't agree that the very existence of this carefree, black-and-white, arm-in-arm procession is sufficient evidence that the battle has been won? "Or do you really think," U. adds after a pause in which I fail to speak, "that this is all just a setup?" A setup for lonely discontents like me, who don't know when to stop com-plaining, who fill in meaning where none was meant.

We argue again as we leave the biggest department store in town. At the door is posted a security guard. Exiting just ahead of us are six young women dressed to perfection. As they walk past the guard, they automatically open their purses, as reflexively as genuflecting. They do it as humbly as submitting to an army checkpoint in a war zone. It strikes me as something they have been accustomed to in school—a ritual performed with the busy, thoughtless preoccupation of a habit assumed in early adoles-cence. They perform it as children remember their manners, like wiping their feet, like curtseying to the headmistress.

It amazes and horrifies me, this bowing down to the gods of Commerce and Security. They debase themselves, lay open their purses that they might shew their pure hearts and be absolved; they expose the intimacy of the kleenex wads and leaking ball-points and small bottles of contact-lens solution and tampax that lie higgledy-piggledy within the secrecy of their silk-lined purses. The priest of a guard nods and mumbles at each as she opens wide, as though he were mumbling a blessing.

I ignore them all. I walk right past the guard and out onto the sidewalk. "No wonder security guards follow you around stores," says U., embarrassed and annoyed. "They can sense your disrespect."

"They are dogging the smell of my atheism," I reply. (Nevertheless, I feel guilty. I have trodden in the temple with my shoes on; I feel like I have blasphemed.)

I sleep fitfully in the New Orleans humidity. I dream that I'm teaching my Uniform Commercial Code class. My students are restless and inattentive, bored to death with the sales of chattels. Suddenly, from somewhere deep in my psyche, polar bears rise. Silent, unbidden, they come to the dissolved walls of the classroom, the polar bears come padding to hear what this law will mean for them. It is snowing in their world. Hunching, they settle at the edge of the classroom, the walls of the classroom melt in the heated power of their breath, their fierce dark eyes are fixed upon me. They hunch and settle and listen, from beyond-language.

I wake up in a cold sweat.

I wake up. Yet large eyes still gleam inquiringly from the foot of the bed. The eyes at the foot of the bed are larger than flashlights. They are polar-bear eyes. I am terrified.

(Why am I so terrified? Some part of me knows that it is intelligent for me to be schizophrenic. It is wise, in a way, for me to be constantly watching myself, to feel simultaneously more than one thing, and to hear a lot of voices in my head: in fact, it is not just intelligent but fashionable, feminist, and even postmodern. It is also wise, I know, to maintain some consciousness of where I am when I am other than the voice itself. If the other voice in my head is really me too, then it means that I have shifted positions, ever so slightly, and become a new being, a different one from her, over there. It gets confusing sometimes, so I leave markers of where I've been, particularly if it's not just a voice but a place that I want to come back to in time. This season, those spots are marked with polar bears.)

I am afraid of their claws and their silence and the accusation in their eyes, the mystery contained in their strong sharp teeth. I am afraid of their smell above all; the meat and blood on their breath, the stiff iciness of their matted fur, the soft grainy pads of the soles of their feet. They smell of even-tempered desperation, of the last resort of pure survival. They come to me in the middle of the night, disguised as insanity itself; they hunch at the foot of my bed, large and cold, warm-hearted and curious. I can taste their meat, the fresh-sliced scent of lung and liver, of still-warm divinations of palpitating heart.

But since I know they are nothing more than, as I have said, markers of where I've been, I get up the courage to calm myself, and settle in for the vision that their presence will have brought. In their turn, the bears give me back my listening, they ring me with their listening, beyond language.

I speak to them of the law: The Law. The law says, the law is. My life, my tissue, my membrane. Connection, suspicion, privacy, the secret wedged in the void. The corrupt entrenchment of my thirst and loneliness. I am a tiny figment, a gear and lynchpin to the law.

I notice suddenly that I am making no sense. I am babbling, though my words are heavy-jawed and consequential. My words are confined and undone; I am tangled in gleaming, bubbled words. I hear the sounds of my own voice but they make no sense. I know the words, but there is no connection, familiar words in an unfamiliar rush; the light from my words is furious and flickering. I am circled in pretense, entwined in nonsense, tangled in cables and connectors. I speak to the distance of emptiness, I speak in circles and signals, I speak myself into the still.

I am seized with golden-weighted, heavy-hearted fear.

I wake up with a dream: a lawyer-shaman in bear mask and leggings and arm bracelets, snakes clutched in each hand, bundles of snakes held aloft. The bear-shaman puts them on the top of a mountainous pyre, a pyramid with a shallow burning bowl at the very top. The bear-lawyer places the snakes in the bowl, which is filled with meal. Smoke rises from the pyramid. The power of the snakes and the meal and the smoke makes me rise, rise, rise. I realize that I will rise higher based on how much I believe that this ritual will work. I am much aware of the power of my belief. I am amazed, as I rise, and the earth grows distant and silvery. I am also aware that I don't go as high as I might, because my consciousness of my amazement is rooted in a sort of disbelief— it lowers me at once. Each doubt that I entertain brings me down, closer to earth. Complete faith frees me to the universe without end. I see the shaman as someone very vulnerable—full of potent magic and pride when given his due, a schizophrenic old fool in embarrassing getup without it.

It's a powerful dream, a good dream for dancing. I take it to the New Year's Day samba party, wearing a new outfit and my just-so baggy, new-but-look-old glitterknit legwarmers. (I am given to a certain amount of display in my dancing, as in my teaching. I am told that, in addition to plotting my funeral, my students scrutinize my clothes, discussing my fashion statements in their carpools and among themselves: my shoes, my watch, the color of the band I have chosen to wear in my hair. I wonder what all this means. I dress myself increasingly with reference to their imagined conversations. I have always been a vain black woman. Now, however, I redress myself, long hours in the mirror every morning, wondering what my students will think, trying to see myself as they must see me; trying to make myself over in a way that will make them like me more. What does all this mean? What complicated oxymoron: a vain black female commercial law professor.)

Anyway, there I am at the samba party, dancing for display, dressed in my little African print sarong, two sets of legwarmers and my baggy blue cotton sweater. I see myself posing and prancing and preening: pas de bourée, pose; double-triple shuffle step, prance-prance-prance; hip-hip-point, *preen*. I look so good.

But that is only for the small-group dances, when the hall is divided into four groups and one quarter of the room dances at a time, as the other three quarters watches. I dance the dance of display in time, in measures, well placed and consciously located, beginning here and ending there. But by the end of the evening, the whole room dances as one group, a rain dance, a timeless, ongoing, unbounded, revivifying, whole-room dance that I take right out onto the street with me. At the end of the evening, everyone's all worked up and shouting, and the music gets cranked up to full volume and the sweat flows in rivers and the whole room moves in unison, transported, ecstatic—that's when I dance the room, I dance to frenzy. I dance beyond myself, beside myself. I dance to join the child in front of me and the man behind. I dance to link the ceiling fans and the floorboards, the mirrors and the windows. I dance because it feels good and there is all the earth's harmony in this feeling so good.

After the party, I go out into the night and head back to my hotel. On the streetcorner there is an old man. He is begging and incanting, frightening passersby. A ragged black man with rusty matted hair and fire-beady eyes, an old man, desperate, hungry, thin, sick, muddy—tapdancing with a begging bowl in hand, the coins jangling as he jumps and shuffles, the wild sad sound of his feet scrambling on the pavement, his old feet scattering whiffs of sound to impervious passersby, the sound of the coins leaping and falling in the cup in timeless accompaniment to the raging desperation of his life-dance, to the jiggling, scraping emptiness of his death-dance, tapdancing, tapdancing to break the heart right open.

The litcrits have left, and the lawyers are starting to arrive in town. Lunch today with my friend Z., a noted property professor. I change hotels, moving from a small room in the French Quarter to a big, glitzy, more expensive hotel in the shopping district, where the Association of American Law Schools will meet. There is a safe in the new room; it makes me suddenly aware of danger. I have a crisis of indecision: whether to leave the room, whether to leave my valuables in the room, whether to leave my valuables in the safe in the room. I note with interest that it is my journals and notebooks that I finally lock up; my words are my only valuables. I put the words that are written on this page in the dictaphone and then put the dictaphone in the safe too. The safe costs four dollars a day. I am insured for up to $10,000 against forcible entry and theft.

Z. is late for lunch; he has just had his wallet taken by an invisible hand on the streetcar. Over a good stiff one, Z. says he looks forward to the day when all personal and financial data will be access-coded by thumbprint. On a cocktail napkin, he draws plans for a microchip that would be implanted under the skin so that one thumb and one thumb only could get into the files of his bank account. I understand the theft of his wallet as a violation of his person. His willingness to do violence to himself, to assume a mechanical identity on behalf of his property, I do not understand. I think: in seeking the physical bounds of unboundable certainty, he has secured himself instead with a prison of psychic stakes.

As I listen, the image of Chase Manhattan marking me with the sign of the O.K. Corral flashing before my eyes, I realize that when Z. wants to implant a computer chip under the skin of his thumb, he is doing what cyberneticians and genetic engineers are trying to do from the inside out: make difference a fixed property, an inherency (or, depending on which side of the boundary of one is to begin with, make sameness a property). Mark the deserving from the not. Moreover, Z. the social engineer (as a nationally renowned property authority) will write laws and model legislation based on the protection of his psychic stakes, spreading his architecture of embattlement against the heathen and the wilderness.

Biology is insistent that no one is more valuable than another. Z.'s laws and anguish perpetuate the social insistence that we wear value, rooted in banked (or embodied) reserves. The mark of the untouchable, the microchip of the well-heeled, the passport of the anointed, the passbook of the condemned. The marking into the flesh of the conviction and religious fervor of our property belief.

After lunch I walk back to my hotel. On the same corner where the old man was tapdancing last night, there stands a large woman with bags full of what looks like trash. She is raging to herself, to another self. She is shouting in two voices—a complete conversation, spun through the recorder of her mind over and over again. I stop to listen. In ten minutes, I hear the same story seven times: over and over, the chronicle of voice number-one coming to borrow a few dollars, of being "sick as a dog," of being in her room vomiting, sickness and fever making her think she was going to die. What's a few lousy dollars, she says over and over. What's the difference to you.

Over and over, the enraged rejoinder of voice number-two: It's not the lousy twenty bucks. It's everything. I've given toys, I've given time, I've paid the bills. It's too much. I don't care if it's your goddamned birthday. I got a birthday too. It's not the goddamned twenty bucks. This is a lousy shame.

The voices of two in one. And yet a third voice, "her" voice, intertwines with the craziness of her split, braids the first two voices with intermittent howls and moans as if to bind the halves like a wound. Each rendition of the story is a little different; the sickness is a little more graphic, the toys purchased are enumerated or not—but each time the hot sneer of "I got a birthday too," the spitting of the "goddamned twenty bucks," and the sorrow of the "lousy shame" are always the climax, then an intermission of loud crying sounds before the tape is played again.

I recall the first time I shifted vision internally and beheld myself with my mind's eye. Unlike the intimacy of my mother's voice, the eye belonged to someone I did not know. The eye beheld that I was "not white"; this awareness did not make me wonder about the source of the eye's vision—I was too caught up in the horrible fascination of the news it brought: I learned, through it, to hate the black mirror image that confronted me in every store window; in public places and in the eyes of others, I was revealed.

In New Orleans, I notice, I am constantly brought back to that time. In New Orleans it is only the black residents who dance in the street; it is only white tourists who can bear to stand and watch. If whites do dance it is in imitation of blacks-who-are-watched. If whites dance it is a separate form of entertainment, like the limbo. It is a seen dance, rather than a felt or a transporting dance.

It has been a long time since I first shifted vision and beheld myself like that. And for a long time, my voices and my visions made war with one another in the fight to rule me.

Now, as I have said, I mark that open space, that shift, with the peace of polar bears. They make strong fashion statements, and they hold for me what I cannot own. Shiny shoes and the need to be seen. Freshly ruffled fur, gleaming with fish oil, sleek with sacrifice and fire, smelling of smoke and bone chips. Polished leather paws, clean-eared and long-whiskered. A different ethic, brought to me from a world beyond difference.

Postscript: Through the Looking Glass

In a courageous moment, I submitted this much of this chapter to a prominent law review. The rejection letter came promptly, although the editors went into unusual and flatteringly thorough detail about how I might wish to revise it for resubmission. [A note to the reader: Logically, what should follow here is the actual letter of rejection; but the editors of Harvard University Press, on the advice of the Press's lawyers, informed me that I could not reprint it, even anonymously, without the authors' permission, which in the circumstances has not been forthcoming. Not to worry, though, for I have plenty of Actual Letters from which to cut and paste. What follows, then, is a carefully crafted and paraphrased composite of rejection after rejection after rejection.]

Your piece has some really great ideas in it, but not once do you give a good clear statement of what the issue is. We understand that your life must seem hard and complicated, but frankly the events you describe are mild and quite ordinary. It is unclear to us why they should leave you on the edge of such self-described psychological trauma. There is nothing in either the content or the calculated calmness of your prose style that indicates any climaxing of emotion. Privileging your status with labels like "complicated oxymoron" sounds self-indulgent. Furthermore, you misdiagnose yourself as "schizophrenic." Schizophrenia is *not* "fashionable," "feminist," or "postmodern"; it is a serious disability affecting millions and we are sure our readers would not appreciate your making so light of it.

If, on the other hand, you genuinely want to confront the risks of mental illness involved in your being a "vain black female commercial law professor," either you should do so by rewriting the piece as an objective commentary, weaving in appropriate references to the law and, if necessary, social science data; or, since you have a very poetic way of writing, you should consider writing short stories. As it is, this piece is far too personal for any legal publication, and furthermore, if you don't mind our saying so, its publication anywhere will risk your being perceived as quite unstable in the public eye. We are confident, however, that with some rewriting, your attempt to express your ideas would be truly successful.

One more thing: by our calculations, the Louisiana meetings of the Modern Language Association and the Association of American Law Schools to which you refer occurred just after Christmas, 1988. Yet in the text you discuss, then footnote, an article dated February 23, 1989. . . . .

On Being the Object of Property

(a gift of intelligent rage)

As I have told you, what I know of my mother's side of the family begins with my great-great-grandmother Sophie. I know that she was purchased when she was eleven by a white lawyer named Austin Miller and was immediately impregnated by him. She gave birth to my great-grandmother Mary, who was taken away from her to be raised as a house servant. I know nothing more of Sophie (she was, after all, a black single mother—in today's terms—suffering the anonymity of yet another statistical teenage pregnancy). While I don't remember what I was told about Austin Miller before I decided to go to law school, I do remember that just before my first day of class my mother said, in a voice full of secretive reassurance, "The Millers were lawyers, so you have it in your blood."

When my mother told me that I had nothing to fear in law school, that law was "in my blood," she meant it in a complex sense. First and foremost, she meant it defiantly; no one should make me feel inferior because someone else's father was a judge. She wanted me to reclaim that part of my heritage from which I had been disinherited, and she wanted me to use it as a source of strength and self-confidence. At the same time, she was asking me to claim a part of myself that was the dispossessor of another part of myself; she was asking me to deny that disenfranchised little-black-girl who felt powerless and vulnerable.

In somewhat the same vein, my mother was asking me not to look to her as a role model. She was devaluing the part of herself that was not-Harvard and refocusing my vision to the part of herself that was hard-edged, proficient, and western. She hid the lonely, black, defiled-female part of herself and pushed me forward as the projection of a competent self, a cool rather than despairing self, a masculine rather than a feminine self.

I took this secret of my blood into the Harvard milieu with both the pride and the shame with which my mother had passed it along to me. I found myself in the situation described by Marguerite Duras in her novel *The Lover:* "We're united in a fundamental shame at having to live. It's here we are at the heart of our common fate, the fact that [we] are our mother's children, the children of a candid creature murdered by society. We're on the side of society which has reduced her to despair. Because of what's been done to our mother, so amiable, so trusting, we hate life, we hate ourselves."[1]

Reclaiming that from which one has been disinherited is a good thing. Self-possession in the full sense of that expression is the companion to self-knowledge. Yet claiming for myself a heritage the weft of whose genesis is my own disinheritance is a profoundly troubling paradox.

A friend of mine practices law in rural Florida. His office is in Belle Glade, an extremely depressed area where the sugar industry reigns supreme, where blacks live pretty much as they did in slavery times, in dormitories called slave ships. They are penniless, illiterate, and have both a high birth rate and a high death rate.

My friend told me about a client of his, a fifteen-year-old young woman pregnant with her third child, who came seeking advice because her mother had advised a hysterectomy—not even a tubal ligation—as a means of birth control. The young woman's mother, in turn, had been advised of the propriety of such a course for herself by a white doctor, some years before. Listening to this, I was reminded of a case I had when I was working for the Western Center on Law and Poverty almost a decade ago. Ten black and Hispanic women were sterilized by the University of Southern California–Los Angeles County General Medical Center, allegedly without proper consent and in most instances even without their knowledge.[2] Most of them found out what had been done to them upon inquiry, after a much publicized news story in which an intern charged that the chief of obstetrics at the hospital pursued a policy of recommending caesarian delivery and simultaneous sterilization for any pregnant woman with three or more children and who was on welfare. In the course of researching the appeal in that case, I remember learning that one quarter of all Navajo women of childbearing age—literally all those of childbearing age ever admitted to a hospital—have been sterilized. (This was the testimony of one of the witnesses. It is hard to find official confirmation for sterilization statistics involving Native American women. Official statistics kept by the U.S. Public Health Service, through the Centers for Disease Control in Atlanta, come from data gathered by the National Hospital Discharge Survey, which cover neither federal hospitals nor penitentiaries. Services to Native American women living on reservations are provided almost exclusively by federal hospitals. In addition, the Public Health Service breaks down its information into only three categories: White, Black, and Other. Nevertheless, in 1988, the Women of All Red Nations Collective of Minneapolis, Minnesota, distributed a fact sheet entitled "Sterilization Studies of Native American Women," which claimed that as many as 50 percent of all Native American women of childbearing age have been sterilized. According to "Surgical Sterilization Surveillance: Tubal Sterilization and Hysterectomy in Women Aged 15–44, 1979–1980," issued by the Centers for Disease Control in 1983, "In 1980, the tubal sterilization rate for black women . . . was 45 percent greater than that for white women. The sterilization rate for all women in the United States is about 17 percent, as compared to about 27 percent in Brazil."[3] Furthermore, a study released in 1984 by the Division of Reproductive Health of the Center for Health Promotion—one of the Centers for Disease Control—found that, as of 1982, 48.8 percent of Puerto Rican women between the ages of fifteen and forty-four had been sterilized.)

As I reflected on all this, I realized that one of the things passed on from slavery, which continues in the oppression of people of color, is a belief structure rooted in a concept of black (or brown or red) antiwill, the antithetical embodiment of pure will. We live in a society where the closest equivalent of nobility is the display of unremittingly controlled willfulness. To be perceived as unremittingly without will is to be imbued with an almost lethal trait.

Many scholars have explained this phenomenon in terms of total and infantilizing interdependency of dominant and oppressed.[4] Although such analysis is not objectionable in a general sense, the description of master-slave relations as "total" is, to me, quite troubling. That choice of words reflects and accepts—at a very subtle level, perhaps—a historical rationalization that whites had to, could, and did do everything for these simple subhumans. It is a choice of vocabulary that fails to acknowledge blacks as having needs beyond those that even the most "humane" or "sentimental" white slavemaster could provide.

In trying to describe the provisional aspect of slave law, I would choose words that revealed its structure as rooted in a concept of, again, black antiwill. I would characterize the treatment of blacks by whites in their law as defining blacks as those who had no will. That treatment is not total interdependency, but a relation in which partializing judgments, employing partializing standards of humanity, impose generalized inadequacy on a race: if "pure will" or total control equals the perfect white person, then impure will and total lack of control equals the perfect black per-

219

son. Therefore, to define slave law as comprehending a total view of personality implicitly accepts that the provision of food, shelter, and clothing (again assuming the very best of circumstances) is the whole requirement of humanity. It assumes also either that psychic care was provided by slaveowners (as if an owned psyche could ever be reconciled with mental health) or that psyche is not a significant part of a whole human.

Market theory always takes attention away from the full range of human potential in its pursuit of a divinely willed, rationally inspired, invisibly handed economic actor. Master-slave relations, however, took attention away from the full range of black human potential in a somewhat different way: it pursued a vision of blacks as simple-minded, strong-bodied economic "actants."[5] Thus, while blacks had an indisputable generative force in the marketplace, their presence could not be called activity; they had no active role in the market. To say that "market relations disregard the peculiarities of individuals, whereas slave relations rest on the mutual recognition of the humanity of master and slave" (no matter how dialectical or abstracted a definition of humanity one adopts) is to posit an inaccurate equation: if "disregard for the peculiarities of individuals" and "mutual recognition of humanity" are polarized by a *whereas*, then somehow regard for peculiarities of individuals must equal recognition of humanity.[6] In the context of slavery, this equation mistakes whites' overzealous and oppressive absorption with projected specific peculiarities of blacks for actual wholistic regard for the individual. It overlooks the fact that most definitions of humanity require something beyond mere biological sustenance, some healthy measure of autonomy beyond anything that slavery could conceive. And it overlooks the fact that both slave and bourgeois systems regarded certain attributes as important and disregarded certain others, and that such regard and disregard can occur in the same glance, like the wearing of horse blinders to focus attention simultaneously toward and away from. The experiential blinders of market actor and slaver go in different directions, yet the partializing ideologies of each makes the act of not-seeing an unsocializing, if unconscious, component of seeing. Restoring a unified social vision will, I think, require broader and more scattered resolutions than the simple symmetry of ideological bipolarity.

So it is important to undo whatever words obscure the fact that slave law was at least as fragmenting and fragmented as the bourgeois world view—and in a way that has persisted to this day, cutting across all ideological boundaries. As "pure will" signifies the whole bourgeois personality in the latter, so wisdom, control, and aesthetic beauty signify the whole white personality in the former. The slavemaster and the burgermeister are not so very different, when expressed in those terms. The reconciling difference is that in slave law the emphasis is really on the inverse rationale: that irrationality, lack of control, and ugliness signify the whole slave personality. Total interdependence is at best a polite way of rationalizing such personality splintering; it creates a bizarre sort of yin-yang from the dross of an oppressive schizophrenia of biblical dimensions. I would just call it schizophrenic—that sounds right to me. Truly total relationships (as opposed to totalitarianism) call up images of whole people dependent on whole people, an interdependence that is both providing and laissez-faire at the same time. Neither the historical inheritance of slave law nor so-called bourgeois law meets that definition.

None of this, perhaps, is particularly new. Nevertheless, as precedent to anything I do as a lawyer, the greatest challenge is to allow the full truth of partializing social constructions to be felt for their overwhelming reality—reality that otherwise I might rationally try to avoid facing. In my search for roots I must assume, not just as history but as an ongoing psychological force, that irrationality, lack of control, and ugliness signify not just the whole slave personality, not just the whole black personality, but me.

Reflecting on my roots makes me think again and again of the young woman in Belle Glade, Florida. She told the story of her impending sterilization, according to my friend, while keeping her eyes on the floor at all times. My friend, who is white, asked why she wouldn't look up, speak with him eye to eye. The young woman answered that she didn't like white people seeing inside her.

My friend's story made me think of my own childhood and adolescence. My parents were always telling me to look up at the world; to look straight at people, particularly white people; not to let them stare me down; to hold my ground; to insist on the right to my presence no matter what. They told me that in this culture you have to look people in the eye because that's how you tell them you're their equal. My friend's story also reminded me how very difficult I had found that looking back to be. What was hardest was not just that white people saw me, as my friend's client put it, but that they looked through me, as if I were transparent.

By itself, seeing into me would be to see my substance, my anger, my vulnerability and my raging despair—and that alone is hard enough to show. But to uncover it and have it devalued by ignore-ance, to hold it up bravely in the organ of my eyes and to have it greeted by an impassive stare that passes right through all that which is me, an impassive stare that moves on and attaches itself to my left earlobe or to the dust caught in the rusty vertical geysers of my wiry hair or to the breadth of my freckled brown nose—this is deeply humiliating. It rewounds, relives the early childhood anguish of uncensored seeing, the fullness of vision that is the permanent turning-away point for most blacks.

The cold game of equality staring makes me feel like a thin sheet of glass: white people see all the worlds beyond me but not me. They come trotting at me with force and speed; they do not see me. I could force my presence, the real me contained in those eyes, upon them, but I would be smashed in the process. If I deflect, if I move out of the way, they will never know I existed.

Marguerite Duras places her heroine in relation to her family: "Every day we try to kill one another, to kill. Not only do we not talk to one another, we don't even look at one another. When you're being looked at you can't look. To look is to feel curious, to be interested, to lower yourself."[7] To look is also to make myself vulnerable; yet not to look is to neutralize the part of myself that is vulnerable. I look in order to see, and so I must look. Without that directness of vision, I am afraid I shall will my own blindness, disinherit my own creativity, and sterilize my own perspective of its embattled, passionate insight.

One Saturday afternoon not long ago, I sat among a litter of family photographs telling a South African friend about Marjorie, my godmother and my mother's cousin. She was given away by her light-skinned mother when she was only six. She was given to my grandmother and my great-aunts to be raised among her darker-skinned cousins, for Marjorie was very dark indeed. Her mother left the family to "pass," to marry a white man—Uncle Frederick, we called him with trepidatious presumption yet without his ever knowing of our existence—an heir to a meatpacking fortune. When Uncle Frederick died thirty years later and the fortune was lost, Marjorie's mother rejoined the race, as the royalty of resentful fascination—Lady Bountiful, my sister called her—to regale us with tales of gracious upper-class living.

My friend said that my story reminded him of a case in which a swarthy, crisp-haired child was born, in Durban, to white parents. The Afrikaaner government quickly intervened, removed the child from its birth home and placed it to be raised in a "more suitable," browner family.

When my friend and I had shared these stories, we grew embarrassed somehow, and our conversation trickled away into a discussion of laissez-faire economics and governmental interventionism. Our words became a clear line, a railroad upon which all other ideas and events were tied down and sacrificed.

As a teacher of commercial transactions, one of the things that has always impressed me most about the law of contract is a certain deadening power it exercises by reducing parties to the passive. It constrains the lively involvement of its signatories by positioning enforcement in such a way that parties find themselves in a passive relationship to a document: it is the contract that governs, that "does" everything, that absorbs all responsibility and deflects all other recourse.

Contract law reduces life to fairy tale. The four corners of the agreement become parent. Performance is the equivalent of passive obedience to the parent. Passivity is valued as good contract-socialized behavior; activity is caged in retrospective hypotheses about states of mind at the magic moment of contracting. Individuals are judged by the contract unfolding rather than by the actors acting autonomously. Nonperformance is disobedience; disobedience is active; activity becomes evil in contrast to the childlike passivity of contract conformity.

One of the most powerful examples of all this is the case of Mary Beth Whitehead, mother of Sara, so-called Baby M. Whitehead became a vividly original actor after the creation of her surrogate contract with William Stern; unfortunately for her, there can be no greater civil sin. It was in this upsidedown context, in the picaresque unboundedness of breachor, that her energetic grief became hysteria and her passionate creativity was funneled, whorled, and reconstructed as highly impermissible. Mary Beth Whitehead thus emerged as the evil stepsister who deserved nothing.

Some time ago Charles Reich, author of *The Greening of America,* and a professor at the University of San Francisco Law School, visited a class of mine. He discussed with my students a proposal for a new form of bargain by which emotional "items"— such as praise, flattery, acting happy or sad—might be contracted for explicitly. One student, not alone in her sentiment, said, "Oh, but then you'll just feel obligated." Only the week before, however (when we were discussing the contract that posited that White-head "will not form or attempt to form a parent-child relationship with any child or children"), this same student had insisted that Whitehead must give up her child, because she had said she would: "She was obligated!" I was confounded by the degree to which what the student took to be self-evident, inalienable gut reactions could be governed by illusions of passive conventionality and form.

It was that incident, moreover, that gave me insight into how Judge Harvey Sorkow, of the New Jersey Superior Court, could conclude that the contract that purported to terminate White-head's parental rights was "not illusory."[8] (As background, I should say that, within the framework of contract law itself, the agreement between Whitehead and Stern seemed clearly illusory. "An illusory promise is an expression cloaked in promissory terms, but which, upon closer examination, reveals that the promisor has committed himself not at all."[9] On the one hand, Judge Sorkow's opinion said that Whitehead was seeking to avoid her obligations: in other words, giving up her child became an actual obligation. On the other hand, according to the logic of the judge, this was a service contract, not really a sale of a child; therefore delivering the child to the Sterns was an obligation for which there was no consideration, for which Stern was not paying her.)

Judge Sorkow's finding the contract "not illusory" is suggestive not only of the doctrine by that name but of illusion in general, and delusion, and the righteousness with which social constructions are conceived and delivered up into the realm of the real as "right," while all else is devoured from memory as "wrong." From this perspective, the rhetorical tricks by which Sara White-head became Melissa Stern seem very like the heavy-worded legalities by which my great-great-grandmother was pacified and parted from her child. In both situations, the real mother had no say; her powerlessness was imposed by state law that made her and her child helpless in relation to the father. My great-great-grandmother's powerlessness came about as the result of a contract to which she was not a party; Mary Beth Whitehead's powerlessness came about as a result of a contract she signed at a discrete point of time—yet which, over time, enslaved her. The contract-reality in both instances was no less than magic: it was illusion transformed into not-illusion. Furthermore, it masterfully disguised the brutality of enforced arrangements in which these women's autonomy, their flesh and their blood, was locked away in word vaults, without room to reconsider—ever.

In the months since Judge Sorkow's opinion, I have reflected upon the similarities of fortune between my own social positioning and that of Sara Melissa Stern Whitehead. I have come to realize that an important part of the complex magic that Sorkow wrote into his opinion was a supposition that it is natural for people to want children "like" themselves. What this reasoning raised for me was an issue of what exactly constituted this likeness? (What would have happened, for example, if Mary Beth Whitehead had turned out to have been the "passed" descendant of my "failed" godmother Marjorie's mother? What if the child she bore had turned out to be recessively and visibly black? Would the sperm of Stern have been so powerful as to make this child "his" with the exclusivity that Judge Sorkow originally assigned?) What constitutes, moreover, the collective understanding of "unlikeness"?

These questions turn, perhaps, on not-so-subtle images of which mothers should be bearing which children. Is there not something unseemly, in our society, about the spectacle of a white woman mothering a black child? A white woman giving totally to a black child; a black child totally and demandingly dependent for everything, sustenance itself, from a white woman. The image of a white woman suckling a black child; the image of a black child sucking for its life from the bosom of a white woman. The utter interdependence of such an image; the merging it implies; the giving up of boundary; the encompassing of other within self; the unbounded generosity and interconnectedness of such an image. Such a picture says there is no difference; it places the hope of continuous generation, of immortality of the white self, in a little black face.

When Sorkow declared that it was only to be expected that parents would want to breed children "like" themselves, he simultaneously created a legal right to the same. With the creation of such a "right," he encased the children conforming to likeliness in protective custody, far from whole ranges of taboo. Taboo about touch and smell and intimacy and boundary. Taboo about ardor, possession, license, equivocation, equanimity, indifference, intolerance, rancor, dispossession, innocence, exile, and candor. Taboo about death. Taboos that amount to death. Death and sacredness, the valuing of body, of self, of other, of remains. The handling lovingly in life, as in life; the question of the intimacy versus the dispassion of death.

In effect, these taboos describe boundaries of valuation. Whether something is inside or outside the marketplace of rights has always been a way of valuing it. Where a valued object is located outside the market, it is generally understood to be too "priceless" to be accommodated by ordinary exchange relationships; if the prize is located within the marketplace, then all objects outside become "valueless." Traditionally, the *Mona Lisa* and human life have been the sorts of subjects removed from the fungibility of commodification, as priceless. Thus when black people were bought and sold as slaves, they were placed beyond the bounds of humanity. And thus, in the twistedness of our brave new world, where blacks have been thrust out of the market and it is white children who are bought and sold, black babies have become worthless currency to adoption agents—"surplus" in the salvage heaps of Harlem hospitals.

> Familiar though his name may be to us, the storyteller in his living immediacy is by no means a present force. He has already become something remote from us and something that is getting even more

227

distant . . . Less and less frequently do we encounter people with the ability to tell a tale properly . . . It is as if something that seemed inalienable to us, the securest among our possessions, were taken from us: the ability to exchange experiences.[10]

My mother's cousin Marjorie was a storyteller. From time to time I would press her to tell me the details of her youth, and she would tell me instead about a child who wandered into a world of polar bears, who was prayed over by polar bears, and was in the end eaten. The child's life was not in vain because the polar bears had been made holy by its suffering. The child had been a test, a message from god for polar bears. In the polar-bear universe, she would tell me, the primary object of creation was polar bears, and the rest of the living world was fashioned to serve polar bears. The clouds took their shape from polar bears, trees were designed to give shelter and shade to polar bears, and humans were ideally designed to provide polar bears with meat.

The truth, the truth, I would laughingly insist was we sat in her apartment eating canned fruit and heavy roasts, mashed potatoes, pickles and vanilla pudding, cocoa, Sprite or tea. What about roots and all that, I coaxed. But the voracity of her amnesia would disclaim and disclaim—and she would go on telling me about the polar bears until our plates were full of emptiness and I became large in the space that described her emptiness and I gave in to the emptiness of words.

There are moments in my life when I feel as though a part of me is missing. There are days when I feel so invisible that I can't remember what day of the week it is, when I feel so manipulated that I can't remember my own name, when I feel so lost and angry that I can't speak a civil word to the people who love me best. Those are the times when I catch sight of my reflection in store windows and am surprised to see a whole person looking back. Those are the times when my skin becomes gummy as clay and my nose slides around on my face and my eyes drip down to my chin. I have to close my eyes at such times and remember myself, draw an internal picture that is smooth and whole; when all else fails, I reach for a mirror and stare myself down until the features reassemble themselves, like lost sheep.

Two years ago, my godmother Marjorie suffered a massive stroke. As she lay dying, I would come to the hospital to give her her meals. My feeding the one who had so often fed me became a complex ritual of mirroring and self-assembly. The physical act of holding the spoon to her lips was not only a rite of nurture and sacrifice, it was the return of a gift. It was a quiet bowing to the passage of time and the doubling back of all things. The quiet woman who listened to my woes about work and school required now that I bend my head down close to her and listen for mouthed word fragments, sentence crumbs. I bent down to give meaning to her silence, her wandering search for words.

She would eat what I brought to the hospital with relish; she would reject what she didn't want with a turn of her head. I brought fruit and yogurt, ice cream, and vegetable juice. Slowly, over time, she stopped swallowing. The mashed potatoes would sit in her mouth like cotton, the pudding would slip to her chin in slow streams. When she lost not only her speech but the power to ingest, they put a tube into her nose and down to her stomach, and I lost even that medium by which to communicate. No longer was there the odd but reassuring communion over taste. No longer was there some echo of comfort in being able to nurture one who nurtured me.

This increment of decay was like a little newborn death. With the tube, she stared up at me with imploring eyes, and I tried to guess what she would like. I read to her aimlessly and in desperation. We entertained each other with the strange embarrassed flickering of our eyes. I told her stories to fill the emptiness, the loneliness, of the white-walled hospital room.

I told her stories about who I had become, about how I had grown up to know all about exchange systems and theories of contract and monetary fictions. I spun tales about blue-sky laws

and promissory estoppel, the wispy-feathered complexity of undue influence and dark-hearted theories of unconscionability. I
told her about market norms and gift economy and the thin ra-
zor's edge of the bartering ethic. Once upon a time, I rambled,
some neighbors included me in their circle of barter. They were in
the habit of exchanging eggs and driving lessons, hand-knit sweaters and computer programming, plumbing and calligraphy. I accepted the generosity of their inclusion with gratitude. At first I
felt that, as a lawyer, I was worthless, that I had no barterable skills
and nothing to contribute. What I came to realize, however, was
that my value to the group was not calculated by the physical
items I brought to it. These people included me because they
wanted me to be part of their circle; they valued my participation
apart from the material things I could offer. So I gave of myself to
them, and they gave me fruit cakes and dandelion wine and
smoked salmon and, in their giving, their goods became provisions. Cradled in this community whose currency was a relational
ethic, my stock in myself soared. My value depended on the glorious intangibility, the eloquent invisibility, of my just being part
of the collective—and in direct response I grew spacious and
happy and gentle.

My gentle godmother. The fragility of life; the cold mortuary
shelf.

The hospital in which my godmother died is now filled to
capacity with AIDS patients. One in sixty-one babies born there,
as in New York City generally, is infected with AIDS antibodies.
Almost all are black or Hispanic. In the Bronx the rate is one in
forty-three. In Central Africa experts estimate that, of children receiving transfusions for malaria-related anemia, "about 1000 may
have been infected with the AIDS virus in each of the last five
years." In Congo, 5 percent of the entire population is infected.
The *New York Times* reports that "the profile of Congo's popula-

tion seems to guarantee the continued spread of AIDS." In the Congolese city of Pointe Noir, "the annual budget of the sole public health hospital is estimated at about $200,000—roughly the amount of money spent in the United States to care for four AIDS patients."[11]

The week in which my godmother died is littered with bad memories. In my journal I made note of the following:

Good Friday: Phil Donahue has a special program on AIDS. The segues are:

(a) from Martha, who weeps at the prospect of not watching her children grow up,

(b) to Jim, who is not conscious enough to speak just now, who coughs convulsively, who recognizes no one in his family any more,

(c) to Hugh who, at 85 pounds, thinks he has five years but whose doctor says he has weeks,

(d) to an advertisement for denture polish ("If you love your Polident Green, then gimmeeya SMILE!"),

(e) and then to one for a plastic surgery salon on Park Avenue ("The only thing that's expensive is our address"),

(f) and then to one for what's coming up on the five o'clock news (Linda Lovelace, of *Deep Throat* fame, "still recovering from a double mastectomy and complications from silicone injections" is being admitted to a New York hospital for a liver transplant),

(g) and finally, to one for the miracle properties of all-purpose house cleaner ("Mr. Cleeean/is the man/behind the shine/is it wet or is it dry?" I note that Mr. Clean, with his gleaming bald head, puffy musculature, and fever-bright eyes, looks as if he is undergoing radiation therapy). Now back to our show—

(h) "We are back now with Martha" (who is crying harder than before, sobbing uncontrollably, each jerking inhalation a deep unearthly groan). Phil says, "Oh honey, I hope we didn't make it worse for you."

Easter Saturday: Over lunch, I watch another funeral. My office windows overlook a graveyard as crowded and still as a rush-hour freeway. As I savor pizza and milk, I notice that one of the mourners is wearing an outfit featured in the window of Bloomingdale's (59th Street store) only since last weekend. This thread of recognition jolts me, and I am drawn to her in sorrow; the details of my own shopping history flash before my eyes as I reflect upon the sober spree that brought her to the rim of this earthly chasm, her slim suede heels sinking into the soft silt of the graveside.

Resurrection Sunday: John D., the bookkeeper where I used to work, died, hit on the head by a stray but forcefully propelled hockey puck. I cry copiously at his memorial service, only to discover, later in the afternoon when I see a black-rimmed photograph, that I am mourning the wrong person. I cried because the man I thought had died is John D. the office messenger, a bitter unfriendly man who treats me with disdain; once I bought an old electric typewriter from him that never worked. Though he promised nothing, I have harbored deep dislike since then; death by hockey puck is only one of the fates I had imagined for him. I washed clean my guilt with buckets of tears at the news of what I thought was his demise.

The man who did die was small, shy, anonymously sweet-featured, and innocent. In some odd way I am relieved; no seriously obligatory mourning to be done here. A quiet impassivity settles over me and I forget my grief.

A few months after my godmother died, my Great-Aunt Jag passed away in Cambridge, at ninety-six the youngest and the last of all her siblings, all of whom died at ninety-seven. She collapsed on her way home from the polling place, having gotten in her vote for "yet another Kennedy." Her wake was much like the last family gathering at which I had seen her, two Thanksgivings ago. She was a little hard of hearing then and stayed on the outer edge of the conversation, brightly, loudly, and randomly asserting enjoyment of her meal. At the wake, cousins, nephews, daughters-in-law, first wives, second husbands, great-grand nieces gathered round her casket and got acquainted all over again. It was pouring rain outside. The funeral home was dry and warm, faintly spicily clean-smelling; the walls were solid, dark, respectable wood; the floors were cool stone tile. On the door of a room marked "No

Admittance" was a sign that reminded workers therein of the reverence with which each body was held by its family and prayed employees handle the remains with similar love and care. Aunt Jag wore yellow chiffon; everyone agreed that laying her out with her glasses on was a nice touch.

Afterwards, we all went to Legal Seafoods, her favorite restaurant, and ate many of her favorite foods.

I have never been able to determine my horoscope with any degree of accuracy. Born at Boston's now-defunct Lying-In Hospital, I am a Virgo, despite a quite poetic soul. Knowledge of the hour of my birth, however, would determine not just my sun sign but my moons and all the more intimate specificities of my destiny. Once upon a time, I sent for my birth certificate, which was retrieved from the oblivion of Massachusetts microfiche. Said document revealed that an infant named Patricia Joyce, born of parents named Williams, was delivered into the world "colored." Since no one thought to put down the hour of my birth, I suppose I will never know my true fate. In the meantime, I read what text there is of me.

My name, Patricia, means patrician. Patricias are noble, lofty, elite, exclusively educated, and well-mannered despite themselves. I was on the cusp of being Pamela, but my parents knew that such a me would require lawns, estates, and hunting dogs.

I am also a Williams. Of William, whoever he was: an anonymous white man who owned my father's people and from whom some escaped. That rupture is marked by the dark-mooned mystery of utter silence.

Williams is the second most common surname in the United States; Patricia is *the* most common prename among women born in 1951, the year of my birth.

In the law, rights are islands of empowerment. To be unrighted is to be disempowered, and the line between rights and no-rights is most often the line between dominators and oppres-

233

sors. Rights contain images of power, and manipulating those images, either visually or linguistically, is central in the making and maintenance of rights. In principle, therefore, the more dizzyingly diverse the images that are propagated, the more empowered we will be as a society.

In reality, it was a lovely polar-bear afternoon. The gentle force of the earth. A wide wilderness of islands. A conspiracy of polar bears lost in timeless forgetting. A gentleness of polar bears, a fruitfulness of polar bears, a silent black-eyed interest of polar bears, a bristled expectancy of polar bears. With the wisdom of innocence, a child threw stones at the polar bears. Hungry in nests, they rose, inquisitive, dark-souled, patient with foreboding, fearful in tremendous awakening. The instinctual ferocity of the hunter reflected upon the hunted. Then, proud teeth and warrior claws took innocence for wilderness and raging insubstantiality for tender rabbit breath.

In the newspapers the next day, it was reported that two polar bears in the Brooklyn Zoo mauled to death an eleven-year-old boy who had entered their cage to swim in the moat. The police were called, and the bears were killed.[12]

In the public debate that ensued, many levels of meaning emerged. The rhetoric firmly established that the bears were innocent, naturally territorial, unfairly imprisoned, and guilty. The dead child (born into the urban jungle of a black welfare mother and a Hispanic alcoholic father who had died literally in the gutter only six weeks before) was held to a similarly stern standard. The police were captured, in a widely disseminated photograph,[13] shooting helplessly, desperately, into the cage, through three levels of bars, at a pietà of bears; since this image, conveying much pathos, came nevertheless not in time to save the child, it was generally felt that the bears had died in vain.

In the egalitarianism of exile, pluralists rose up as of one body, with a call to buy more bears, control juvenile delinquency, eliminate all zoos, and confine future police.

In the plenary session of the national meeting of the Law and Society Association, the keynote speaker unpacked the whole incident as a veritable laboratory of emergent rights discourse. Just seeing that these complex levels of meaning exist, she exulted, should advance the discourse significantly.[14]

At the funeral of the child, the presiding priest pronounced the death of Juan Perez not in vain, since he was saved from growing into "a lifetime of crime." Juan's Hispanic-welfare-black-widow-of-an-alcoholic mother decided then and there to sue.

How I ended up at Dartmouth College for the summer is too long a story to tell. But there I was, sharing the town of Hanover, New Hampshire, with about two hundred prepubescent males enrolled in Dartmouth's summer basketball camp, an all-white, very expensive, affirmative-action program for the street-deprived.

One fragrant evening I was walking down East Wheelock Street when I encountered about a hundred of these adolescents, fresh from the courts, wet, lanky, big-footed, with fuzzy yellow crewcuts, loping toward Thayer Hall and food. In platoons of twenty-five or so, they descended, jostling me, smacking me, and pushing me from the sidewalk into the gutter. In a thoughtless instant I snatched off my brown silk headrag, my flag of African femininity and propriety, my sign of meek and supplicatory place and presentation. I released the armored rage of my short nappy hair (the scalp gleaming bare between the angry wire spikes) and hissed: "Don't I exist for you? See me! And deflect, godammit!" (The quaint professionalism of my formal English never allowed the rage in my head to rise so high as to overflow the edges of my text.)

They gave me wide berth. They clearly had no idea, however, that I was talking to them or about them. They skirted me sheepishly, suddenly polite, because they did know, when a crazed black person comes crashing into one's field of vision, that it is impolite to laugh. I stood tall and spoke loudly into their ranks: "I have my rights!" The Dartmouth Summer Basketball Camp raised its collective eyebrows and exhaled, with a certain tested nobility of exhaustion and solidarity.

I pursued my way, manumitted back into silence. I put distance between them and me, gave myself over to polar-bear musings. I allowed myself to be watched over by bear spirits. Clean white wind and strong bear smells. The shadowed amnesia; the absence of being; the presence of polar bears. White wilderness of icy meateaters heavy with remembrance; leaden with undoing; shaggy with the effort of hunting for silence; frozen in a web of intention and intuition. A lunacy of polar bears. A history of polar bears. A pride of polar bears. A consistency of polar bears. In those meandering pastel polar-bear moments, I found cool fragments of white-fur invisibility. Solid, black-gummed, intent, observant. Hungry and patient, impassive and exquisitely timed. The brilliant bursts of exclusive territoriality. A complexity of messages implied in our being.

Notes · *A Word on Categories* ·
Acknowledgments · *Index*

Notes

1. The Brass Ring and the Deep Blue Sea

1. *Icar v. Suars,* 7 Louisana Rep. 517 (1835).
2. "MacNeil/Lehrer News Hour" (PBS television broadcast), May 10, 1990. See also Anthony Flint, "Bell at Harvard: A Unique Activism," *Boston Globe,* May 7, 1990, p. 1, describing the resignation of Professor Derrick Bell from the faculty of Harvard Law School "until a black woman was considered for tenure."

2. Gilded Lilies and Liberal Guilt

1. Eugene Genovese, "Don't Mess with Mammy," *Washington Post,* October 27, 1974, p. C5.
2. Theresa Laurino, "I'm Nobody's Girl," *Village Voice,* October 14, 1986, p. 18. See also Kathy Dobie, "Black Women, White Kids: A Tale of Two Worlds," *Village Voice,* January 12, 1988, pp. 20–27. Compare Frances Anne Kemble, *Journal of a Residence on a Georgia Plantation in 1838–1839,* ed. John Scott (New York: Knopf, 1984), p. 279: "While the men discussed about this matter, Mrs. B[ryan] favored me with the congratulations I have heard so many times on the subject of my having a white nurserymaid for my children. Of course, she went into the old subject of the utter incompentency of Negro women to discharge such an office faithfully; but, in spite of her multiplied examples of their utter inefficiency, I believe the discussion ended by simply our both agreeing that ignorant Negro girls twelve years old are not as capable or trustworthy as well-trained white women of thirty."
3. David Lurie and Krzysztof Wodiczko, "Homeless Vehicle Project," *October,* 47 (Winter 1988), 54.

4. "A Homeless Woman Gives Birth in Subway," *New York Times*, March 22, 1989, p. B6.
5. Lloyd Cutler, "Pro-Life? Then Pay Up," *New York Times*, July 7, 1989, p. A29.
6. Jay Mathews, "Earthquake Swells Ranks of Homeless," *Washington Post*, October 27, 1989, p. A14.
7. 424 U.S. 1 (1976), p. 39. The Supreme Court states:

"While the independent expenditure ceiling thus fails to serve any substantial governmental interest in stemming the reality or appearance of corruption in the electoral process, it heavily burdens core First Amendment expression . . . Advocacy of the election or defeat of candidates for federal office is no less entitled to protection under the First Amendment than the discussion of policy generally or advocacy of the passage or defeat of legislation.

"It is argued, however, that the ancillary governmental interest in equalizing the relative ability of individuals and groups to influence the outcome of elections serves to justify the limitations on express advocacy of the election or defeat of candidates imposed by §602(e)(1)'s expenditure ceiling. But the concept that government may restrict the speech of some elements of our society in order to enhance the relative voice of others is wholly foreign to the First Amendment." Ibid., pp. 47–49.
8. §71(a), *Restatement of the Law, Contracts (2d)* (St. Paul: American Law Institute, 1982) provides: "To constitute consideration a performance or a return promise must be bargained for." §79 further provides: "If the requirement of consideration is met, there is no additional requirement of (a) a gain, advantage, or benefit to the promisor or a loss, disadvantage, or detriment to the promisee, or (b) equivalence in the values exchanged; or (c) 'mutuality of obligation.'"
9. Robert Ellickson, "Cities and Homeowners' Associations," *University of Pennsylvania Law Review*, 130(1982), 1562. In encouraging consideration of a system of local elections in which voting power would be based on the "economic stake" in a community, Ellickson writes: "Suppose that voting power in a suburb were to be reallocated from one-vote-per-resident to one-vote-per-acre. That reallocation would strengthen prodevelopment forces relative to antidevelopment forces because owners of undeveloped land would gain in political power. Assume more housing would be built. If exclusionary practices had previously pushed housing prices above competitive levels, housing prices would fall. It is possible that the gains low-income families would obtain from the drop in housing prices would outweigh other losses they would sustain from residing in a suburb that conferred voting power according to a formula that was facially disadvantageous to them. In other words, an apparently regressive voting system may have progressive distributional consequences."

10. See 131 *Congressional Record* S5727 (daily ed. May 9, 1985), statement of Jessica Lange.

11. Jean Baudrillard and Sylvère Lotringer, "Forget Baudrillard," in *Forget Foucault* (New York: Semiotext(e), 1987), p. 86.

12. John M. Brockman, "Bitburg Deconstruction," *Philosophical Forum,* 7(1986), p. 160.

13. Marlise Simons, "Women in Brazil Are Now Finding Out Sterilization May Save Their Jobs," *New York Times,* December 7, 1988, p. A11.

14. See *U.A.W. v. Johnson Controls, Inc.,* 886 F.2d 871, 898–99 (7th Cir. 1989).

15. See, e.g., *Smith v. Superior Court,* 151 Ariz. 67, 725 P.2d 1101 (1986).

16. *State v. Brown,* 284 S.C. 411, 326 S.E.2d 410(1985).

17. See generally Winthrop Jordan, *White over Black* (Chapel Hill: University of North Carolina Press, 1968), pp. 136–178 ("castration [for blacks] was dignified by specific legislative sanction as a lawful punishment in Antigua, the Carolinas, Bermuda, Virginia, Pennsylvania, and New Jersey," p. 154); John Dollard, *Caste and Class in a Southern Town* (Garden City: Doubleday, 1957), pp. 134–172 (published originally in 1937, the author ominously and ambiguously reports that the mythology of exaggerated black potency is "further suspect because the same point seems to be coming up with respect to the Jews in Germany"; p. 161).

18. See, e.g., "Judge Suggests Castration for Convicted Sex Offender," *Los Angeles Daily Journal,* January 24, 1990, p. 26.

19. "Plan to Sterilize Women is Debated," *New York Times,* September 25, 1988, p. 35.

20. Sacvan Bercovitch, "Hawthorne's A-Morality of Compromise," *Representations,* 24 (1988), pp. 21.

21. See *De Shaney v. Winnebago County Department of Social Services,* 109 S. Ct. 998, 1007 (1989); also Comment, "*De Shaney v. Winnebago County:* The Narrowing Scope of Constitutional Torts," *Maryland Law Review,* 49 (1990), 463.

22. Carl Wellman, "The Growth of Children's Rights," *Archiv fur Rechts und Sozialphilosophie,* 70 (1984), 441.

23. "Tower Takes Vow He Will Not Drink If He Is Confirmed," *New York Times,* February 27, 1989, p. A1.

24. §243(a), Lanham Act, 15 U.S.C.S. §21125(a) (1988).

25. The "expectation interest" in contract law is the promisee's "interest in having the benefit of his bargain by being put in as good a position as he would have been in had the contract been performed." §344(a), *Restatement of the Law, Contracts (2d)*.

26. John Stuart Mill, *On Liberty,* ed. David Spitz (New York: Norton, 1975), p. 6.

3. The Death of the Profane

1. "When 'By Appointment' Means Keep Out," *New York Times,* December 17, 1986, p. B1. Letter to the Editor from Michael Levin and Marguerita Levin, *New York Times,* January 11, 1987, p. E32.
2. *New York Times,* January 11, 1987, p. E32.
3. See generally *Blyew v. U.S.,* 80 U.S. 581 (1871), upholding a state's right to forbid blacks to testify against whites.
4. "Attorney Says Affirmative Action Denies Racism, Sexism," *Dominion Post,* (Morgantown, West Virginia), April 8, 1988, p. B1.
5. These questions put me on trial—an imaginary trial where it is I who have the burden of proof—and proof being nothing less than the testimony of the salesman actually confessing yes yes I am a racist. These questions question my own ability to know, to assess, to be objective. And of course, since anything that happens to me is inherently subjective, they take away my power to know what happens to me in the world. Others, by this standard, will always know better than I. And my insistence on recounting stories from my own perspective will be treated as presumption, slander, paranoid hallucination, or just plain lies.

    Recently I got an urgent call from Thomas Grey of Stanford Law School. He had used this piece in his jurisprudence class, and a rumor got started that the Benetton's story wasn't true, that I had made it up, that it was a fantasy, a lie that was probably the product of a diseased mind trying to make all white people feel guilty. At this point I realized it almost didn't make any difference whether I was telling the truth or not—that the greater issue I had to face was the overwhelming weight of a disbelief that goes beyond mere disinclination to believe and becomes active suppression of anything I might have to say. The greater problem is a powerfully oppressive mechanism for denial of black self-knowledge and expression. And this denial cannot be separated from the simultaneously pathological willingness to believe certain things about blacks—not to believe them, but things about them.

    When students in Grey's class believed and then claimed that I had made it all up, they put me in a position like that of Tawana Brawley. I mean that specifically: the social consequence of concluding that we are liars operates as a kind of public absolution of racism—the conclusion is not merely that we are troubled or that I am eccentric, but that we, as liars, are the norm. Therefore, the nonbelievers can believe, things of this sort really don't happen (even in the face of statistics to the contrary). Racism or rape is all a big fantasy concocted by troublesome minorities and women. It is interesting to recall the outcry in every national medium, from the *New York Post* to the *Times* to the major networks, in the wake of the Brawley case: who will ever again believe a black woman who cries rape by a white man? (See Chapter 9.) Now shift the frame a bit, and imagine a white male facing a consensus that he lied. Would there be a difference? Consider Charles Stuart, for example, the white Bostonian who accused a black man of murdering his pregnant wife and whose brother later alleged that in fact the brothers had conspired to murder her. Most people and the media not only did not claim but actively resisted believing that Stuart represented any kind of "white male" norm. Instead he was written off as a troubled weirdo, a deviant—again even in the face of spousal-abuse statistics to the contrary. There was not a story I could find that carried on about "who will ever believe" the next white man who cries murder.

4. Teleology on the Rocks

1. Robert McFadden, "Police Seek New Witnesses to Howard Beach Attack," *New York Times*, January 6, 1987, p. B1.
2. Samuel Freedman, "In Howard Beach, Pride and Fear in a 'Paradise,' " *New York Times*, December 23, 1986, p. B4. Joyce Purnick, "Koch, Seeking Racial Talk, Gets Irate Reception at Queens Church," *New York Times*, December 29, 1986, p. B3.
3. Guy Trebay, "Howard Beach Memoirs," *Village Voice*, January 6, 1987, p. 16.
4. "A 'we-they' analysis . . . justifies a disadvantage that we (the majority) want to impose on ourselves to favor them (the minority). This type of thinking, however, leaves the choice of remedy and the time frame for that remedy in the hands of the majority; it converts affirmative action into a benefit, not a right. It neglects the possibility that the disadvantaged minority may have a moral claim to a particular remedy.

   "The inner-circle commentators rarely deal with issues of guilt and reparation. When they do, it is often to attach responsibility in a scapegoat, someone of another time or place, and almost certainly of another social class than that of the writer. These writers tend to focus on intentional and determinable acts of discrimination inflicted on the victim by some perpetrator and ignore the more pervasive and invidious forms of discriminatory conditions inherent in our society. This 'perpetrator' perspective deflects attention from the victim-class, the Blacks, Native Americans, Chicanos, and Puerto Ricans who lead blighted lives for reasons directly traceable to social and institutional injustice." Richard Delgado, "The Imperial Scholar," *University of Pennsylvania Law Review*, 132 (1984), 570–571.
5. Vernon Reid, "Visible Man," *Village Voice*, January 6, 1987, p. 15.
6. "Emphasizing utility or distributive justice as the justification for affirmative action has a number of significant consequences. It enables the writer to concentrate on the present and the future and overlook the past . . . The past becomes irrelevant; one just asks where things are now and where we

ought to go from here, a straightforward social-engineering inquiry . . . But . . . it robs affirmative action programs of their moral force in favor of a sterile theory of fairness or utility. No doubt there is a great social utility to affirmative action, but to base it solely on that ground ignores the right of minority communities to be made whole, and the obligation of the majority to render them whole." Delgado, "The Imperial Scholar," p. 570.

7. *New York Times,* December 29, 1986, p. B3.

8. Daniel Berrigan and Thich Nhat Hanh, *The Raft Is Not the Shore* (Boston: Beacon Press, 1975), p. 38.

9. "Who, if not us, will question once more the objective status of this 'I', which a historical evolution peculiar to our culture tends to confuse with the subject? This anomaly should be manifested in its particular effects on every level of language, and first and foremost in the grammatical subject of the first person in our languages, in the 'I love' that hypostatizes the tendency of a subject who denies it. An impossible mirage in linguistic forms among which the most ancient are to be found, and in which the subject appears fundamentally in the position of being determinant or instrumental of action.

"Let us leave aside the critique of all the abuses of the cogito ergo sum, and recall that, in my experience, the ego represents the centre of all the resistances to the treatment of symptoms.

"It was inevitable that analysis, after stressing the reintegration of the tendencies excluded by the ego, in so far as they are subjacent to the symptoms that it tackled in the first instance, and which were bound up for the most part with the failures of Oedipal identification, should eventually discover the 'moral' dimension of the problem." Jacques Lacan, "Agressivity in Psychoanalysis," in *Ecrits: A Selection,* trans. Alan Sheridan (New York: Norton, 1977), pp. 23–24.

10. See generally Phillip Boffey, "Health Experts Fault U.S. on Response to AIDS," *New York Times,* August 13, 1987, p. A20.

11. See generally Kenneth Clark, *Prejudice and Your Child* (Boston: Beacon Press, 1955), and *Dark Ghetto* (New York: Harper and Row, 1965); William Grier and Price Cobb, *Black Rage* (New York: Basic Books, 1968); James Comer and Alvin Poussaint, *Black Child Care* (New York: Simon and Schuster, 1975).

12. See generally Phillip Selznick, "Law, Society and Moral Evolution," in *Readings in Jurisprudence and Legal Philosophy,* ed. Phillip Shuchman (Boston: Little, Brown, 1979), pp. 947–949.

13. See generally Alice Miller, *The Drama of the Gifted Child,* trans. Ruth Ward (New York: Basic Books, 1984).

14. "An example relevant to the development of 'legal reification' can be found in any first grade classroom. It is 8:29 and children are playing, throwing food, and generally engaging in relatively undistorted communication. At

8:30 the teacher . . . calls the class to attention: it is time for the 'pledge of allegiance.' All face front, all suffer the same social rupture and privation, all fix their eyes on a striped piece of cloth. As they drone on, having not the slightest comprehension of the content of what they are saying, they are nonetheless learning the sort of distorted or reified communication that is expressed in the legal form. They are learning, in other words, that they are all abstract 'citizens' of an abstract 'United States of America,' that there exists 'liberty and justice for all,' and so forth—not from the content of the words but from the ritual which forbids any rebellion. Gradually, they will come to accept these abstractions as descriptive of a concrete truth because of the repressive and conspiratorial way that these ideas have been communicated (each senses that all the others 'believe in' the words and therefore they must be true), and once this acceptance occurs, any access to the paradoxically forgotten memory that these are mere abstractions is sealed off. And once the abstractions are reified, they can no longer be criticized because they signify a false concrete." Peter Gabel, "Reification in Legal Reasoning," *Research in Law and Society,* 3(1980), 26–27.

15. *New York Times,* December 29, 1986, p. B3.
16. "Apology on Beach Protest," *New York Times,* January 22, 1987, p. A3.
17. *New York Times,* December 23, 1986, p. B4, col. 6.
18. "Inner rage tends to burn out our connections to the real world. It tends to overwhelm reason and to destroy the faces and beings of others. In our anger we can only see ourselves. The inability to imagine the experience of the stranger, of the other, was exactly what made the Holocaust possible. The Nazi success in dehumanizing their victims has left us with such rage that we too can dehumanize, erase the individual faces of others. We must find a way to let our anger burn freely, openly without consuming or perverting . . . otherwise we remain victims forever." Ann Roiphe, "The Politics of Anger," *Tikkun,* 1(1987), 21–22.
19. "The judge in imposing a sentence normally takes for granted the role structure which might be analogized to the 'transmission' of the engine of justice. The judge's interpretive authorization of the 'proper' sentence can be carried out as a deed only because of these others; a bond between word and deed abtains only because a system so social cooperation exists. That system guarantees the judge massive mounts of force—the conditions of effective domination—if necessary. It guarantees—or is supposed to—a relatively faithful adherence to the word of the judge in the deeds carried out against the prisoner. . . . If the institutional structure—the system of roles—gives the judge's understanding its effect, thereby transforming understanding into 'law,' so it confers meaning on the deeds which effect this transformation, thereby legitimating them as 'lawful.' A central task of the legal interpreter is to attend to the problematic aspects of the integration of role, deed, and word, not only where the violence (i.e., enforcement) is lacking for mean-

ing, but also where meaning is lacking for violence." Robert Cover, "Violence and the Word," *Yale Law Journal*, 95(1986), 1619, 1629.

20. Robert McFadden, "3 Youths Charged in Racial Attack Ordered Held Without Bail," *New York Times*, December 24, 1986, p. B4.

21. *New York Times*, December 29, 1986, p. B3.

22. See Chapter 3. The microcosm to which I am referring is the experience of being excluded, not that of not being able to get into Benetton's per se. My particular choice of stores was an unfortunate reflection of the degree to which Manhattan's traditional eccentricity and cultural richness have been consumed by silly enterprises—row upon row of privatized public spaces, dedicated to "moneyed frivolity" and "fabulousness, an attitude inspired by greed, marked by Gucci buckles, and rampant in Benetton stores." Margot Mifflin, "Heimel Maneuver," *Village Voice*, January 27, 1987, p. 55.

23. It is in understanding the degree to which black buying power is nevertheless a sustaining component in even the most parasitic white economies that reveals the logic behind the controversial boycott of white-owned businesses, called for by some black leaders in the wake of Howard Beach. "The Rev. Calvin O. Butts 3d of the Abyssinian Baptist Church said in one of the interviews: 'We're talking about getting the kind of respect that comes from the power of our vote and our buying power.'" Ronald Smothers, "Racial Violence Focus of Blacks in Day of Protest," *New York Times*, January 22, 1987, p. B3.

24. For an analysis that elevates precisely this thinking to normative principles of "good intentions" in the law, see Larry Simon, "Racially Prejudiced Governmental Actions," *San Diego Law Review*, 15 (1978), 1041.

25. "It is common for racial minorities, especially those who find themselves relatively isolated in predominantly white institutions, to have white colleagues express stereotyped or derogatory views either by way of direct statements or by unstated but implicit assumptions . . . It is obvious to the minority person that the speaker has not intended a racial slight—his tone is friendly and candid—and that he is unaware of the attitudinal source of the inadvertent derogation. And when other whites are present, they are unlikely to hear or be sensitive to the connotations of the demeaning remark." Charles Lawrence, "The Id, the Ego, and Equal Protection: Reckoning with Unconscious Racism," *Stanford Law Review*, 39 (1987), 341n100.

26. "Undoubtedly, something that is not expressed does not exist. But the repressed is always there—it insists, and it demands to come into being. The fundamental relation of man with this symbolic order is precisely the same one which founds this symbolic order itself—the relation of non-being to being." Jacques Lacan, "Sign, Symbol, Imaginary," in *On Signs*, ed. Marshall Blonsky (Baltimore: Johns Hopkins Press, 1985), p. 209.

27. Joan Petersilia, *Racial Disparities in the Criminal Justice System*, prepared for

National Institute of Corrections, U.S. Department of Justice (Santa Monica: Rand, June 1983), pp. 44, xxiv.

28. Black attempts to invert this imagery have been logical but largely lost efforts. See generally Floyd Flake, "Blacks Are Fair Game," *New York Times,* June 19, 1987, p. A35.

29. *New York Newsday,* June 17, 1987, p. 5.

30. Ibid., p. 40.

31. "You Have To Think in a Cold-Blooded Way" *New York Times,* April 30, 1987, p. B6.

32. See generally Richard Restak, "The Law: The Fiction of the Reasonable Man," *Washington Post,* May 17, 1987, p. C3; George Fletcher, *Los Angeles Times,* May 17, 1987, part 5, p. 1.

33. "Jury Selection Begins in Trial of Bernhard Goetz," *Los Angeles Times,* March 24, 1987, part 1, p. 4.

34. *New York Newsday,* June 17, 1987, p. 40.

35. Kenneth Clark, "In Cities, Who Is the Real Mugger?" *New York Times,* January 14, 1987, p. 19.

36. See also Richard Delgado, "Words That Wound: A Tort Action for Racial Insults, Epithets and Name-Calling," *Harvard Civil Rights—Civil Liberties Law Review,* 17 (1982), 133.

6. The Obliging Shell

1. Julie Johnson, "Prospect of Racial Parity Called Bleak," *New York Times,* August 8, 1989, p. A13.

2. Theresa Miller, "An Anti-Integrationist's Critique of School Desegregation: Making the Case for Black Colleges" (unpublished manuscript on file at University of Wisconsin Law School, Madison), citing "College Outlook Grim for Blacks 25 Years after Barriers Fell," *Chronicle of Higher Education,* September 2, 1987, p. A88.

3. "Equity in Higher Education Still Eludes Blacks, Urban League Says," *Chronicle of Higher Education,* January 20, 1988, p. A31.

4. 109 S. Ct. 706 (1989), p. 730.

5. Ibid., p. 727 (emphasis added, citation omitted), quoting *Regents of California v. Bakke,* 438 U.S. 296–97 (1978; Powell, J.).

6. Ibid, p. 725.

7. §243, *Restatement of the Law, Contracts (2d)* (St. Paul: American Law Institute, 1982); §2–202, *Uniform Commerical Code,* in *Selected Commercial Statutes* (St. Paul: West, 1989).

8. 109 S. Ct. 2180 (1989).

9. Al Kamen, "Sharply Divided Court Eases Way for Challenges to Affirmative Action Plans," *Washington Post,* June 13, 1989, p. A4; "Clarification," *Washington Post,* June 15, 1989, p. A3.

10. Peter Applebome, "'65 Rights Act Now a Tool for Whites," *New York Times,* August 8, 1989, p. A10.
11. §§215–216, *Restatement of the Law, Contracts (2d).*
12. "Ujaama Incident a 'Gripping Study' in Race Relations," *Stanford University Campus Report,* January 18, 1989, pp. 1, 19.
13. Board of Trustees, Stanford University, *Final Report on Recent Incidents at Ujaama House* (1989), p. 2.
14. See, e.g., Regina Austin, "Employer Abuse, Worker Resistance of the Tort of Intentional Infliction of Emotional Distress," *Stanford Law Review,* 41 (1988), 1, exploring the tension between the ideal of free-market worker independence and the reality of workplace harrassment based on factors of race, class, and gender. In the examination of informal resistance techniques employed by subordinates against abusive authority, Austin attempts to identify a program that would "universalize the conflict of the workplace, and . . . shift the focus of the dispute from the narrowly economic to the broadly cultural and political" (p. 49). She provides a nuanced discussion of the mechanics of coercion and control; and illuminates specifics of oppression that are traditionally dismissed or made invisible by assumptions of inevitability or disciplinary necessity. The discussion recaptures, from the discursive inexpressibility of the experience of humiliation, real words of outrage. It models a discourse of moral issue and, literally, of legal claim.
15. Stanford Trustees, *Final Report,* p. 2.
16. Bruce Lambert, "Rockettes and Race: Barrier Slips," *New York Times,* December 26, 1987, pp. 25, 27.
17. Michael Winerip, "A City Struggles over an Honor for Dr. King," *New York Times,* January 19, 1988, p. B1.
18. *Baltimore Sun,* November 29, 1988, p. D4.
19. I have tried to do a fair amount of reading on the subject since then. By no means do I want to imply, in my recounting of S., any implication that this was all there was to her story or that her story explains transsexuality: there is a whole range of transsexuality beyond S. herself, as well as an S. who exists beyond my limited characterization or experience of her.
20. Lena Williams, "Uneasy Mingling: When Small Talk at Parties Tackles Large Racial Issues," *New York Times,* October 21, 1988, p. A15.

7. Fire and Ice

1. Ronald Smothers, "Blacks, after Howard Beach, Unite on Goals, Split on Policy," *New York Times,* January 12, 1987, p. B2.
2. Margaret Taylor, "A Court Fails, an Old Woman Dies, and the Police Stand Trial," *New York Times,* March 19, 1987, p. A26.
3. Dennis Heuesi, "Bumpurs Case Charge Reinstated," *New York Times,* November 26, 1986, p. B6.

4. Selwyn Raab, "Trial of Officer in Bumpurs Case Starting with Request for No Jury," *New York Times*, January 12, 1987, p. B2.
5. Remarks of Commissioner Benjamin Ward at City University of New York Law School, November 1985, audiotape on file at CUNY Law School.
6. *New York Times*, November 21, 1987, p. B3.
7. *Fact Sheets on Institutional Racism* (New York: Council on Interracial Books for Children, 1982).
8. Remarks of Ward; Selwyn Raab, "Ward Defends Police Actions in Bronx Death," *New York Times*, November 3, 1984, p. A27.
9. *New York Times*, November 3, 1984, November 21 and 26, 1986; remarks of Ward.
10. Selwyn Raab, "Civilian Describes 'Struggle' Before Shooting of Bumpurs," *New York Times*, January 14, 1987, p. B2.

8. The Pain of Word Bondage

1. See generally Richard Delgado et al., "Fairness and Formality: Minimizing the Risk of Prejudice in Alternative Dispute Resolution," *Wisconsin Law Review*, 6 (1985), 1359.
2. "Whatever else they learned in school, black children came to understand, as their parents had, that their color marked them as inferior in the eyes of whites, no matter how they conducted themselves. 'We came to understand,' a black woman would recall of her youth, 'that no matter how neat and clean, how law abiding, submissive and polite, how studious in school, how churchgoing and moral, how scrupulous in paying our bills and taxes we were, it made no essential difference in our place.'" Leon Litwack, "'Blues Falling Down Like Rain,'" in *New Perspectives on Race and Slavery in America*, ed. Robert Abzug and Stephen Maizlish (Lexington: University of Kentucky Press, 1986), p. 118.
3. Peter describes the law of formalized hierarchical social arrangements as deriving from "externalized" and "totemic source[s] of unification" in which each person experiences his or her authentic being as a privatized non-self that is denied recognition and that is therefore "invisible" or unconscious: it is known or comprehended only though the experienced bodily tension that derives from not being-oneself and through a continual obsessive and pre-conscious fantasy life that reaches a dim awareness in moments of distraction . . . The 'visible' or conscious self that is enacted in behavior is experienced as a 'public' or 'outer' synthesis of as-if performances which is at once lived as passively undergone to the degree that it lacks any sense of its own agency and yet is 'owned' to the degree that each person feels this self as 'I'." Peter Gabel, "The Bank Teller," *Tikkun*, 2 (1987), p. 48–49.
4. Mary Ann Caws, "Literal or Liberal: Translating Perception," *Critical Inquiry*, 13 (1986), 55.

5. Mark Tushnet, "An Essay on Rights," *University of Texas Law Review*, 62 (1982), 1386.

6. Demanding that needs "be satisfied—whether or not satisfying them can today persuasively be characterized as enforcing a right—strikes me as more likely to succeed than claiming that existing rights to food and shelter must be enforced" (ibid., p. 1394). See also Alan Freeman, "Legitimizing Racial Discrimination Through Anti-Discrimination Law: A Critical Review of Supreme Court Doctrine," *Minnesota Law Review*, 62 (1978), 1049.

7. For a discussion of the transformative significance of black music and literature, see Mari Matsuda, "Looking to the Bottom," *Harvard Civil Rights—Civil Liberties Law Review*, 22 (1987), 335.

8. Michael Ignatieff, *The Needs of Strangers* (London: Chatto and Windus, 1984), p. 38.

9. Ibid., p. 53.

10. Gabel, "The Bank Teller," p. 28.

11. Mark Tushnet, *The American Law of Slavery* (Princeton: Princeton University Press, 1981), pp. 37–42. Tushnet's analysis is premised, in part, on an understanding of the law of slaveholders as creating a system of enforceable expectations and limited rights for slaves.

12. Gabel, "The Bank Teller," p. 29.

13. "In the discussion of law, there is an ever-renewed conflict between those who see it as a functional necessity and others who invest it with hope and promise. The former accept law as a given, as fact, at best as an instrument of practical problem-solving. For the legal idealist, on the other hand, law connotes a larger moral achievement." Phillip Selznick, "Law, Society and Moral Evolution," in *Cohen and Cohen's Readings in Jurisprudence and Legal Philosophy*, ed. Phillip Schuman (Boston: Little, Brown, 1979), p. 930.

14. See Mary Jo Frug, "Reading Contracts: A Feminist Analysis of a Contracts Casebook," *American Law Review*, 34 (1985), 1065; Karl Klare, "Contracts, Jurisprudence and the First-Year Casebook," *New York University Law Review*, 54 (1979), 876.

15. See Catherine MacKinnon, "Feminism, Marxism, Method and the State: An Agenda for Theory," *Signs*, 7 (1982), 515; Frances Olsen, "The Family and the Market: A Study of Ideology and Legal Reform," *Harvard Law Review*, 96 (1983), 1497.

16. 3 Cai. R. 175 (N.Y. Sup. Ct. 1805).

17. Søren Kierkegaard, cited in Karl Jaspers, *Existentialism from Dostoevsky to Sartre* (New York: New American Library, 1972), p. 176.

18. See Derrick Bell, "Social Limits on Basic Protections for Blacks," *in Race, Racism and American Law* (Boston: Little, Brown, 1980), p. 230.

19. See William Simon, "Legal Informality and Redistributive Politics," *Special Issue, Clearinghouse Review*, 19 (1985), 384; E. Johnson, "The Justice System of the Future: Four Scenarios for the Twenty-First Century," *Access to*

Justice and the Welfare State, ed. Mauro Cappalletti (Alphen aan den Rijn: Sijthoff, 1981), p. 183; Jerold Auerbach, *Justice Without Law?* (New York: Oxford University Press, 1983).

20. Carl Jung, *Psyche and Symbol: A Selection from the Writing of C.J. Jung* (Garden City: Doubleday Anchor Books, 1958), p. 214.

21. §2–202, *Uniform Commercial Code,* in *Selected Commercial Statutes.*

22. Robert Williams, "The Algebra of Federal Indian Law: The Hard Trail of Decolonizing and Americanizing the White Man's Indian Jurisprudence," *Wisconsin Law Review,* 7 (1986), 290; see also *Dred Scott v. Sandford,* 60 U.S. 383 (1857).

23. Derek Goodwin, "Raiders of the Sacred Sites," *New York Times Magazine,* December 7, 1986, p. 65.

24. Christopher Stone, "Should Trees Have Standing?—Toward Legal Rights for Natural Objects," *Southern California Law Review,* 45 (1972), pp. 453, 455.

25. See generally John M. Brockman, "Bitburg Deconstruction," *Philosophical Forum,* 7 (1986), 160.

26. Dinesh Khosla and Patricia Williams, "Economies of Mind: A Collaborative Reflection," *Nova Law Review,* 10 (1986), 621.

27. James Jones, *Bad Blood* (New York: Free Press, 1981).

28. Lewis Hyde, *The Gift: Imagination and the Erotic Life of Property* (New York: Vintage, 1983), p. 139.

29. Kenneth Stampp, *The Peculiar Institution* (New York: Knopf, 1956), pp. 250–251.

30. *Dred Scott v. Sandford,* 60 U.S. 383 (1857), at 407.

31. Stampp, *The Peculiar Institution,* p. 198.

32. See generally Winthrop Jordan, *White over Black* (Chapel Hill: University of North Carolina Press, 1968), pp. 136–178; John Dollard, *Caste and Class in a Southern Town* (Garden City: Doubleday, 1957), pp. 134–172.

33. "You must teach your children that the ground beneath their feet is the ashes of our grandfathers. So that they will respect the land, tell your children that the earth is rich with the lives of our kin." Chief Seattle of the Suquamish, 1854 speech in response to a U.S. offer to enter into a treaty for tribal lands, in Williams, "The Algebra of Federal Indian Law," p. 292.

34. Almost every culture in the world has its share of such tales: Plains Indian, Inuit, Celtic, Siberian, Turkish, Nigerian, Cameroonian, Brazilian, Australian, and Malaysian stories—to name a few—describe the phenomenon of the power mask or power object. Moreover, the unmasking can occur in a number of less-than-literal ways: killing the totemic animal from whom the sourcerer derives power; devaluing the magician as merely the village psychotic; and, perhaps most familiarly in our culture, incanting sacred spells backwards. See Joan Halifax, *Shamanic Voices* (New York: Dutton, 1979); James Frazer, *The Golden Bough* (London: Macmillan, 1963); Claude Lévi-

Srauss, *The Raw and the Cooked* (New York: Harper and Row, 1969); Michael Taussig, *Shamanism, Colonialism, and the Wild Man* (Chicago: University of Chicago Press, 1987); Weston La Barre, *The Ghost Dance* (New York: Dell, 1978).

35. "In exactly the same way that the South imagines that it 'knows' the Negro, the North imagines that it has set him free. Both camps are deluded. Human freedom is a complex, difficult—and private—thing. If we liken life, for a moment, to a furnace, then freedom is the fire which burns away illusion." James Baldwin, *Nobody Knows My Name* (New York: Dell, 1970), p. 99.

9. Mirrors and Windows

1. "Police, Marshals and Chicken Lure Fugitives into Custody," *New York Times*, December 16, 1985, p. B17.
2. E. Diamond, "The Brawley Fiasco," *New York Magazine*, July 18, 1988, p. 22.
3. "Evidence Points to Deceit by Brawley," *New York Times*, September 27, 1988, p. A1, italics added.
4. M. Cottman, "Abrams' Brawley Update: There Might Be No Crime," *New York Newsday*, July 15, 1988, p. 5.
5. Robert McFadden "Brawley Made Up Story of Assault, Grand Jury Finds," *New York Times*, October 7, 1988, p. 1.
6. *New York Times*, September 27, 1988, p. A1.
7. "What first signalled to me that a Black girl was about to become a public victim was hearing the *name* of an alleged rape victim—Tawana Brawley— given on a local radio news show. Since when does the press give the name of any rape victim, much less one who is underage? Obviously when the victim is Black, and thus not worthy of the same respect and protection that would be given a white child." Audrey Edwards, "The Rape of Tawana Brawley," *Essence*, November 1988, p. 80.

   As NAACP attorney Conrad Lynn observed, "State law provides that if a child appears to have been sexually molested, then the Child Protective Services Agency is supposed to take jurisdiction and custody of that child. Now, Tawana Brawley was 15 at the time of the incident. If that had been done, as I proposed early on, the agency would have given her psychiatric attention and preserved evidence, if there were evidence . . . But there was a state decision that the agency shouldn't be involved." Editorial, "What Happened to Tawana Brawley's Case—and to Attitudes about Race and Justice," *New York Times*, October 9, 1988, p. E8.
8. E. R. Shipp, "A Flamboyant Leader of Protests," *New York Times*, January 21, 1988, p. B6.
9. M. A. Farber, "Protest Figure Reported To Be a U. S. Informant," *New York Times*, January 21, 1988, p. B1. "Mr. Sharpton said that he—not investiga-

tors—had put a recording device on his phone, but only to serve as a 'hot line' for people turning in crack dealers" (p. B6).

10. "Roy Innis Pushes Al Sharpton: Fracas at 'Downey Show' Taping; Boxing Match Planned," *Washington Post*, August 11, 1988, p. D4.

11. A. Bollinger, "Tawana's Mom to Get 'Black Army' Escort," *New York Post*, June 3, 1988, p. 7.

12. Howard Kurtz, "New York Moves Against Brawley Lawyers," *Washington Post*, October 7, 1988, p. A1.

13. Pete Hamill, "Black Media Should Tell the Truth" *New York Post*, September 29, 1988, p. 5.

14. "The Victims of the Brawley Case," *New York Times*, September 28, 1988, p. A22.

15. "One witness said Mr. King 'would watch her exercise' and talked to the girl 'in a real sexual way,' sometimes describing her as a 'fine fox.'" *New York Times*, September 27, 1988, p. A16.

16. "Then it was off to the airport cafeteria for a strategy session and some cheeseburgers with advisers Alton Maddox, C. Vernon Mason and the Rev. Al Sharpton. 'The fat one, he ate the most,' said Carmen, the cashier. 'He and the skinny one [an aide] bought about $50 or $60 of cheeseburgers, orange juice, chocolate cake, pasta salad and pie,' she added." J. Nolan, "Traveling Circus Has 'Em Rollin' in Aisles," *New York Post*, September 29, 1988, p. 4.

17. Joy Kogawa, *Obasan* (Boston: David Godine, 1981), p. 1.

18. Edwards, "The Rape of Tawana Brawley," p. 80.

19. *Washington Post*, August 11, 1988, p. D4.

20. Under the caption "Robin Givens: Waiter, a Tonic with Slime for the Lady," even *Ms* magazine wrote: "We sympathized with the fights. We understood the divorce. But this crazy libel suit we don't get. Was it his personality and his pecs, or did you just want the bucks all along?" E. Combs and M. Suh, "Women Who Made Us Cringe," *Ms*, January-February 1989, p. 96.

21. Brawley To Get Muslim Name," *New York Times*, October 11, 1988, p. B3.

10. Owning the Self in a Disowned World

1. "Tales of the Farmyard," *Economist*, July 8, 1989, p. 75.

2. Christopher Daly, "Woman Charged in Death of Own Fetus in Accident," *Washington Post*, November 25, 1989, p. A4.

3. "Missouri Fetus Unlawfully Jailed, Suit Says," *New York Times*, August 11, 1989, p. B5.

4. Victoria Churchville, "D.C. Judge Jails Woman as Protection for Fetus," *Washington Post*, July 23, 1988, p. 1.

5. "Proposal for Woman's Sterilization Draws Protest," *New York Times*, September 26, 1988, p. 30.

6. Ronald Sullivan, "Mother Accuses Sperm Bank of a Mixup," *New York Times,* March 9, 1990, p. B1.
7. *Marciniak v. Lundborg,* Wisc. Sup. Ct., No. 88–0088, 58 U.S.L.W. 2460, February 13, 1990.
8. William Robbins, "Court to Decide Missouri Prisoner's Right to Father Child," *New York Times,* February 20, 1990, p. A19.
9. *International Herald Tribune,* February 28, 1990, p. 1.
10. All quotes about Maxine Thomas from Roxane Arnold and Terry Pristin, "The Rise and Fall of Maxine Thomas," *Los Angeles Times,* May 6, 1988, part 2, pp. 1–3.
11. Dorothy Gilliam, "Mixed Rewards of Success," *Washington Post,* December 30, 1986, p. 1.
    Despite persistent public images to the contrary, black birth rates "declined from 153.5 per 1000 women in 1960, to 81.4 per 1000 women in 1984." T. B. Edsell, "Race in Politics," *New York Review of Books,* December 22, 1988, p. 24.
12. This representation is made so often that it has entered the stratosphere of needing-no-citation, but here is a random sample: "One factor [accounting for the decreasing numbers of black men enrolled in college] is the growing number of black families that are headed by young, impoverished, similiterate single women, poor role models for daughters and no model at all for sons." "Blacks on Campus," *Los Angeles Times,* February 13, 1989, part 2, p. 4.

11. Arm's-Length Intimacies

1. "Ursine Ennui," April or May or June 1989. This is a quotation without a cite. It is a real quote—I cut it out of a San Francisco Bay Area newspaper myself and everything. I just don't remember which paper, and searches of every conceivable data base have turned up nothing. Some people might insist, therefore, that my persistence in using it is a sure sign (a) that my work is unscholarly, or (b) that this is not a real quote and I am either a liar or hallucinating. I, however, prefer to think of it as an open invitation to the reader to participate in the construction of authority.
2. Isabel Wilkerson, "New Funeral Option for Those in a Rush," *New York Times,* February 23, 1989, p. A16.

12. On Being the Object of Property

1. Marguerite Duras, *The Lover,* trans. Barbara Bray (New York: Harper and Row, 1986), p. 55.
2. *Madrigal v. Quilligan,* U.S. Court of Appeals, 9th Circuit, Docket No. 78–3187, October 1979.

3. "Decline in Births Eases Brazil's Population Worries," *New York Times*, August 8, 1989, p. A9.
4. See generally Stanley Elkins, *Slavery* (New York: Grosset and Dunlap, 1963); Kenneth Stampp, *The Peculiar Institution* (New York: Knopf, 1956); Winthrop Jordan, *White over Black* (Chapel Hill: North Carolina University Press, 1968); Mark Tushnet, *The American Law of Slavery* (Princeton: Princeton University Press, 1981).
5. "Actants have a kind of phonemic rather than a phonetic role: they operate on the level of function, rather than content. That is, an actant may embody itself in a particular character (termed an acteur) or it may reside in the function of more than one character in respect of their common role in the story's underlying 'oppositional' structure. In short, the deep structure of the narrative generates and defines its actants at a level beyond that of the story's surface content." Terence Hawkes, *Structuralism and Semiotics* (Berkeley: University of California Press, 1977), p. 89.
6. Tushnet, *American Law of Slavery*, p. 69.
7. Duras, *The Lover*, p. 54.
8. See generally *In the Matter of Baby "M," a Pseudonym for an Actual Person*, Superior Court of New Jersey, Chancery Division, Docket No. FM–25314–86E, March 31, 1987. This decision was appealed, and on February 3, 1988, the New Jersey Supreme Court ruled that surrogate contracts were illegal and against public policy. In addition to the contract issue, however, the court decided the custody issue in favor of the Sterns, but granted visitation rights to Mary Beth Whitehead.
9. Joseph Calamari and Joseph Perillo, *Contracts*, 3rd ed. (St. Paul: West, 1987), p. 228.
10. Walter Benjamin, "The Storyteller," in *Illuminations*, ed. Hannah Arendt, trans. Harry Zohn (New York: Schocken, 1969), p. 83.
11. Bruce Lambert, "Study Finds Antibodies for AIDS in 1 in 61 Babies in New York City," *New York Times*, January 13, 1988, p. A1, col 2–3. "Study Traces AIDS in African Children," *New York Times*, January 22, 1988, sec. A, p. 6. James Brooke, "New Surge of AIDS in Congo May Be an Omen for Africa," *New York Times*, January 22, 1988, p. A1.
12. James Barron, "Polar Bears Kill a Child at Prospect Park Zoo," *New York Times*, May 20, 1987, p. 1.
13. *New York Post*, May 22, 1987, p. 1.
14. Patricia J. Williams, "The Meaning of Rights," address at the annual meeting of the Law and Society Association, Washington D.C., June 6, 1987, on file at the University of Wisconsin Law School.

A Word on Categories

As I write, my editor at Harvard University Press is waging something of a struggle with the people at the Library of Congress about how this book is to be categorized for cataloging purposes. The librarians think "Afro-Americans—Civil Rights" and "Law Teachers" would be nice. I told my editor to hold out for "Autobiography," "Fiction," "Gender Studies," and "Medieval Medicine." This battle seems appropriate enough, since for me the book is not exclusively about race or law but also about boundary. While being black has been the most powerful social attribution in my life, it is only one of a number of governing narratives or presiding fictions by which I am constantly reconfiguring myself in the world. Gender is another, along with ecology, pacifism, my peculiar brand of colloquial English, and Roxbury, Massachusetts. The complexity of role identification, the politics of sexuality, the inflections of professionalized discourse—all describe and impose boundary in my life, even as they confound one another in unfolding spirals of confrontation, deflection, and dream.

A final note about some of my own decisions on categories: I wish to recognize that terms like "black" and "white" do not begin to capture the rich ethnic and political diversity of my subject. But I do believe that the simple matter of the color of one's skin so profoundly affects the way one is treated, so radically shapes what one is allowed to think and feel about this society, that the decision to generalize from such a division is valid. Furthermore, it is hard to describe succinctly the racial perspective and history that are my concern. "Disenfranchised" will not do, since part of my point is that a purely class-based analysis does not comprehend the whole problem. I don't like the word "minority" (although I use it) because it implies a certain delegitimacy in a majoritarian system; and if one adds up all the shades of yellow, red, and brown swept over by the term, we are in fact not. I prefer "African-American" in my own conversational usage because it effectively evokes the specific cultural dimensions of my identity, but in this book I use most frequently the term "black" in order to accentuate the unshaded monolithism of color itself as a social force.

Acknowledgments

I wish to thank the following persons for their invaluable conversation, inspiration, friendship, and encouragement:

Barbara Babcock, Joyce Backman, Katherine Baur, Derrick Bell, Jewell Bell, Sacvan Bercovitch, Beryl Blaustone, Paulette Caldwell, Marguerite Cartwright, Denise Carty-Benia, Rhonda Copelon, Bobbi Cordano, Kimberle Crenshaw, Richard Delgado, Jennifer Elrod, Martha Fineman, Nancy Fraser, Peter Gabel, Thomas Grey, William Hing, Sharon Hom, Barbara Johnson, George Joseph, Dinesh Khosla, Homer Larue, Charles Lawrence, Howard Lesnick, Mari Matsuda, Maureen McCafferty, Vanessa Merton, Kirin Narayan, Gary Patterson, Michael Peirce, Richard Perry, Benita Ramsey, Celina Romany, Blanca Silvestrini, Bernestine Singley, Ellen Tarry, Lindsay Waters, Matthew Wilkes, Carol Williams, and Rob Williams.

Index